PLAY
POWER

RICHARD NEVILLE

PLAY POWER

Exploring the
International
Underground

RANDOM HOUSE NEW YORK

To
My Mother
and Father

Acknowledgments

The initial inspiration for *Play Power* came from my publisher, Ed Victor. Not only was he acutely sympathetic to the numerous problems encountered en route, but he insisted that I abandon any pose of academic neutrality and write instead with my own voice.

Many people helped me complete this book. Peter Buckman, Germaine Greer, Martin Sharp, Deborah Rogers, Mohamed and Lee – have lent houses to hide away in, made available books and documents otherwise unobtainable – or helped me in countless other ways. Thanks to Jane de Mendelsohn of *BIT* and Harvey Matusow for their data on Turkish pot-trail casualities. Thanks to Rosemary Pettit for her early research assistance and for her conscientious dispatches from the Asian front. Thanks to everyone at *OZ*: Andrew Fisher, Felix Dennis, Jon Goodchild, Brigid Harrison and Bridget Murphy, who for so long tolerated a distracted editor. Thanks to Ian Stocks, Tina Liber, Tina Date, Michelene Victor and Andrew who helped during proof stages.

Play Power would never have been undertaken without the loyalty and help of Louise Ferrier, who contributed to it more than I can ever repay.

This book would never have reached the publishers without the perseverence and encouragement of Jim Anderson, who gave invaluable assistance at every stage in the preparation of the manuscript, acting as an editor throughout. He constructed the Underground Press chart (page 155) and researched much of the material for the chapters on the Underground Press, Drugs, the directory of publications and the Headopoly Game. I look forward to his first book, *Gay Power*.

CONTENTS

PROLOGUE

Power
Flower

They want bread? ... Oh, they've got plenty of that, said Timothy, let them wear flowers. Fuck your flowers, said Stokeley, we want ... Revolution? offered the Marx brothers, Danny, Rudi and Tariq. No! sang the Beatles in three catchy versions. None of which, responded the man in the burgundy vest, will equal the impact of cigarillos — the revolution in smoking pleasure.

*

'Whenever you ring me,' he said, 'ask for Pete the Coyote.' And whenever I did, no one had ever heard of him. It was the week before Christmas 1968 and Pete the Coyote, along with other members of San Francisco's Hell's Angels had flown to London with his immense gaudy bike to check out the traction. When I met them, they were stacked into a lush little room at the Beatles' Savile Row headquarters, only mildly subdued by George Harrison's efforts to evict them ('He said we ain't got manners.'). Ken Kesey had travelled with the Angels and was in the room tape recording the visiting Dutch magician Simon Vinkenoog, now babbling with mellifluous extravagance. Meanwhile, Pete the Coyote was laying it down: 'The cybernetic age entails a change in our frame of reference, man. The traditional spatio-temporal concepts are inadequate ... the digital computer is easing us into the electronic/automotive age just as the steam engine pivoted us into the industrial revolution. In those days it was gin. It flowed like water. Kids were suckled on it, societies campaigned against it. Now it's acid. LSD is for us what gin was for the Victorians. It lubricates our acceptance of a new age ... ' A Hell's Angel? With his grim eye shades, weathered leather, and stale Levis, he should have been talking about rebuilding his Harley Davidson or wrenching out some girl's teeth with a pair of rusty pliers.

*

You can't drop just *any* flowers from an aeroplane. Some disintegrate upon landing, others drift off to infinity. That's why they have to be tested. At a crowded yippie meeting in Lower Manhattan, Abbie Hoffman regretted that his free-fall flower experiments from a nearby rooftop had been interrupted by suspicious winos; nevertheless he recommended sturdy daisies. Above the Central Park be-in the next day, the tiny specks spewed from a light aircraft only to float gently away past Fifth Avenue.

They must have used prissy primroses.

*

I arrived late at the home of the man behind *The Black Dwarf*. It was obviously a solemn occasion. The living room was strewn with hand-picked London militants. The man in the chair was speaking heavy Marx in a German accent. It was Mr (deadly) Ernest Mandel, editor of Belgium's left wing *Le Gauche*, and a respected socialist economist. In measured tones, he precisely minimised the contribution of 'libertarian elements' in the Paris uprising and spoke of the subsequent influx of recruits to 'the party'; of the seriousness of revolution and the importance of being ideological. He had come to praise Marx, and proceeded to bury him. In the discussion which followed, tense for those involved, three hours were spent arguing over the definition of 'neo-capitalism'. Ken Tynan was the first to leave, in despair.

One man's revolution is another man's purgatory.

CARRY
ON
MOTHERFUCKERS

Up
Against
the
Wall,
Mr
Chips

The headmaster of Eton resigned. 'The stress and strain on a headmaster have clearly increased,' he said. No one commented on the stress and strain of being a school boy. It seemed that some of the pupils had been toting guns and smoking pot. In the same month the second master of Rugby told the *Daily Telegraph* that 15 boys had been rusticated in the past two years for drug offences. Another press report alleged that over 30 pupils had been dismissed for being 'hippy rebels'. After St Paul's had expelled several boys over marijuana, I met one of them at the office of Release, the London drug-bust organisation ('dial 01-603 8654 day or night with love'). He was fifteen.

At fifteen I wore khaki shorts and a boater to school, cheer-led the football team, failed Latin and hummed *Memories are Made of This* during cadet drill. This young man, with his bright purple kerchief and friendly cool, talked amiably of eradicating compulsory sport and religion, abolishing prefects and punishment, putting an end to the arbitrary authority of masters ... and I listened, uncomfortably conscious of being one of the mid-way generation, still-born into a limbo of chairman's reports, vicars on television and invitations to become a railway guard for a life of fun, travel and adventure, £12 per week. My generation—I am almost thirty—was already pubertal by the time Carl Perkins, pot and a kind of easy sex all happened. Our God was still in business, our Elvis in the army, our future in the Positions Vacant columns.

We had to learn to waltz before learning not to.

Don't be concerned, it will not harm you,
It's only me pursuing something I'm not sure of,
Across my dream, with nets of wonder,
I chase the bright, elusive butterfly of ... [1]

Although we are still only *half* liberated — secretly savouring the smell of brown ale, boot polish and Brylcreem — our once furtive sub-culture has come out of the shadows, on to the hit parades, into the headlines and at the local Odeon. The bright elusive butterfly has landed on the shoulders of the fifteen-year-olds.

A summer's night; strolling at a pace which overtakes two girls in front. Both have sleeping bags slung over their backs, fringe leather jackets, mock Aztec jewellery and Eastern carpet shoulder bags. 'Hello,' smiles one of them, 'isn't it a good idea to say hello to strangers? No one ever does. We just said good evening to an old man and he freaked out completely.'

We walk together awhile. One is sixteen, the other a year older. They have just hitched down from Yarmouth, bound for Cornwall. 'You won't be able to sleep in the pill boxes there any more,' I warn them, 'the council has filled them in with oil.' 'That's all right,' says the younger of the two, 'we'll con some straight.' We exchange good nights, one of them asking rhetorically, 'Do you smoke?' as she slips into my hand a pebble of hash.

A casual meeting. Two young chicks. Nothing extraordinary; except a reminder that girls like this are everywhere and they're not going to grow up and marry bank managers.

'One of the most astonishing sights of the May revolution was thousands of school children marching to the slogan

[1] Bob Lind, 'Elusive Butterfly.' Fontana TL 5340.

"Power is in the streets, not in Parliament".'[2] On May 10, 1968, French high schools declared a national strike in support of their elder brothers at the Sorbonne, nearly 9,000 joining in the demonstrations, manning the barricades and bloodying the ambulances. French lycées are now uncamouflaged training grounds for a repeat performance. In American schools, it is said that Che Guevara is 13 years old and not doing his homework. Already there have been several successfully co-ordinated school strikes and the angriest Underground newspapers are often members of HIPS—the High School Independent Press Service.

A report to a London teachers' association in 1969 revealed how classroom anarchy is driving out teachers. The symptoms of a discipline collapse were listed as: chronic misbehaviour, breaches of school rules, challenges to teachers' authority, disturbances of lessons, lateness, incorrect dress, vandalism, and general deterioration in the tone of the school. In other words, it's goodbye to Goodbye Mr Chips. 'This appears to be mainly due to an increase in neurotic types of children,' comments the report.[3]

Neurotic types of children. That depends on your perspective. Maybe these children saw what it was like to be *normal*, on the ten o'clock news—and didn't like it.

A
Buzzard
in
Macy's

'The world was split into two camps, armed to the teeth and

[2] Patrick Seale & Maureen McConville. *Red Flag, Black Flag; French Revolution* 1968. Ballantine, 1968.
[3] Report prepared by working party of London's branch of the Association of Assistant Masters and presented to the Association's annual meeting, January 1969.

mutually hostile,' droned our school history masters when outlining causes of the First World War: a text-book world view that is not inappropriate today. The two camps have become generational; an over-simplification, but those who are actually a part of either camp will know what is meant. Nowadays the weapons are more refined. The Big Bertha of both sides is culture—one inherited, the other do-it-yourself. From the outside looking in, the radical youth Movement seems determined to destroy civilisation as we know it. From the inside looking out, it is civilisation which is destroying itself.

A unique feature of today's Youthquake—as *Vogue* once dubbed it—is its intense, spontaneous internationalism. From Berlin to Berkeley, from Zurich to Notting Hill, Movement members exchange a gut solidarity; sharing common aspirations, inspirations, strategy, style, mood and vocabulary. Long hair is their declaration of independence, pop music their esperanto and they puff pot in their peace pipe.

Even divisions *within* the Movement are broadly consistent. The terms New Left, Underground, and 'militant poor' are loosely applicable throughout the wide and scattered domain of youthful insurgency. Sometimes these categories generously overlap, at other times, less generously, they conflict. The *New Left* is comprised largely of the 'alphabet soup' of student protest, (SDS, SNCC, NACLA, RSA, BLF, RSSF, etc.) with just occasionally a dash of LSD.

That unpopular label, *Underground*, embraces hippies, beats, mystics, madmen, freaks, yippies, crazies, crackpots, communards and anyone who rejects rigid political ideology ('it's a brain disease') and believes that once you have blown your own mind, the Bastille will blow up itself. The *militant poor*, whose struggles require a separate book, include Europe's radical young workers, blacks, and assorted ethnic communities emerging in the United States.

In different areas, at different times, a different compound of these categories becomes the agency of disruption. The actions of the New Left are said to be 'political'. The antics of the Underground are said to be 'cultural'. In fact, both sociological manifestations are part of the behaviour pattern of a single discontented body. The days of nine to five radicalism are over. The hippie who has brown rice for breakfast, and the student who burns his examination paper are both learning to live the same revolution.

There is one quality which enlivens both the political and cultural denominations of Youth protest; which provides its most important innovation; which has the greatest relevance for the future; which is the funniest, freakiest and the most effective. This is the element of play, and it will be examined more specifically in the final chapter.

Apart from the lightning evolution of a counter culture, the One Great Youth Unifier has been Vietnam. In the UK and US outrage at the war grew naturally out of CND and civil rights movements—considerably nurtured by an oafish political rationale and horrendously inept generalship. It is naive to assume, however, that US withdrawal from Vietnam would anaesthetise youth protest. Symbols are easily replaceable. Anything can be made into an issue— an irritating State occasion, the awkward presence of a police car, the untimely sacking of a university lecturer, the discovery of 'confidential' student files, a fenced-in vacant lot. All can trigger off a youthful show of force.

One law of Movement dynamics is that the Movement is never contained by political events—it is propelled by them.

Another law of Movement dynamics is that one thing leads to another—in geometric progression. Imagery knows no boundaries. Specific national characteristics impose a certain complexion on insurrectional activity, but the differences are becoming less obvious than the similarities.

19

For instance: The first draft card was burned in 1965. This single act rapidly assumed forest fire proportions, consuming even the bodies of three Americans, who in the same year, ignited themselves on the steps of the Pentagon. A few years later, a Czech student, Jan Palach became a national hero when he adopted the same form of protest against the Russians. Even in Lund, in placid Sweden, students were charged with desecration, during a performance of Tuli Kupferberg's *Fucknam* in which actors set alight the American flags which adorned the monstrous papier maché penises in which they were parading. The stars and stripes have been lit up all over Europe and we may not see them go out again in our lifetime. In 1969, when all these early incendiary gestures were being sung and danced to on West End and Broadway stages in the production *Hair*, Berlin school children demonstrated that they had not forgotten the lesson of the blazing draft cards by putting their report cards to the torch.

Mass media is partly responsible for today's extraordinary generational self-consciousness. It follows that the Movement regularly identifies mass media's instruments as objectionable:

Amsterdam 1966 Masses of provos and construction workers besiege offices of the *ex*-fascist newspaper *De Telegraaf*.
London 1967 Hundreds of hippies attempt to block deliveries of the *News of the World*. Angry hand-bills reveal editor's home address and ask demonstrators to post pot to him. (Weeks later, his residence is searched by drugs squad.)
Germany 1968 Students sack Springer press office in Munich and raid distribution centres in all key cities. Police throw up barricades around every office.
New York 1968 Thirty hippies storm live TV discussion. At first, it was considered part of the show, ' ... but when one hairy type shouted that it was fine to hear a certain four-letter word on television and uttered it, doubts crept in.'[4]

[4] *The Times*, June 27, 1968.

20

New York 1969 Demonstrations outside offices of *New York Times* for its failure to cover Movement news.

One surprising exception: There were no demonstrations against mass media during the 1968 Paris uprising. This was regretted however, and the Cohn-Bendits have noted that this 'is a point to remember for the future and one that we will be sure to take care of.'[5]

On the eve of the celebrated Vietnam demonstration in London in October 1968, the press cried 'wolf!' so often, it began to sound like an old lady yelling 'rape!—please'. On its front page, *The Times* warned readers that demonstrators planned to take over several of the city's key buildings, including newspaper offices. The *Evening News* breathlessly followed this up by announcing that the BBC was to be invaded. It even dispatched its ace reporters, suitably disguised, to demonstrate the weaknesses in Auntie's defences. The BBC retaliated by storming the washrooms of the *Evening News* with similar ease, televising the result. Despite this handy pair of blue-prints, no move to occupy either building was made by demonstrators.

Among other symbols of oppression to come under fire by Movement radicals are department stores—although not literally, as this headline from a German Springer newspaper implies: FURNITURE STORE IN FLAMES: IS THIS DEMONSTRATION? IS THIS DISCUSSION?[6] The fire as it turned out was the result of a bungled burglary by a petty criminal. While such deception is typical of Springer policy, the editor had correctly sensed the fire's emotional connotations. Members of the Berlin Kommune K, the nucleus of which has sparked off Berlin's most flamboyant confrontations, distributed to the public leaflets which suggested philosophically that many such fires should be started in Berlin, and saw the blaze as 'the crackling image of Vietnam'. Fifteen buildings were listed (and spaces left

[5] *Obsolete Communism, The Left Wing Alternative.* McGraw-Hill, 1969.
[6] *Bild*, April 1968.

for additional suggestions) including of course, America House and the Springer Offices. Eight members of the Kommune were indicted on charges of inciting arson, and the trial was used by them as a further forum for ridicule, riot and rhetoric.

In New York at about the same time, April 1968, I was present at a yippie meeting in Union Park at which a department store loot-in was being planned. 'We'll choose a shop. About twenty of us will go in, select the stuff we want, hand the cashier a flower and head towards the door ... '

A militant Lower East Side group, the Black Mask, once staged a mill-in at Macy's during the Christmas rush. Demonstrators flooded into the store disguised as shoppers, floor walkers and counter assistants. Stock was either spoiled, stolen, swapped around or given away. Half starved dogs and cats were let loose in the food department. A berserk buzzard flew around the crockery section, smashing china and terrorizing sales girls. Accomplices ensured that respectable middle class shoppers were mistakenly roughed up and arrested.[7] Inspired by such chaos, a London group swept into Selfridges one Christmas with their key man dressed as Santa Claus. 'Free presents' were pressed into surprised but eager hands. Not long afterwards, shoppers were treated to the spectacle of police confiscating toys from small children, and arresting Santa Claus.

Paint
it
Black

On many an ageing would-be drop-out's bookshelf, among the crisp volumes of McLuhan, Cleaver and Marcuse, lies a yellowing copy of *Protest*, a look back in embarrassment at the angry young men on both sides of the Atlantic. 'The

[7] Based on a report in London's *King Mob Echo*.

only logical spokesmen of our age ... ' boasts the blurb, they ' ... revolted against the assumed conformities, bland hypocrisies and comfortable conceits of modern society.' The English team included Kingsley Amis, John Osborne and Colin Wilson (who themselves these days lack neither comfort nor conceit). US stars included Jack Kerouac and Allen Ginsberg. *Protest* was published in 1958, the same year that CND was formally launched in England, and nascent rumblings were heard on US campuses, which until then had been pre-occupied with such questions as—'Is God Dead?' or 'Is Eisenhower Alive?'[8] When the Beat era is recalled, it is customary to dig up a passage from Norman Mailer's so-called definitive essay *The White Negro* and juxtapose it significantly with a slice of psychiatry from Robert Linder's *Rebel Without Cause*. Despite its overuse, *The White Negro* has aged somewhat better than its author, who at the time presciently estimated the significance of the beats, whom he described as a sociological *'ménage-à-trois* ... [where] the bohemian and the juvenile delinquent came face to face with the Negro, and the hipster was a fact in American life.'

Not only American life. Media cultification was gearing into its brash new phase. Beatniks happened elsewhere — even in Australia where there were not even aborigines to come face to face with (all being safely secreted on punitive reservations). It should be recorded here, that despite, or perhaps because of, Australia's remote and unexciting image, the You Beaut land is compulsively tuned in to the rest of the world, thirstily absorbing the pop products of its culture and sociology; a half way market between England and America.

A minority of crazies — tantalisingly magnified by the media mirror — had shattered the silence of their big brothers with jazz and anarchy, junk and mysticism,

[8] The answer was 'yes'. He scored an 85 in a round of golf on March 10, 1959.

poverty and promiscuity. The Beats showed it was possible, even glamorous, to throw the gauntlet at the lifestyle of IBM.

Hampstead was said to be London's Greenwich Village, which was New York's Montmartre, which was Paris' Tangier. Jack Kerouac and Kingsley Amis appeared together on University panels to discuss: Is there a Beat Generation? Wrote Jack Newfield: 'More than anything else, the Beat generation was a portent, the first wind of a new storm, a coded signal that America's youth were starting to gag on conformity, materialism and silence.'[9]

Meanwhile, back at Trafalgar Square, John Osborne became a member of the Direct Action Committee which sponsored the first of the Aldermaston marches, later taken over by the Campaign for Nuclear Disarmament and which by 1961 had 5,000 people lying determinedly outside the Ministry of Defence. In *Bomb Culture* Jeff Nuttall compassionately, if innaccurately, chronicles the rise and fall of British Conscientious Objection, with its beery, bearded, Jelly Roll Morton atmosphere; where characters lurch about 'ill with anxiety about the bomb', dizzily establishing Golders Green Committees for the Abolition of Nuclear Weapons. Looking back on the battling Mods and Rockers of the early sixties ('every London hospital was crowded to overflowing with motor cycle casualties') Nuttall is convinced that the violence of this essentially hedonistic life style was the consequence of living with the prospect of a nuclear holocaust.

The poets blamed the Bomb, but people don't care about dying if the whole world's going to die with them. Duffle coats and CND badges symbolised a new generational identity. For the young, being sad about the Bomb was fun.

It was in the early sixties, while Mr and Mrs *Saturday Evening Post* thrilled to the election of the first telly president, JFK, that their sons and their daughters, who were

[9] *A Prophetic Minority*. New American Library, 1966.

neither starving hysterical nor naked, saw that 'the best minds of [its] generation' were being destroyed by iniquities more immediate than a nuclear mirage. In February 1960, four black students sat at a Woolworth's segregated counter in Greensboro, North Carolina and ordered coffee. It never came, but the next day sixteen other students sat beside them and lunch counters have never been the same since. By May the following year, the first batch of Freedom Fighters had left Washington DC for New Orleans on integrated buses. 'We Shall Overcome' echoed from southern Main Streets to Tin Pan Alley; a white man, John Howard Griffin blacked his skin and revealed for the remaining sceptics what it was like to be 'cast on the junkheap of second class citizenship'. In October 1962, James Meredith was admitted to the University of Mississippi. In March 1964 LBJ announced a War on Poverty (waged with even less success than his War on Commie Aggression).

Despite the national furore provoked by early radical activism, the protesters were mild-mannered, patriotic and religious—they sat-in with a bible in one hand and the Constitution in the other, both tear stained. Recalling the black man's part in those early days, Dick Gregory in London in 1968 said: 'We marched down the street and got shot at because we were black. And for some reason we felt ashamed because we were aggravating the situation to make the white folk shoot black folk. To get rid of some of the shame, we went to the police station and prayed for the sheriff ... '[10] It was clear that attack was the only means of survival.

In December 1964, the Free Speech Movement erupted from the University of California's Berkeley campus. It was the beginning of the end for the impotent paradox of liberalism. The FSM rose to expose the contradiction

[10] At the same meeting, Gregory explained that their first big mistake was to desegregate the washrooms first. It ruined the greatest thing the blacks had going for them—the myth of the giant cock.

between democracy's rhetoric and the Pentagon's reality. It was time to close the hypocrisy gap.[11]

Vote
Provo
for
Better
Weather

In Amsterdam in the mid-sixties, a new kind of revolt happened. Called Provo, it spawned imitators throughout Europe, and it inspired the Underground already emerging through pop, poetry and pot in Britain and the US. Provo was a rebellion without obvious cause. No Dutch soldiers were dying in Vietnam. No ethnic or social groups were being unduly victimised. 'In fact', noted one local commentator, 'there was a lack of any concrete inducement to protest against the established order.'[12] Except of course, the very existence of established order itself. It was the idea of Provo to *provoke* — spontaneously, flexibly, relentlessly — which meant choosing hyper-retaliatory situations and reaping the consequences, even if they proved to be political.

The Provotariat was raised in the anti-smoking circuses of Robert Jasper Grootveld, who began by painting K (for Kancer) on every tobacco hoarding in sight (undeterred by a 60 day gaol sentence) and later conducted flippantly blasphemous black masses against the weed at his 'smoke temple'. Police were also being taunted by the game, Marijhu, in which cigarette machines were crammed with

[11] 'There is a time when the operations of the machine become so odious' make you so sick at heart that you can't take part, you can't even tacitly take part. And you've got to put your bodies upon the gears and upon the wheels, upon the levers, upon all the apparatus, and you've got to make it stop.'
From Mario Savio's famous pre-sit-in speech.
[12] A.A.D. Nuis, in *Delta*, Autumn 1967. Published quarterly by Delta International Publication Foundation J.J. Viottastraat 41, Amsterdam ZI.

26

fake marijuana cigarettes in Day-Glo packets. Grootveld established a venue for his happenings by the statue of Liverdje ('The little rascal') on the Spui, which had been donated to the city by a cigarette company. It was here on Saturday nights amidst the irreverent carnival congregations of bored dissident and extrovert youth that the first issue of *Provo* was distributed—and confiscated. *Provo* paid homage to anarchism as the 'inspirational source for resistance', contained bomb recipes and initiated a vigorous campaign against the forthcoming marriage of Princess Beatrix to ex-Nazi Claus von Amsberg. (For the occasion the Mayor tactfully commandeered the Anne Frank House for use as a temporary police station.) For the wedding day, the Provos' plans anticipated the ridicule strategy used by the yippies three years later at the Chicago Democratic Convention:

—During the Psalms, the church organ to emit laughing gas.
—Hidden loudspeakers would blare forth the sounds of machine guns. Watch the police fire back.
—Horses always bolt at the smell of lion manure. It would be collected from the zoo and strewn along the procession route. Oh what fun to see the runaway golden coach, with Beatrix and Claus clinging desperately to each other.

The massive police contingent enticed by such plans, prevented their execution. But the Provos were not disarmed. One TV watcher recalls:

'Then all at once the picture grew hazier and hazier until the whole screen was white. A break in transmission—not a bad idea either. But suddenly the carriage with the newly weds emerged from the mist, and when I grasped what had happened, I was overcome with emotion. Other people, with more guts than me, had brought it off, were throwing smoke bombs into living rooms all over Europe, the Soviet

27

Union, United States, Japan, and were being pursued far along the canals and beaten up in doorways by policemen falling over each other to get at them. Others were being shoved up against bridge railings by mounted police, held tight by reins looped around their necks, and kicked senseless by spurred riding boots.'[13]

But basically Provo was anti-violent. The originality of the movement was its early assessment of the dehumanising consequences of approaching technology, and the 'White Plans' were a desperate bid to stem the tide of automation.

White Bicycles: Thirty provos painted their bikes white and announced they belonged to everyone. City traffic to be banned. Others were invited to bring their bicycles to the Spui at midnight on Saturday, where they would be painted free. Urged on by insurance companies and manufacturers, the police confiscated the bikes on the pretext that they might be stolen.

White chimneys: Compulsory smokeless zones.

White chickens: (chicken = kip = Dutch slang for policeman.) The policeman to become the disarmed social worker of the future. 'He will carry matches and contraceptives, as well as Royal Dutch Oranges and chicken drumsticks for the starving … '[14]

White Housing: Young families and students to occupy and improve condemned residences.

White wives: Not a parallel to the common property white bicycle plan, but a suggestion for free contraceptive clinics and abortions for all.

White corpse: An anti-automobile plan to dramatise accidents. 'As soon as the ambulance has removed the sad remains, the murderer himself, using the chisel and hammer, must hack out the silhouette of his victim one inch deep in the asphalt under supervision of police. Next he must fill the hollow with white mortar.'

[13] Harry Mulisch, *Delta*, op. cit.
[14] *Provo* 9.

The first issue of *Provo* had anticipated that the movement would be the 'final loser'. The editor, Roel van Duyn, predicted that the sun would rise in the West before there would be revolution in Holland, and the First International Provo Convention at Borghaven Castle in November 1966 was also the last. But the immediate repercussions of this curious, short-lived anarchistic explosion were remarkable. Both the mayor of the city and the chief of police were fired. In the municipal elections of June 1966, the Provos won a seat on the council with thirteen thousand votes, although most of their adherents were under voting age. By May a year later, Provo was considered a cliché, and it was formally disbanded. 'The stopping of Provo means total decentralising,' said their second council electee, Luud Schimmelpenninck, 'now everyone can run by himself.'

Early in 1970, some city dwellers discovered Gnomes at the bottom of their garden. A tough, new, imaginative student left pressure group, The Gnomes declared an independent republic in Amsterdam, the 'Orange Free State,' and set up 12 separate 'Ministries.' Former Provo, Roel van Duyn, re-incarnated himself a Gnome and became 'ambassador' to Amsterdam. Financed by a bank's clerical error, the group fought against technology by planting trees in unexpected places, uprooting cars during rush hour and stealing official chairs from such enemy Trolls as the city mayor.

Amsterdam is still a city brimming with possibilities, a seething European Headopolis where countless wanderers celebrate their exile, smoke pot freely in the clubs Kosmos and Fantasio and, joining forces with the gentle locals, fruitfully multiply into a new community.

From Love-in to Cash-in

Recalling the genesis of the UK Underground is not to

chronicle a history of *ideas* but to relive a pageant of public events. This is because the cultural politics of the Psychedelic Left, in its formative stages, were akin to those 'getting-to-know-you' games once played at parties to relax and mingle the guests before they got down to the serious business of having a good time. The initial task was to inaugurate a communal experience, to abolish loneliness, finally to eradicate the Victorian Depression ethic of virtuous sacrifice and to remind the world that—in the words of Paolo Lionni—'love need not remain a banal cliché but is and must be a constantly original and divine verb.'

In London in 1967, every Friday night until dawn, shimmering flower children, splashed with Day-Glo, spotted with marcasite, clad in diaphanous re-vamped negligées, tarted-up Grenadier Guards jackets, in tat and glitter from the markets of Asia and the stalls of Portobello Road, in anything as long as it was beautiful, tripped inside a monstrous basement or queued outside, bedazzling the passing traffic. This was UFO, Unidentified Flying Object or Underground Freak Out, in Tottenham Court Road, where Arthur Brown sang suspended, head-gear aflame, swaying across the crowds in an eerie pendulum. Or where youth jerked joyfully to the Pink Floyd, Procul Harum, the Soft Machine and the Bonzo Dog Doo Dah Band, or were transfixed by molten 'high' slides and theatrical side shows. The throbbing psychedelics were occasionally punctuated by sad flashbacks to a beatnik heritage—the tired jazz trio 'improvising' to a Pathé newsreel, or the men in black polo neck sweaters swearing at 'the system' in a style imagined to be Pinteresque and proving to be pedestrian.

The seeds of London's first psychedelic circus were sown as far back as June 1965 at the famous Albert Hall 'Cosmic Poetry Visitation Accidentally Happening Carnally' where London's incubating hippies tuned in to Allen Ginsberg, Simon Vinkenoog, Christopher Logue, Lawrence Ferlinghetti etc. and discovered much to their surprise

30

that 7,000 others were in a similar state of gestation. 'Hippie' was a new word, then being tentatively employed by the *San Francisco Chronicle* to warn its readers of the neo-beatnik drift into the streets of the Haight-Ashbury. Its evolution nurtured by Provo and a new exotic bohemianism across the Atlantic, *IT* ('the first real attempt to create a London community' – Miles, manager of the Indica bookshop) was launched in October 1966. Over the next few months the directors and friends of the paper, a hippie mafia, engineered the most spectacular of London's Underground happenings.

When trouble occurred, everyone homed-in on UFO. It was the Underground's living equivalent to *The Times* letters column. When *IT* was raided by the police, readers rushed to this psychedelic basement and crowded sympathetically around the editor, who read aloud from proofs of the forthcoming issue. Hampstead liberals, ruffled by the threat to liberty of the press, joined the throng. Expecting Oxbridge Union wisdom and witty motions from the Chair, they turned away, confused by sparklers, light shows and an orgasmic Suzy Creamcheese. Again we tumbled into UFO when its co-founder John 'Hoppy' Hopkins was gaoled for possession of cannabis. 'The man who drives UFO is in the hands of the enemy,' roared *IT*, 'realize that they drink and get high and feel great, and you do other things and get high and they shit on you.' The next day inmates of the Circle Line watched the Provo-like enactment of the death and resurrection of *IT*, which in the person of a poet volunteer, was carted in a coffin from the Whitehall Cenotaph to Portobello Road, via the tubes. When Mick Jagger was sentenced to three months' imprisonment for possessing four mild amphetamine tablets, the anger spilled out from Tottenham Court Road to lamplit street meetings.

The early days of UFO were an externalised acid trip – traumatic, familial, euphoric – but journalists were soon to headline it as London's answer to Haight-Ashbury, and the sensitive clientele vanished in the wake of German film crews, the iron cross boys, and drunken shore leave sailors, who mistook the girls' freedom and flamboyance for an invitation to forcibly abduct them from their friends.

> 'Maybe to-night is kissing night. Don't just
> kiss your lover to-night, kiss your friends.'
> *Public announcement at UFO*

Some months after the success of UFO the perspiring heavies at Covent Garden vegetable markets were titillated by a nightly spectacle of flower children tiptoing daintily through the turnips in search of the Electric Garden—one of the more extravagant and less successful of the mushrooming psychedelic venues. Although you could see a haunting celluloid version of Dante's *Inferno* and Fritz Lang's *Metropolis*, Eric Burdon plus an oriental floor show, all at once, the Electric Garden was short circuited by the 'bad vibrations' sensed by Yoko Ono on the opening night. They came from rival Underground entrepreneurs. Later the Electric Garden was annexed by 'less commercial elements' renamed Middle Earth and kept firmly shut on UFO nights. Those who were socially marooned by the demise of UFO (Oct 67) were absorbed by Jim Haynes' Arts Laboratory and a revitalized Middle Earth. Sensationalised love-ins erupted from venues as diverse as Alexandra Palace[15] and the Duke of Bedford's Woburn Abbey Estate. The occasional hot-dog stand man held his own hippie circus and got rich quickly. But neither aristocracy nor roadside impresario could— by any stretch of journalistic fantasy—be considered Under-

---

[15] The most talked about of these was the *IT* benefit, 'Twenty four hour Technicolour Dream.' Seven thousand ravers at a guinea a head turned up to record their new found spontaneity for handy randy BBC cameras, yet only £1,000 found its way into the *IT* coffers. With classic subterranean cool, no one ever asked what happened to the rest, but the following weeks saw a surprising number of new business ventures sprouting from the undergrowth.

ground hosts. Those public freakouts which were initiated and promoted by the Underground itself were genuinely permissive and were recognized as alive and significant by those who participated.

'The three day Festival of the Flower Children faded out at Woburn Abbey, home of the Duke of Bedford yesterday, to the tinkling of necklace bells and cash registers ringing up more than £20,000 profits.'
Daily Telegraph, 29.8.67

'I thought it was going to be a flower show with competitions, prizes and lots of flowers.'
Duchess of Bedford, *The People*.

'It has been the pop festival of the year. It has been wonderful.'
Mr Cyril 'Flower' Power, general manager of the company which promoted the event. *Daily Sketch*.

'It is not a love-in. It's a cash-in. A hot dog is costing 1/9d... We are disgusted.'
Guest in flowered tunic. *Sunday Mirror*.

A
Rough
Trip
For
Us
All

Allen Ginsberg had been one of the conspirators in the promotion of the Albert Hall poetry reading, and two years later in January 1967, having in the meantime immersed himself in the Ganges, he helped to launch yet another cataclysmic voyage of human discovery—the world's first Human Be-in. It was pleonastically heralded by a street leaflet as ' ... a union of love and activism previously

33

separated by categorical dogma and label mongering, will finally occur ecstatically when Berkeley political activists and hip community and San Francisco's spiritual generation and contingents for the emerging revolutionary generation all over California, meet for a *gathering of the tribes*.' Over 10,000 turned up and turned on. The Be-in's birth-in was a love riot in fancy dress. People participated as confederate soldiers, pirates, gypsies, witch doctors, three-eyed magicians, 20's film stars, cowboys and Indians (both Red and Bengali), and real life Hell's Angels shocked reporters by brandishing flowers and tambourines and looking after lost children. A man floated down from a helicopter, others converged on San Francisco's Golden Gate Park in custom styled hearses, ambulances and laundry vans. The Grateful Dead, Big Brother and the Holding Company, The Jefferson Airplane and The Quicksilver Messenger Service lulled the crowds with pioneering acid rock. A dazed Santa Claus liberally threw LSD capsules and marijuana to the winds. An overawed *Time Magazine* recorded, 'The huge crowd was peaceful ... an amazing tribute to Haight-Ashbury.' More accurately, it was a tribute to LSD which had begun to suppress local aggression on an ever-increasing scale.

Many of those present were graduates from Ken Kesey's notorious acid tests. Begun in August 1965, the tests continued until LSD was declared illegal in October 1966, by which time it was estimated that 10,000 — the same number as the park celebrants — had ingested the drug in sugar lumps, punch, coffee or cookies. It was at these intensive social environments, initially in a garage and later moving to the Fillmore Auditorium, that stroboscopic light shows were allegedly invented and the whole pulsating minutiae of electronic party gadgets perfected.

Eight years before, Jack Kerouac had preached to college audiences of the 'two kinds of beat hipsters — COOL: bearded, sitting without moving in cafés, with their unfriendly girls dressed in black, who say nothing; and HOT:

34

crazy, talkative, mad shining eyes, running from bar to bar only to be ignored by the cool subterraneans.'[16] Ken Kesey with his Merry Pranksters and Hell's Angels speeding through La Honda in that radiant International Harvester schoolbus, believed to be powered with LSD, with the hero of Kerouac's *On the Road*, Neal Cassady at the wheel, were obviously spiritual progeny of the hot variety.[17] Yet they were descendants, not duplicates, for the hippies were fundamentally a different breed of cat. 'The hip person, the 'hipster' had to work for it,' wrote Tuli Kupferberg, 'the hippie is to the manner born ... the change from hip to hippie was a change from hard to soft.' Timothy Leary helped in the softening. With his colleague, Richard Alpert, he dropped out thousands by means of college lectures, the *Psychedelic Review* (published by the Castalia Foundation, financiers of group LSD experiments), and his amazing Psychedelic Roadshows, which he took to New York, where audiences were invited to 're-live the myth of Jesus Christ ... the resurrection has been a rough trip for us all.'

One of the first batch of acid converts, the Thelin brothers, ex-Eagle scouts and stock investors, opened the world's first psychedelic shop, in Haight-Ashbury on January 1st 1966. At that time, they said, 'you might see maybe fifteen people with long hair and strange dress walking down the street on a good day.' In less than eighteen months this figure had multiplied a thousand fold or more, depending on which account you read. *Time Magazine* estimated 50,000 hippies in the Bay area alone. *Newsweek* predicted 100,000 would swarm into Haight-Ashbury for the summer of '67. Leary was interviewed by *Playboy*, evaluated by

[16] *The Village Voice Reader*. Doubleday, 1962.

[17] Tom Wolfe. *The Electric Kool-Aid Acid Test* (Farrar, Straus & Giroux, 1968) describes a party where Kesey, Kerouac and Cassady meet together for the first time: 'Kesey and Kerouac didn't say much to each other ... Cassady in between them, once the mercury for Kerouac and the whole Beat Generation and now the mercury for Kesey and the whole—what?— something wilder and wierder out on the road. It was like hail and farewell. Kerouac was the old star. Kesey was the wild new comet from the West heading christ knew where.'

35

Diana Trilling in *Encounter* and featured in dozens of magazines and TV documentaries. The slogan 'Haight is love' reverberated from Atlanta to Hawaii, from Colorado to the East Village. Woolworths sold hippie wigs, airmen daubed hippie insignias on their fighter planes, agencies offered charter tours of hippie locales, correspondents in German newspapers revealed that 'hippies are not human beings' and protested at their desecration of sidewalk cafés.

The Grubbla in Stockholm, Futenzoki (Crazy Tribe) in Tokyo and scattered youth groups all over the world did the hippie thing. There was intense international feedback. Timothy Leary, with customary enthusiasm, has written: 'For the last few years, America has been on a Magical Mystery Trip, planned and guided by Englishmen ... the American Psychedelic movement is almost completely a British import.' Leary traces it back to the British Raj (of all things): 'They went there to mind a colony but many of them got their minds colonised by smiling Krishna, the aphrodisiac Love God ... the English in India got turned on.' Which would have been news to Rudyard Kipling, the Indians and Her Majesty's Army ...

Contemporary British reinforcement of the US psychedelic scene is less obscure. The Beatles released 'Sergeant Pepper' with its cryptic track '*L*ucy in the *S*ky with *D*iamonds'. Paul McCartney contributed towards the £1,800 full page advertisement in *The Times*, calling for the legalisation of marijuana, and announced that he had discovered God through LSD, although it later transpired that he meant the Maharishi. Parliament was told that 'No honourable member has not at some time taken a soft drug,' (H. P. G. Channon, Southend West) and Mick Jagger, arrested after a tip-off from the *News of the World*, was acquitted after a flagrant sub-judice editorial in *The Times*.

Towards the end of 1967, the first flush of hippiedom was on the wane. In the UK, brave little be-ins were washed out in Slough, Hull and the West Country. Sid Rawle, the leader of an ultra-hippie cult, the Hyde Park Diggers, was

36

gaoled for six weeks for non-payment of maintenance to his wife. (She: 'I'll give him beautiful thoughts.') Frankie Vaughan launched a campaign to stop the spread of hippie influence. 'Hippies are leeches on society,' he said at a public meeting, rejecting a proferred chrysanthemum from a leech in the audience. In Redditch, Worcestershire, the Establishment hit back at hippies by banning bells from the Gaumont Cinema. UFO closed down a month later, so did the world's first psychedelic shop, after a loss of £2,140. The Thelin brothers proclaimed the death of the hippie movement and made plans for an open coffin to be borne through the streets of Haight-Ashbury filled with remnants of beads and beards. They also announced the birth of the freebies ('we want to concentrate on how it feels to be free every minute of the day'), a new movement which expired soon after reaching the afternoon editions.

The hippie movement wasn't dead, of course, it was merely the end of the phase of press glamorisation and the dulling of the universal love ethic which had characterised a generation's over-enthusiastic response to its own sense of collective identity. The graphic obituary came with the double murder in October '67 of East Village hippies Linda Fitzpatrick and James 'Groovy' Hutchinson. She was a wholesome upper class drop-out, he was an amiable tattooed drifter who had 'beguiled Linda into life in hippieland.' *Newsweek* reported after the murder: 'Almost overnight, the East Village seemed aswarm with parents searching for some of the 9,000 runaway children believed to be leading the hippie life in New York.' Although there had been other hippie murders, such as that of Haight-Ashbury's celebrated pusher, Superspade, it was Linda and Groovy who symbolised to the press, public and hippies alike, the bitter finale of flower power. Their deaths proved, according to one New York hippie, 'that you can't find love in Sodom and Gomorrah.' An accusation which met with scant sympathy from those who believed it was the hippies who founded Sodom and Gomorrah in Haight.

Breezy obituaries of hippiedom predicted that 90% of the 250,000 domestic flower children would 'return from whence they came', many carrying an 'insatiable need for drugs'. Imagine their surprise when two years later, 500,000 of them turned up at the Woodstock Festival. Civil authorities were so scared when they heard reports of how many people were on their way to hear the quintessence of American rock music, that they decided to declare the Festival site a disaster area ... a move which proved unnecessary. There was not even a hint of the animal violence and senseless destruction, which would logically have been expected from such a large crowd. A large *normal* crowd. But these were 'neurotic' types of children ...

Yippee!

But in that busy October month of 1967 while flower power wilted, a new movement was born. It was not to hit world headlines until the following August, when America, in the form of Mayor Daley of Chicago, was taunted into revealing its true colours and the strategy of revolution was dragged into a new dimension of bawdy comic fantasy. This was the Youth International Party ('Yippee! Yippee! Say it loud and you'll see what we mean.') which was to absorb the thousands of hippies who did not opt for the only other major alternative—a retreat into the exploratory isolation of communal living. The most publicised event of the October march on the Pentagon was Norman Mailer's arrest on the steps thereof, but the most significant was the inauguration of the (then unnamed) yippie strategy. Marshall Bloom's report in *Liberation News Service* was as portentous as it was enthusiastic:

'Something's happening, and you won't know what it is, General Jones, because you think that only Angry Mothers and bearded students march, and that hippies stay in

38

Haight-Ashbury and the East Village. Look out your window on October 21 and freak out at what will be marching towards the Pentagon:

Not only thousands of straight, concerned citizens but a whole huge separate hippie flowery march. Quick! Grab a shot of scotch, maybe even a double shot, General, if it helps you, because you won't know how to deal with what you're going to see and hear:

Swamis, indian men, people with water pistols (passed out free), noise makers, hundreds of skulls on poles, flower banners. And groups. The Jefferson Airplane, Mother Earth, Med Rivers, The Fugs, CIA Change and The Rhinoceros. And thirty theatre groups, including the Bread and Puppet Theatre and the Surrealist Minority ... all stopping along the way to do guerilla play-fare.

And there aren't going to be any 'leaders' or 'marshalls' like there will be with the rest of the March, General, so there won't be any individuals you can order. Abbie Hoffman, who is helping to arrange it, says that the hippie parade will be entirely separate. At 11 a.m. everyone who is at the Jefferson Memorial will just start marching across the Bridge.'

Whether actual events surpassed or disappointed these expectations, depends on your reading of 'How I Lost the War at the Pentagon', in Abbie Hoffman's important joke, *Revolution for the Hell of It*, where he describes attempts to exorcise and levitate the building, concluding 'the peace movement has gone crazy and it's about time'. The essence of future yippie confrontation was here. The ingenious exploitation of media: sensationally exaggerated advance publicity which no one believed but which inevitably created the sort of mood which was bound to precipitate those events anyway. The children who gaily unzipped the flies of military police guarding the Pentagon would soon be throwing money on to the floor of the New York Stock Exchange and nominating a pig for President.

The yippies are politicised acid freaks, or as Paul Krassner once put it: 'they're hippies who've been hit on

39

the head by a policeman.' Doped, they stumbled into politics backwards. Instead of painstakingly acquiring a textbook ideology and seeking to feed society into its vision machinery, the yippies found their politics and their freedom through a lifestyle. They extracted their world view from an intense, electrifying generational communion, which taunted authority, and like a poultice, brought out the worst of it. By abolishing the distinction between theory and action, the yippies were to challenge not only the cliché hypocrisies of the White House and the Pentagon, but also the dogged, atavistic weekend-seminar ploys of the stolid New Left.

The
Devil
to
Pay

On the Thursday afternoon of Easter 1968, Rudi Dutschke was shot in the head, jaw and chest as he left the Berlin headquarters of the SDS (German Socialist Students' Federation). Over the next four days the country exploded with a fury unknown since the last days of the Second World War: horrific clashes occurred with police, and in a dozen cities the Springer press was stormed. It was less than a year before, during the Shah of Iran's visit that thousands of young people had been shaken from their dreamlike involvement in Konrad Adenauer's 'Economic Miracle' to swell the ranks of the Extra Parliamentary Opposition (APO). These riots gave APO a new solidarity and pumped extra potency into its most active ingredient, the SDS. After the earlier demonstrations, the Director of Police was packed off on a permanent vacation and both the Senator of Internal Affairs and the Mayor of Berlin resigned. While some of the components of the Extra Parliamentary Opposition wish merely to revitalise parliament, the most militant seek to overthrow it altogether and replace it with a loose, decentralised network of councils comprised of workers and intellectuals. Support for APO has been stimulated by despair of the antiquated German educational system, the outlawing of the Communist party, the tacit complicity of the government in the Vietnam war, and the dictatorial National Emergency Laws, which in May 1968, propelled 50,000 people into the streets.[18]

As his promoters are ever fond of emphasising, Marx has made something of a comeback in the past two years, but it has been the three brothers of the same name who have given the youth movement its infectious irresponsibility, channelling it in the most unexpected directions. Like the yippies who appeared consistently before the former House Un-American Activities Committee (HUAC) and its successor, dressed as Indians, Viet Cong, Santa Claus and Hallowe'en witches ('to cast a spell on the proceedings'), Teufel and Langhans, founders of Kommune K, dressed for court as if for a masquerade ball which the trials more or less became.

Prosecutor: 'It is normal procedure here that the accused stand up.'

Teufel: 'Unfortunately I don't feel like standing here all the time. Since I have so many court cases, it would be bad for my health ... '

They consented to be medically examined only if 'the members of the court and public prosecutor will also have a psychiatric examination ... ' (Teufel). 'The same persons will have to undergo an intelligence test of which all the results will have to be extensively published' (Langhans).

At one time, Teufel was expelled from the SDS for 'sham radicalism' and the fact that he was welcomed back five months later, indicated more of a change in the mood of

---

[18] Under these laws, the Government can, in cases of self-imposed emergency, curtail travel, tap telephones and intercept mail, restrict parliament, and grant every citizen the Wallace-like right to 'resist attacks on the constitutional order.'

the politicos than any sobering of the communalists. The day before Dutschke was shot, an Arts Laboratory was founded in Berlin, to be, like its UK antecedents, a centre for happenings, fun, the new culture and madness. The German Underground press derives more from hippie journalism than from the grey earnest periodicals so beloved of the New Left.

The idea of people living together creatively in cheap apartments had spread (by October 1969 there was said to be at least 100 communes in Berlin) and there was a manifestation of other activity associated with the Underground side of the revolution, such as the creation of integrated social work schemes which tackled everything from local evictions to adventure playgrounds.

In 1968 there appeared everywhere in Berlin the slogan 'A gun in your right hand — a joint in your left', and Felix Scorpio reported in *IT* on April 11th, 1969:

'Of course, the real change on the scene here has been the dope revolution. In the last six months everybody has turned on, all the Communards are stoned out of their heads, leaving only the straight, unimaginative ideologues to make the speeches. Berlin is alive with heads dropping acid and STP in cinemas, parks, buses, and this too is a kind of revolution, and an interesting antithesis to America, where pot came first and politics followed. Here the mellow influence of the holy weed has really blown many minds — some of them into oblivion, others into a rethink over that whole dogmatic bit.'

If pot is a belated addition to the protest scene, there is another manifestation which is chillingly contemporary: violence. The injuries of police were said to outnumber, for once, those of the demonstrators six to one, when students and 'rockers' rioted in November 1968. A German Underground newspaper commented: 'One hundred and thirty cops now have a hole in their head. Few can complain about that.' In other centres of rebellion, Molotov cocktails were

42

everywhere, and an SDS spokesman has warned that those not prepared to throw them 'do not belong with us'. Judges have been threatened with acid (sulphuric) and American buildings have been damaged.

The gun and the joint: both smouldering.

The
New
Left Bank

Following the Easter riots in Germany, French student militants called meetings of support. They declared that Dutschke's would-be murderer was not a solo fascist, but all those 'carrying on a monstrous slander campaign' against students protesting Vietnam. In fact, write the Cohn-Bendits, 'the action of the German students had repercussions far beyond the borders of the Federal Republic. One result was the 22nd March Movement—for the first time French students found a common platform and forgot their factional differences.'[19] And so, the movement, in an atmosphere of daily conferences and debates, beginning with a wholesale rejection of the examinations system, moved on to occupy the Sorbonne, swept up 50,000 university and school students (who one night, built 61 barricades) in bloody battles with the police, later escalating, by mid-May 13th to a general strike of 10 million workers, which paralysed France both emotionally, and for a time, administratively.

Each man learns his own lessons from the events of Paris. It showed that the workers, the classic agency of change, had not been beguiled by promises of a whiter washing day and colour television. The supposed vanguard of capitalism's overthrow, the Communist Party, was seen to be a nervous adjunct of repression. For thousands, one night behind the barricades proved a more effective political

[19] *Obsolete Communism* (op. cit.).

43

education than fifteen years in the library. For young
people everywhere, who experienced Paris through hearsay
and the Sunday papers, the unique and most heartening
aspect of that joyful inferno was the spontaneous, fluid and
libertarian manner in which it was stoked up. That same
characteristic which confounded and irritated the 'more
mature' observers – the team from the London *Observer*
called it, 'the extravagant camouflage of poetry, sex and
nonsense.'[20]

Camouflage? Or a vivid proclamation, breathtaking in
its implications, that the kids were not interested in a bigger
slice of the cake – only in stuffing it down everyone's throat.

In Paris, London and Berlin, Cohn-Bendit talked Marx,
but acted vaudeville. 'There is only one reason for being
a revolutionary ... ' say the brothers Bendit, in *Obsolete
Communism*, their own record of events, ' ... it is the best
way to live.' An observation no doubt confirmed by Danny's
own swashbuckling experiences, not the least of which,
according to informed rumour, was to have laid, while a
student at Nanterre, the daughter of a member of de
Gaulle's cabinet.

Two days after the occupation of the Sorbonne, Jean-
Jacques Lebel, France's first homegrown hippie, who had, a
year before, shocked tourists at St Tropez with a production of a Picasso play which incorporated nudes, psychedelic slides and on-stage urination, stormed into the Théâtre
de France at the Odéon, to participate in the grandest
'happening' of his career. The Odéon occupation is dismissed as the 'tourists' revolution' but it was the first time
the revolt engulfed non-university territory. The wardrobe
department was ransacked and dozens faced the tear gas
dressed as centurions, pirates and princesses. The Théâtre
came into the streets. Confused, all-night, ruleless debates
took place in an atmosphere which turned the Odéon into a
cross between a doss house and an Arts Laboratory. Lebel

[20] *Red Flag, Black Flag* (op. cit.).

aimed at demolishing 'even the Left', and was 'trying to, beginning to, reinvent the concept of life, language and political expression itself'.

Long before May 1968 in almost every other West European city, there were exchange centres for Underground newspapers, massive pop-music freak-outs, communal crash pads and a billowing hash scene. Paris stayed drab fifties, and beat. In November 1967, I watched a batch of English psychedelic missionaries try to turn on the French at the Palais des Sports with an explosive mixture of pop, plastics and poetry, but the young Parisians soaked themselves glumly in beer and called for Johnny Hallyday. And yet, in those mystical days of May, the walls of Paris were suddenly emblazoned with slogans—a mixture of the surreal and psychedelic—'we are inventing a new and original world. Imagination is seizing power ... I take desires for reality because I believe in the reality of my desires ... Ten days of happiness already.' The ghost of Trotsky may have been parading the banks of the Seine, but he was stoned.

Students from the Beaux-Arts produced 350 original designs and 100,000 reprints in a few weeks. They lacked the dazzling, electric immediacy and technical originality of hippiedom's counterparts, but they were innovatory in both content and method of production—anyone could submit designs, everyone could vote which ones to produce. The poets of Paris were the International Situationists, who have attained a similar state of frenzied anti-doctrinal comic anarchism to the yippies, though suckled on Dada, not LSD. They hit the streets with their spray cans and clowned seriously over the Sorbonne loudspeaker system.

In November 1966, this same freak show of anarchists, in the wake of the apathy of the 16,000 undergraduates of Strasbourg University, had manipulated their own election to the left-wing students' union and founded a society for the rehabiliataion of Karl Marx. They plastered the walls of the city with a surrealist comic strip, *The Return of the*

Duritti Column (later published throughout the international Underground press) and announced plans for dissolving the students' union. The most provocative incident, the one which made world headlines, was the publication and distribution of a pamphlet which, as the preface to the English edition put it, 'pours shit on student life and loves (and a few other things)':

'Art is dead, but the student is a necrophiliac. He peeks at the corpse in ciné clubs and theatres, buys its fish fingers from the cultural supermarket. Consuming unreservedly, he is in his element; he is the living proof of all the platitudes of American market research; a conspicuous consumer, complete with induced irrational preference for Brand X (Camus, for example) and irrational prejudice against Brand Y (Sartre, perhaps).'

'These students have insulted their professors,' thundered the Rector of the University in reply, 'they should be dealt with by psychiatrists.' The International Situationists dealt with the Rector by closing the student psychiatric clinic. The Strasbourg incident was the first rumblings of European student revolt.

The Autonomes of Zurich

After Paris, student uprisings spread with a velocity and a geography difficult to document fully. Although the fact that the insurgents are usually described as students meant little even in Paris, a great proportion were aimless youths, beats, travellers, mercenaries and criminals.

Take, for example, what happened when 10,000 young people attended a Jimi Hendrix concert in Zurich. The music—the usual delirious, steamy mixture of black power and masturbation—ended after midnight; public transport had closed down and to keep warm, people made bonfires in the street out of garbage. Without warning, Zurich's police force attacked, swinging their truncheons, and unleashing their dogs. The police violence and brutality (a cliché of generational clashes these days) so shocked the staid city elders that they gave the victims permission to use an empty chain store as a meeting place. Thousands of young people flocked to it, and in a welter of all-night discussions, echoing the events at the Odéon in Paris, it was decided they wanted a youth centre, and they gave the City Council two weeks to find a permanent place. The council's offer of two workmen's huts on the outskirts of Zurich was declined, and two weeks later the police removed everyone from the store by force.

After two nights of rioting (200 in hospital and 250 in gaol), eighteen public figures published a manifesto calling for an end to the 'pogrom against youth', and for the establishment of Autonomous Youth Centres.[21] These 'Autonomes', as they came to be called, published hundreds of posters, said to be wittier and more acidic than the French ones, as well as 100,000 copies of a youth newspaper distributed free.

'But
what
can
a
poor
boy
do...?'

In 1968, with the French Government no longer in full

[21] For a fuller account see Bradley Martin, *IT*, October 18–31, 1968.

possession of its faculties, a British Surrealist Group distributed a manifesto headed: 'WE NEED YOU, COHN-BENDIT BECAUSE ... We are fed and watered by the State's Almighty Hand, and do exactly as we are told ... We are superior to all foreigners who are (a) oppressed, (b) untrustworthy, (c) violent, (d) backward, (e) far away ... Although we don't believe in God, we let him make our laws and frighten our children ... We are very, very frightened.' To these would-be impresarios of revolution, the 'State's Almighty Hand' in the form of the British Broadcasting Corporation delivered not only Cohn-Bendit, but over a dozen other young student leaders as well. From Belgrade to Berlin, Milan to Madrid, New York to Tokyo, the BBC had ransacked the world's barricades for its forum on student power, and on a balmy afternoon at White City, there seemed to be more professional 'leaders' than there could ever be masses to follow them.

However, the Herculean task of promoting student revolution in England was not left entirely to the BBC. Dashing envoys from the Latin Quarter appeared in London, including students from the College des Beaux-Arts, who planned to launch a poster co-operative at Chalk Farm's Roundhouse in imitation of their own successful precedent. At the request of some of these destitute expatriates, the Free France Committee was launched to relieve their distress. With mail-outs, hand-bills, and a one-night stand at the Mermaid Theatre, several hundred pounds were raised, with which those of us involved were forever packing off 'fugitive' young Frenchmen on midnight planes to Zurich, only to find them turning up in Kings Road a few days later, cheerfully demeanoured, and much better dressed than before.

In March, hundreds had been arrested when anti-Vietnam demonstrators attempted to storm the American Embassy in Grosvenor Square. A few weeks later, there was a violent fracas at Essex University, after which three students were suspended, inciting *The Times* to editorialise:

48

'There is a feeling these days that students are getting above themselves.' An opinion not shared by art students at Hornsey and Guildford, who promptly occupied their respective colleges. On 10th May the French took over the Latin Quarter, and a few days later, the English took over the student canteen at Crouch End Hill.

Hornsey was a personal affair. Political cliques who swooped ambitiously into its circumference were archly directed elsewhere, although the press was accepted with naïve enthusiam: 'We worshipped sexy Kathy Olsen of the *Express*.'[22] But some students were affected enough by the six week occupation to reject totally the élitism entailed in the concept of 'art colleges' and indeed, art itself: 'I say shit on their art world … It is totally irrelevant to the lives and struggles of the great mass of population and it is the inheritance of the years of acceptance of the myth of the "artist" as being the lone spirit, free from the mundane pursuits that govern most people's lives, and born radical, the free liberal thinker, sitting up high creating his works in an attempt to communicate the ideas of a superior mind to the philistine public.'[23] So wrote Kim Howell, whom I was later to meet at a time he was taking 'art' in the form of cinema back to his own community, a Welsh mining village, and enjoining the people there to shoot-their-own-thing.

Britain's Underground, while generally ambivalent toward student disruptions, warmed to Hornsey (the sitters-in designed a front and back cover of *IT*), somehow sensing an affinity of purpose. Later that year, the Underground's snowballing 'new culture' enterprises curiously complemented the aesthetic agitation of the art collegiates —the explosion of Arts Laboratories. Jim Haynes had launched his experimental workshop in Drury Lane in July 1967. By the end of 1969 over 150 Arts Lab organizations had been announced, to be linked together by

[22] *The Hornsey Affair*. Penguin Educational Special, p. 50.
[23] *ibid*, p. 71.

49

a videotape network and financed by a Trust.[24] These centres, like the art college sit-ins, are a rejection of the chic gallery, dilettantish, whiz-kid, polka-dotted art-as-a-commodity philosophy, and in the case of Guildford art college, student sitters-in have their ranks swelled by visitors from the local Arts Lab, Hare Krishna chanters *et al.*

It is by interlacing the country with such outposts of cultural revolution that the Underground has consolidated itself in the UK in the past two years ... Arts Labs, local underground magazines, crash pads and BIT the 24-hour information and co-ordinating service, which is little more than a telephone surrounded by stoned optimists, all suffering, as someone once said of an unfortunate actor, from delusions of adequacy.

Legalise Pot rallies, free pop concerts and burgeoning head shops are evidence of an evolving counter community; not as sensational as the Amsterdam legal-pot paradises or the US hippie-cop confrontations, but in their own plodding evolutionary way, providing a solid, communal basis for the ultimate and inevitable change in lifestyle.

Those in London on October 27, 1968, for the massive anti-Vietnam march who had long hair or a vaguely intemperate air had difficulty in dining at Lyons Cafeterias[25] or Wimpy bars, or even acquiring taxis. Shops and banks were ostentatiously boarded up, newspaper offices were under extra guard — all in response to the front page promise in *The Times* that 'a small army of militant extremists plans to seize control of certain highly sensitive installations and buildings in central London ... '[26] an

[24] A detailed list of Arts labs, and related phenomena, by regions; can be obtained from BIT Information Service, 141 Westbourne Park Road, London W.II. BIT now links up with US switchboards and boasts an Intergalactic Medical Service, and a Food Commune run by "2 lovely liberated ladies" who serve porridge daily for 8 pence.

[25] In September 1969, after the London Street Commune squatters were removed from 144 Piccadilly, Ronald Lyon donated £1,000 to the Police Benevolent Fund, 'in thanks for the police action'.

[26] *The Times*, September 5, 1968.

allegation which injected into the massive anti-Vietnam demonstration, a delicious aura of importance.

The London School of Economics was intermittently under siege. Early in 1969, militant students forced its closure for several days when they demolished iron barriers installed by the administration: a lesson not wasted on the authorities at Essex University, who, when libertarians defiantly conducted a Revolutionary Festival there in February 1969, discreetly faded into the cloisters. There were no threats, no police, no wardens – a situation which left the militants, according to a not unsympathetic report in *Solidarity*[27] – 'baffled and frustrated. For the first time in its history the movement could no longer assert its identity and demands in a purely negative sense.'

A year later, some students took the hint and tried to accentuate the positive. The outcome provides a salutary guide to the comparative skills of US and UK revolutionaries. Not long after rioting Californian students set fire to a branch of the Bank of America and destroyed it completely, three Essex students set out to do the same to Barclays Bank and failed even to light their molotov cocktails, much less their objective. They were sent to borstal reform school.

The administration's persistence in this matter was part of a pattern of general toughening in response to nationwide disturbances resulting from the discovery of secret student files. Liverpool University suspended nine students for participating in a two-week occupation. One boy was expelled, and when told of his sentence produced an imitation pistol and fired three caps at the Disciplinary Board. They are said to have immediately dived under the table. The appalling paradox of 100,000 homeless people and 500,000 vacant homes – many of which were scheduled to remain empty for years – gave rise to the London Squatters' Committees. These groups of young radicals,

[27] *Solidarity* No. 18. Vol. 5.

notably in Ilford and Notting Hill, began moving home-less families into unoccupied premises and invited the councils to provide rentbooks, receiving instead bailiffs and private detectives with private armies. Redbridge Council in Essex, spent over £2,000 wrecking remaining unoccupied cottages under their control. Despite the shaggy, bearded appearance of the squatters and the com-munality of their living arrangements (enforced by the necessity of permanently defending their occupied territory), the press and even the police were relatively sympathetic. Yet when hippies applied the same technique—not to homeless families, but to themselves—the long arm of the law reached over the barricades and through the front door.

In London's Drury Lane, there is an abandoned build-ing, scarred by fire, bandaged with sheets of shiny gal-vanized iron. Emblazoned in red on a crumbling, peeling pillar is the slogan: THIS WAS HOME. Not a time-worn testimonial from a grateful guest of this onetime flourishing hotel, but an epitaph to an Underground communal squat-in. Weary of the dozens of drop-outs using the Arts Laboratory as a permanent crash pad, and inspired by the success of the squatters' movement, Jim Haynes finally broke into the condemned hotel at which he had 'stared stupidly' for two years, and with the help of drop-outs began cleaning, painting and redecorating the building. Fifty police and two reporters soon arrived, flushing out the two hundred non-paying guests. Now the building stands use-less and deserted, an ugly memento of bureaucratic idiocy.

An even less successful Underground squatting venture occurred in St Ives in Cornwall, where 400 local residents surrounded a decayed council house occupied by the floating beat population, a traditional feature of the St Ives landscape. This beatnik's Alamo was the culmination of months of harassment from the council (who had filled the concrete defence bunkers on the beach with bricks and oil) and vigilante groups of residents (who roamed the streets after pub closing time in angry gangs) all bent on eradicating 'promiscuity' from their otherwise idyllic village. The beatniks involved are the last surviving examples in England of a species rapidly becoming extinct, and should be protected by a Wild Life Association, not exterminated.

Czechago

'Our children have come home,' chortled election advertisements in the US press, when Senator Eugene McCarthy knocked LBJ asunder in the New Hampshire Primary (March 1968), 'suddenly they have come back in the mainstream of American life.' But the mainstream turned out to be a lonely tributary, which ran its hopeful and uncertain course to the Democratic Convention in Chicago, where, having stranded a multitude of disillusioned navigators, it dried up. Besides, many children had not come home at all. They were preparing for Chicago in ways less reassuring to those who regard party politics as the secular equivalent of the search for the Holy Grail. While other dissident groups were still brooding over blueprints,[28] the yippies, determined to fuse together New Left and hippie elements, were already engaged in a headlong assault on the media:

Over the remaining months, the yippies' Youth International (let's have a ... ') Party—a chimera without any political tradition or ostensibly, any coherent philosophy, operating from a dilapidated New York office, without financial resources, without a network or even a

[28] (The day after a yippie-police clash at Grand Central Station, Easter 1968), Abbie Hoffman, Jerry Rubin and Paul Krassner went to Chicago to meet New Left & Black groups, who were then formulating Convention week tactics. The Walker report wryly recalls: 'So while the "Left" continued to debate whether or not they were coming to Chicago and what they were going to do when they got there, the yippie organisers took a positive attitude—they were coming, to be sure, with music and myth and with their threats to disrupt the city.' *The Walker Report. Rights in Conflict.* Signet Books, 1969.

branchline of brother organisations, without a master plan or a master—helped mobilise not only the thousands who poured into Mayor Daley's city in August, but indelibly branded the imaginations of millions who experienced Chicago second hand. The secret weapon? Understanding media. Unlike most radical groups, eschewing the press or issuing them with dry facts and pompous resolutions, later wondering why they're not published or complaining of distortion if they are, the yippies *relied* upon that distortion, and exploited it; comprehending its myth-making potential and resolutely weaving a seductive spell of fiction and fantasy which, by the very act of publication, gained a compelling credibility.[29]

Among the fantasy-realities the yippies predicted for their Festival of Life: the simultaneous burning of draft cards by 100,000 people; the collection of everyone's money in communal barrels to buy food for all; the infiltration of right-wing crowds with short-haired yippies who would make pro-yippie speeches and statements; the disruption of traffic by staging a mass stall-in of vintage cars on the express ways; the shanghai-ing of delegates in cars disguised as cabs in order to dump them in Wisconsin or other places far from the Convention; the use of yippie call-girls who would seduce delegates and dose their drinks with LSD; the insinuation of agents into the kitchens of Convention hotels to drug the food; the staging of sensational rock concerts ('Definitely coming! The Beatles, Bob Dylan, The Doors, The Who, The Monkees and the Smothers Brothers'); the release in the streets of greased pigs, one of which would be nominated for President ('and we will kill and eat him. And we will say to America: "You nominate a President and he eats the people. We nominate a President and we eat him." '); the capture of all petrol

[29] This is not to underplay the role of the National Mobilization Committee to End the War in Vietnam which after the Pentagon demonstration was asking its members as early as November '67, 'Can we do better at the Democratic National Convention in Chicago?' (*Liberation Magazine*) and invited 250 delegates to a preliminary meeting in Illinois in March '68.

stations in order to flood the sewers and set the city alight; 10,000 naked bodies floating in Lake Michigan and mass copulation on lakeside beaches; the bombardment of the Convention Amphitheatre with mortar fire; the recruitment of a battalion of sexually athletic yippie males to rape the wives and daughters of convention delegates.

There were set-backs. McCarthy's youthdrive, LBJ's de-escalation of the war and his exit from political life, the grandiose if belated entrance of Robert Kennedy ... all drained incentive from the yippie cause. But in June came Kennedy's death, bestowing upon the yippies the kiss of life and a will to survive resistance from both the New Left — whose attitude to the psychedelic left was once compared to that of the little old lady who, upon catching sight of a looning longhair, muttered, 'then I'm *for* the war'—and from the hippie communities who feared a massacre:

'You enter at your peril.' Lawrence Lipton.

'The non-violent course followed by Gandhi and Martin Luther King is an ideal toward which we must strive. The alternative may be an unprecedented period of barbarism. I'm not going to Chicago this August'. Eugene Schoenfield, M.D. (alias Dr Hip-pocrates)

'This is an urgent appeal to your readers to do their summer grooving in the mountains or at the sea rather than at the Yippie Convention in Chicago.' Digger Bill, writing in the *East Village Other*.

For 10,000, the promise of free rock groups, Hubert Humphrey and the slaughter of Pigasus, if nothing else, was a greater enticement than Digger Bill's scenic counter-attractions.

The débâcle of Chicago[30] finally revealed to millions of TV-watching Americans that hippiedom meant more than wearing beads to the neighbourhood barbecue, and that student protest was more than a new kind of pantie

[30] See Appendix (i) Doing it on the Road.

55

raid. They saw their sons and their daughters (beyond their command) getting their heads bashed in, not merely to sabotage the election of a computerised superstar, but also to flaunt religiously an alternative mode of existence. The two sides were ranged against each other like protagonists in a medieval morality play. Who represented Good, and who Evil? Mayor Daley (an Irish Catholic who went to mass every morning, rarely drank and disclaimed violence) and his merry men? 'This Puritan with absolute powers', said *The Times* of London, 'was outraged by the yippies and hippies in Lincoln Park. Heaven alone knows what dark and terribly immoral things he thought were going on under the trees.'[31] On their part, the hippie-yippies were equally outraged by Mayor Daley and the dark immoral things going on under every American's nose. Their attitude to the values of Wall Street, White House and Pentagon were exquisitely symbolised by the refreshment they tendered Chicago's overworked police force — sandwiches filled with shit.

Abbie Hoffman has likened the yippies' participation in the Convention to a high powered commercial bursting into the middle of a dreary TV epilogue. 'We were an advertisement for revolution. We were a high degree of involvement played out against the dull field of establishment rhetoric.'[32] Judging from consumer reaction, the yippie 'advertisement' was a copywriter's dream.

**Test
Drive
a
Revolution
Today**

'Revolution' became the most popular consumer product

[31] *The Times*, August 31, 1968.
[32] *Revolution for the Hell of It.* Dial Press, 1968.

since the T-model Ford ... *test drive one today. Out accelerate your rivals in a special custom-built vehicle or choose from three basic 'Revolution' styles — all part of the famous 'Movement' range:*

1 *Student Internationale: with New Left drive, collapsible steering and comfy sit-in support for fellow travellers.*
2 *Acid-Cool Underground model: On full 'speed' the only sound you can hear is the top 40.*
3 *Ghetto Guerrilla: Black powered, brakeless, best used when destination seems impossible.*

As the sixties sizzled to a close, 'revolution' was on everybody's lips, which in many cases was where it remained. Banks advertised vacancies for bearded accountants ('although long hair might be vetoed on the grounds that it gets caught in our computers.'), Omar Sharif played Che Guevara in a 20th Century Fox wide screen quickie. (Fox prided itself on its objectivity and visual accuracy. Close attention to Fox's detail, however, observed Jeffrey Shero, writing in *Rat*, reveals that Sharif is wearing US Army issue buttons), and the Beatles, Rolling Stones and even Elvis Presley pressed the switch marked 'Social Conscience' on their Moog electric sound synthesisers. Intrepid teams of reporters who had once 'lifted the lid off the great hippie hoax' found themselves being hastily dispatched to sit-ins and strikes, left-wing conventions and occupied gymnasiums to prepare their 'horrific exposés of revolting students'.

In April 1968, Columbia became the first private university in the US to be captured by students. Five buildings were seized for a week. A college dean was held prisoner for 26 hours. The President's office was occupied, and confidential files xeroxed and published in the Underground press. Other novelties, later to become standard features, included the autonomous barricading by the previously undemonstrative black students in Hamilton (renamed Malcolm X) Hall, a goodwill visit by hundreds of High School students from the local community (Harlem) and that silver-haired head of Stephen Spender, cautiously

57

peeping over the barriers. Of Columbia, a post-graduate student had observed that 'a powerful, prestigious, patrician American university had in ten days been shaken to its knees,'[33] and over the next two years, as the 60's lurched to its climax, there was, to borrow a phrase from Mr. Jerry Lee Lewis, *a whole lotta shakin' goin' on.* Within two months of Chicago, 200 Berkeley students were being arrested for protesting the regent's refusal to credit Eldridge Cleaver's experimental lecture course. November found 600 police swarming into San Francisco State College during three days of turmoil over the firing of a Black Panther teacher. In January 1969, the US correspondent of the *Guardian* reported that ' ... a series of protests to dramatise demands for greater control of curricula by members of racial minorities has mushroomed into a full scale revolution marked by guerrilla warfare.'[34] But he hadn't seen anything yet. Within a few days of this assessment, Governor Reagan declared a state of 'extreme emergency' on the Berkeley campus, and over the next six months, America's universities exploded like a chain of fireworks factories:

The mid- west

Demands for a black studies department at the Wisconsin State University, Madison, were met with tear gas, fixed bayonets and the State Governor's flair for the obvious "national student unrest is being directed by someone who has different ideologies than we have." – *The Times* February 14).

---

[33] Arnold Beichman, *Encounter*, July 1968.
[34] The *Guardian*, January 21st, 1969.

The
deep
south

One thousand black students at the Southern University, Baton Rouge, Louisiana, traded rocks, bottles, fire bombs and tear gas with hundreds of police after a campus visit by former student H. Rap Brown.

The
east

On the anniversary of the first Columbia upheaval, 100 militant members of the Afro-Asian Society (later renamed the Black Liberation Front) made a particularly picturesque impact when they occupied the Willard Straight Hall at Cornell University. After a massive student strike and bungled efforts by fraternity jocks to rout them, the blacks came out of the building and on to the cover of *Newsweek*, draped with bandoliers; brandishing rifles, shotguns and homemade spears.

All
over

In May, over 200 colleges throughout the US were reported to be in the throes of uncontrolled student demonstrations, centering in most cases around civil and minority rights, Vietnam and the draft, and faculty links with military and business research requirements. Sometimes, the adminis-

59

trations conclusively repulsed the students with tough, swift action as at the Second Columbia[35] and San Francisco State College, while on other occasions their generalship was distinctly Italian. When 400 students occupied the central administration building of it-couldn't-happen-here Harvard, which until the SDS occupation had managed to camouflage its links with the CIA and the Pentagon (napalm was invented in its chemical laboratories, and tested on its football fields), President Pusey's instinctive and unoriginal response, was to call in the police, who indiscriminately clubbed everyone in sight, including one spectator in a wheelchair, and hurled students down a stone staircase. The august campus was plunged into such a state of shock and solidarity, that within ten days almost all the SDS demands were conceded.[36]

Long time favourite flashpoints of youth rebellion were not entirely upstaged by these insurrectionary incursions into virgin territory. The local community in Berkeley turned a long unwanted vacant allotment into a playground and people's park, planting apple trees, shrubs, turf and corn, building swings and sandboxes. The University, jolted into a display of proprietary rights, foiled the pirate gardeners with an eight foot high barbed wire fence—the sort of device already proven to have inflammatory effects upon students by the Governors of the London School of Economics. Berkeley became a city under siege, with one onlooker killed, another permanently blinded, over a thousand injured, many of them shot in the back with bird

---

[35] Where on May 2nd '69, the President rapidly cleared an occupied building by initiating court procedures.

[36] The University agreed to:

1 Begin negotiations with the government to drop the Reserve Officers Training Corps as an accredited course of study.
2 Encourage faculties to 'share the interests' of black students.
3 Increase efforts to build new homes for Cambridge and Boston residents dislocated by university expansion.
4 Ensure rents charged in Harvard-owned houses are below the market level.
5 Continue its attempt to get criminal charges against the rebellious students who took over the hall dropped.

60

or buck shot; helicopters, tanks, and 2,500 National Guardsmen with fixed bayonets and 700 demonstrators bundled off to the courts.

As in the case of Harvard, Cornell and Columbia, the term 'student' covers a multitude of agitators and of the twelve who formed The Committee of the Peoples' Park, only one turned out to be an undergraduate. Hippies, yippies, street-people, SDS professionals and their girl friends, drifters, drop-outs, women liberators and band wagoneers — too heterogeneous a group to be trapped successfully in a newspaper headline, they are all stock characters in the protest parade.

In the last few years there has not only been more protest, but it's been more committed. Paul Jacobs' and Saul Landau's *New Radicals* of 1966 (who felt it 'pitiable that people need artificial stimulants to "turn on" ' ... emphatically could not 'accept sex without a deeper commitment to the other partner' and who 'when they picket the White House to decry the brutal war in Vietnam ... warn also that the Viet Cong will betray the South Vietnamese people') seem by present standards as out of style as an army of drum majorettes and mastodons. Now, 'we are all Vietcong'. On that historic occasion in February 1960 in Greensboro, North Carolina, a handful of pacifist blacks at a lunch counter demanded whitey's coffee. In May 1969 the same town had become a battlefield for 100 *armed* negro students holding out against helicopters, nausea gas and rifle fire from the encircling National Guard. In Berkeley it had once been a fight for free speech. Five years later it was a fight to free land. 'The Telegraph Avenue community which has long been in the forefront of the nation's youth revolt, built a park, People's Park, on land the University said it owned because it had a piece of paper. Land in this society is owned by men rich enough to afford such pieces of paper ... Either the land belongs to the University or the land belongs to the people.'[37] A sentiment echoed by

[37] *Outcry* No. 2 — a newspaper published from 'Occupied Berkeley'.

London's Piccadilly squatters who, four months later, occupied an 18th-century mansion not far from Buckingham Palace.[38] At the time, both 144 Piccadilly and People's Park were empty and wasting, awaiting the hack inspiration of speculators. In London, the people had nowhere to sleep. In Berkeley, they had nowhere to plant flowers The community confiscated the land for the people. On it, they stayed together. And played together.

Paradise
Now

Against this background of international youth rebellion, which terrified the rest of the world into cultifying such safe, established, mature family figures as astronauts and yachtsmen, society was subverted in another way. By a new culture which is alive, exciting, fun, ephemeral, disposable, unified, unpredictable, uncontrollable, lateral, organic and popular.

The old culture is infinitely divisible, élitist, remote and detached — Nazis wept over Wagner then turned on the gas. Counter-culture is warm, total and all-involving. Hippies dream through a light show, then turn-on each other. In Chicago, the yippies did not oppose the Democrats with an isolated political programme, but with an alternative way of *life*. This merging of politics and way of life, is fundamental to the Underground, and also entails total commitment to this new culture. 'Revolution must break with the past, and derive all its poetry from the future' — The International Situationists. 'Our programme is cultural revolution through a total assault on culture, which makes use of every tool, every energy and every media we can get our collective hands on … our culture, our art, the music, newspapers, books, posters, our clothing, our homes, the way we walk and talk, the way our hair grows, the way we smoke dope

[38] See THE POLITICS OF PLAY.

62

and fuck and eat and sleep—it's all one message—and the message is FREEDOM'—John Sinclair, Ministry of Information, White Panthers.

Accept a fundamental behavioural and political unity and most other distinctions begin to crumble. The desire to end authoritarian divisions between people is manifested in the creation of Action Committees (Paris), Affinity Groups (New York), and Kommunes (Berlin), where everyone participates in the decisions affecting them. Schoolboys are seeking to abolish prefects. Soldiers have formed unions to check the authority of officers. Women are uniting to overthrow male dominance. That is why the happening is an archetypal Underground (anti) art form, because it jells a *variety* of seemingly distinct categories. It is where the Muses—art, poetry, dance, music and drama—have an orgy, with the audience joining in, and the whole operation essentially unrepeatable, beyond preservation, in constant flux and out of anyone's full control.

A girl appears on the stage naked to the waist. In front of her belly is a TV-sized movie screen. It lights up with a film about caber tossing, undoubtedly boring in any other context. Through the screen bursts an inflated plastic tube, which, fed between the girl's legs, snakes into the front stalls. As the great phallus thrusts deeper into the dense corps of the audience, the girl stands mute and expressionless. With the hint of a smile, she produces a razor and severs the base, eliciting an involuntary chorus of masculine groans. Smoke billows through the resulting aperture. A previously unnoticed object above her head repeatedly explodes. The happening is over.

Counter-culture is a brain child of the new technology. Light shows require sophisticated electronic equipment, from adjustable stroboscopes to multi-injector projectors finely synchronised with the rhythms of rock and roll. And just as rock depends on a *group*, so products of the new culture are symbiotic; they work better all together. The most memorable experiences underground are when you connect to the music, to the light show, happening and movie simultaneously, while being stoned and fucking all at the same time — swathed in stereo headphones, of course.

Underground theatre groups are breaking new ground in other ways, embodying the international, equisexual, tribal, nomadic lifestyle implicit in the Movement (e.g. The Exploding Galaxy, The Human Family (UK), La Mama Troupe, The Living Theatre (US)).

When the Living Theatre celebrated *Paradise Now* in London in June 1969, the critics tumbled triumphantly over each other in their bid to demonstrate that Julian Beck & Co. failed to conform to the classical requirements of legitimate theatre. They can't act, they can't dance, they can't sing, snorted Fleet Street, tying blinkers to its motor car and galloping forth to measure the hurricane with a slide rule. The night I saw *Paradise Now*, Judith Malina didn't kick her legs as high as Ginger Rogers in *Mame*, angry black Rufus didn't deliver blank verse with the taut aplomb of Sir John Gielgud, but within ten minutes, most people had abandoned their seats and were roaming the auditorium tense, confused, excited and wholly involved. The Living Theatre is counter-culture in action. It is commonly judged miraculous if British audiences even humalong, like Butliners at a jamboree, yet the Roundhouse guests were randomly engaging each other and the cast in belligerent debate; some stripping, others kissing, some in a trance, others fleeing in a state of shock. This was not a cosy night at the opera—a few laughs, a few tears, home to pay the baby-sitter, a witty post-mortem over supper, back to the grind in the morning, and that's that.

The man I saw spat upon will never be quite the same. One member of the cast, frustrated by the frigidity of one section of the audience pranced about threateningly like a caged ape, shouting, 'You really scare me ... you really scare me ... ' finally spitting at a gentleman in a brown suit and drooping moustache. The man lunged furiously forward (as we are trained to do), grabbing the actor, ready to strike. Suddenly, several other members of the cast materialised, immediately assessed the situation and began to spit upon each other.

'Look at this! Spit! Does it hurt? Is it painful? It's just water. Did you want to kill him?' The spectacle of the cast of the Living Theatre bathed in each other's phlegm, and brown suit's horrified realisation of the implications of his deadly and futile aggression was far beyond entrapment in the grey, review pages of the quality Sundays.

The intensity of suppressed racial animosity has never been exposed so clearly (at least for me) as in the confrontations between the audience and the black members of the cast. The power of this experiment was not verbal, its eloquence not divisible into cogent packages of 'acting ability' 'choreography' or 'voice projection'. But when the white lady in the front row reacted to black taunts with a savage jab at the actor's balls to which he did not retaliate, one boggled at the patience and restraint of black pride and ached for the sins of one's own race—a tragedy more important than Hamlet's oedipal procrastinations. *Paradise Now* is the culmination of the troupe's years of theatrical explorations and the first work totally their own. Every performance is different, and like Heraclitus' river, you never step into the same flow twice. One's experience of it is contingent upon that random collection of variables—the audience.

This principle of indeterminacy is endemic in the Underground.[39] One of the more devoted pioneers of creation by chance has been John Cage, whose extensive efforts *not* to compose his own compositions, are legendary.

[39] Derived, like so many other inspirations, from Dada and Surrealism (cf. nudity, hoaxes, toys, satirical uniforms and laughter). Just as their anti-art antics were an attempt to go beyond art, so the anti-ideological anti-politics of the Yippies/Situationists attempt to go beyond politics.

He has made a science of the elimination of self, allowing the inspiration for the sounds he produces depend upon such things as imperfections in the paper used, the toss of a coin, the weather and whatever happens to be on the local radio station during the concert. 'You have a beautiful mind,' Cage once told a fellow composer, 'but it's time you threw it away.' Explaining his predeliction for chance, Cage has said: 'The whole idea of chance operations is that the field of awareness that's now open to us is so big that if we are not careful we'll just go to certain points in it, points with which we're already familiar. By using chance operations, we can get to points with which we are unfamiliar.'[40]

Interestingly, despite the tendency of our empiricist Western education system to suggest the opposite, chance plays an important part in the discovery of new ideas. In *The Use*[41] *of Lateral Thinking*, Edward de Bono has shown the connection of chance with the breakthroughs of modern science: indeterminate factors being instrumental in the invention of the wireless, penicillin, photography and the X-ray.[42] William Burroughs, Brion Gysin and a plethora of imitators offer cut-up novels and other self-creative delights, although the success of chance methods in these cases, except as an aid against media brainwashing, depends on the flair of those involved. The indeterminacy principle in both science *and* art have been effectively welded by recent cybernetic artist-mechanics deriving from Jean Tinguely — who talks of 'the functional use of chance' and encourages accidental events to assist in the construction of his humanoid machines which in themselves can create a drawing, a play, a tune or a poem. Because of the complexity of the random factors, repetition is near impossible. Machines can

[40] Calvin Thompkins. *The Bride and the Bachelors: The Heretical Courtship in Modern Art*. Viking Press, 1965.

[41] Edward de Bono. *New Think: The Use of Lateral Thinking in the Generation of New Ideas*. Basic Books, 1968.

[42] See also Nigel Calder: *Technopolis, Social Control of the Uses of Science* MacGibbons & Kee, 1969.

create in the purest sense, untroubled by distracting human emotions.

It should be re-affirmed that the creation of a counter-culture, in itself a haphazard, chancy and unpredictable affair, has profound political implications. For while the Establishment, with its flair for survival, can ultimately absorb *policies*, no matter how radical or anarchistic (abolition of censorship, withdrawal from Vietnam, Legalised Pot, etc.), how long can it withstand the impact of an alien culture? — a culture that is destined to create a new kind of man?

Outwardly by their appearance, inwardly by blasting their minds with drugs, rock and roll and communal sex; by abolishing families, nationalities, money and status, those of the new generation are disqualifying themselves from becoming somnambulating flunkeys of the power structure. The most intelligent of the young are dropping out. The brighter graduates ignore the contracts proffered by big business ('40% of college students show a lack of concern about making money' — *Fortune Magazine*, January '69). John Paul Getty writes panicky hard-sells for national glossies, urging young people to become businessmen — 'it's fun and rewarding' — and army recruiting advertisements have become positively desperate. Meanwhile, into the world, children are being born like they never have before. 'We want our son to be free, unprogrammed and completely unidentified with the state,' says one child's young father, who delivered the baby himself, and told no one except the Underground press. That means no birth certificate, no schooling unless the child wants it, no taxation, no official record of his existence. These children will be tranquillised by hash, lullabied by rock and roll, educated by the community. And if one of them is ever discovered by the bureaucracy? 'He will tell them he's from another planet,' advises one father.

And in a sense, he will be.

GROUP
GROPE

'The more I revolt, the more I make love.'

Wall graffiti

'Once upon a time, there was a beautiful chick. One day, she went on a demonstration at a local draft board. She carried a sign which read: FUCK THE DRAFT. All the secretaries at the local draft board screamed a little when they saw the beautiful chick's sign. So a recruiting sergeant with a strong stomach went up to the beautiful chick and asked her to please censor her sign, because the local draft board secretaries ... well, you know. So the beautiful chick dug what the sergeant was saying. She left the picket line and disappeared. A little while later she came back and now her sign read: FUCK THE D***T.'

Peace and Freedom News

'A hand on your cock is more moral — and more fun — than a finger on the trigger.'

Lawrence Lipton, *Radio Free America column, Los Angeles Free Press*

'That chick is one of the greatest anarchists of all time. She brought down a government with just one little pussy ... I can't do it with 2,000 students.'

Jean-Jacques Lebel on Christine Keeler

'It's more than just politics. You know, it's not just our demonstrations that all Germany is frightened of. It's because we're not afraid to go to bed with each other.'

Fritz Teufel

'We believe that people should fuck all the time, anytime, whomever they wish. This is not a program demand but a simple recognition of the reality around us.'

From a yippie pamphlet

Every spring, Chelsea has its flower show, Paris flaunts its fashions, New York has its garbage strike, and the press promotes its sexual revolution. On cue, as a premeditated interlude from the serious things of life, it manifests itself in bolder advertisements, franker films, dirtier books and a giddy profusion of bum and tit magazines, outrageous clothes and theatrical free-for-alls. This sexual revolution has been running for as long as I can remember, but its celebrated permissiveness, which flows fulsomely enough on to the TV screens seems rarely to spill over into the living room. The marginal increase in society's promiscuity quotient, detected by various pollsters[1] is not about to shatter the foundations of Christendom. In a brief investigation, I once discovered that an unmarried couple could still *not* (without lying), book a double room at Claridge's, obtain a chalet at a Butlin's holiday camp, migrate to Canada or book a double berth on a P & O liner ('The Government might get us for encouraging immorality,' said the embarrassed booking clerk, when pressed for an explanation.) For all their frenzied documentation of erectile phenomena, *Time* and *Newsweek* still bromide their copy with asterisks. *Playboy*, the most triumphant of the prophets of Eros, is also the most false. Neither babies nor pubic hair impair its perpetual spray-tanned landscape of thighs and silicone-swelled mammary glands.

For some, however, there is a *genuine* sexual revolution. Consciousnesses which are being 'expanded' by forbidden stimulants are undergoing modifications of another sort. There is a change in sexual style. A shift in the structure of human relationships. Seduction is obsolete. According to *The Shorter Oxford Dictionary* to 'seduce' means to tempt, entice or beguile someone to do wrong. Not even the churches consider pre-marital lovemaking wrong these days, and the prospect of having to 'tempt, beguile or entice' today's

[1] Typical is one carried out in south-east Leicestershire by school medical officer, Dr William Kind. The poll detected an 18 per cent increase in young women verbally pre-disposed to pre-marital sex since 1963 — but this almost always meant relations with their fiancé. There was actually a 10 per cent decline in the number of women who would approve 'with *any* consenting party.' The *Sunday Times* still headlined the poll on the front page as: 'GIRLS BECOMING MORE RECKLESS' (February 9, 1969).

freewheeling girls to bed is, well ... imagine having to entice Janis Joplin.

Underground sexual morality is, in its own way, as direct as the Old Testament. If a couple like each other, they make love. Table for two, boxes of chocolates, saying it with flowers, cementing it with diamonds—the flashy paraphernalia of spring courtship—seem as dated as Terry-Thomas in a smoking jacket. The ancient rituals do not apply. In Eric Berne's *Games People Play*, the first Sexual Game is LET'S YOU AND HIM FIGHT: 'The woman manœuvres or challenges two men into fighting, with the implication or promise that she will surrender herself to the winner.' Nowadays she would surrender to both—at once—and the men to each other. Surrender? Military phraseology provides more than ever, an inadequate metaphorical vocabulary for the free flows of physical affection between today's youth. One cannot offer verifying statistics. The sons of Kinsey have not yet emerged from their Underground researches to disclose that hippiedom is Peyton Place without the lies or Polynesia without the superstitions; where Jimi Hendrix meets Fanny Hill in a see-through—but they will. And yet it is not the promiscuity—a characteristic common to brothels and rabbit warrens—which is significant. It could just be possible that the sexual candour of the radical generation is indicative of a healthier, more honest overall relationship, the longing for which was naïvely embodied in that ridiculed anti-warcry, 'All You Need Is Love'.

The Beverley Sisters reflected their times with the hit: 'Love and marriage ... love and marriage. Go together like a horse and carriage.' Now it is The Beverley Sisters who have gone, together with their horse and carriage, and it is currently seen to be not impossible for love and marriage to survive independently. *Come travelling lady, stay awhile* ... sings Leonard Cohen, *Until the night is over/I'm just a station on your way/I know I'm not your lover* ... which seems a less deluded sentiment and one that expresses

73

the warm mixture of compassion and playful pragmatism which characterises the love-making style of a generation. In earthier language, a New York Underground editor, Paul Krassner, once gave a hint of the new sexual consciousness with an obituary of his favourite comedian: 'Lenny Bruce and John F. Kennedy had something in common. They were both great cocksmen. I couldn't help thinking, amongst other thoughts one has at the death of a friend, that there must have been a special throb of mourning among all the ladies who had been limited partners in the countless less-than-one-night stands of comedian and President alike.' So the randy skeleton is removed from the cupboard and hung trophy-like over the fireplace. It's groovy to be carnal. And there's nothing more carnal than the Underground, although to communicate its unique sexual atmosphere is like trying to teach a blind man to play hopscotch.

I meet a moderately attractive, intelligent, cherubic 14-year-old girl from a nearby London comprehensive school. I ask her home, she rolls a joint and we begin to watch the mid-week TV movie. It is *The Woman of the Year*, and Spencer Tracey, almost against his will, finds himself in Katharine Hepburn's apartment. (He kisses her, flashes his look of 'there's a volcano bubbling inside me' and hurriedly leaves.) Comes the Heinz Souperday commercial, a hurricane fuck, another joint. No feigned love or hollow promises. (Tracey, at work the next morning, reads a note from Katharine: 'You left your hat. What's the hurry?' He smiles, and the wheels of matrimony grind into operation.) A farewell kiss, and the girl rushes off to finish her homework.

'One looks forward to being buried with a hard-on.'
Angelo d'Arcangelo – *The Homosexual Handbook*.

74

The first public declaration of a private revolution in sexual attitudes came with the hippie environments, outdoor love-ins and indoor freak-outs, which in 1967 began reverberating from Golden Gàte Park to Tottenham Court Road, from Prins Hendrikade to Formentera. At UFO, although it took the morbid libido of the *News of the World* actually to unearth a couple 'intimate on the floor, as hundreds of other youngsters milled around them ... so normal and everyday that it wasn't even a peep show,' the atmosphere *was* overwhelmingly and cheerfully sexual. A few hundred yards away in Soho clubs, tight-lipped accountants guiltily watched stag movies—at UFO young boys and girls could see the same kind of films and laugh uproariously.

At the yippies' Easter be-in in New York I witnessed a similar mood of easy eroticism. Strangers kissed, young mothers breast-fed children, and an occasional couple fucked on the grass.[2]

On the Leidesplein in Amsterdam, one must be respectably dressed, wealthy and unaccompanied to see a strip show, while at the nearby Paradiso the topless Indian girls swaying to the music are as natural as the sales of Lebanese hash. The films, happenings and theatrical sideshows at Underground venues are as uninhibited as the audiences. At London's first Arts Lab (which closed in October 1969) it was not unknown for a play to reach its climax at the same time as the audience is reaching theirs, all unconcernedly intertwined with each other.

William Reich believed that happiness and goodness are directly related to sexual well-being. Unless a culture is sexually healthy, all efforts to build a good society are

---

[2] A year later it was the odd gang bang. 'A young long-haired girl stripped and danced in the warm rain ... her friends stood by while a dozen young men raped her in an animal frenzy. Of the hundreds who gathered to watch, no one helped her, no one cared. Someone even stole her clothes. As she staggered around dazed and muddy, all she wore was a four-letter word painted on her forehead: "Love".' The *Sunday Mirror* reporting an incident in Central Park, Easter 1969. Raped?

doomed to fail. While everyone has his own idea of what constitutes sexual fitness, many believe that the Underground freedom from inhibition is the first step *en route* to a new, freer and happier civilization. Meanwhile, if nothing else, the libertarian sex ethic boosts recruitment: 'I'm only in the Movement to meet chicks and get laid anyway,' as Krassner again puts it.

There are, of course, communal groups dedicated to pursuing the sexual revolution to its extreme conclusion, but more often they constitute, as with drugs and art, a fringe and unresolved affair. Julian Beck of the Living Theatre, which tries to represent in its lifestyle as near as possible a microcosm of the new society, has said:

'There is in the community a great deal of free sex and inter-community sex. There are many short-lived love affairs within the community: there are also peripheral or outside love affairs of a transient sort – when they become very steady or very close then the person usually comes into the community. There is a reasonable amount of multiple party sex – three four five six people … sex. There is a reasonable amount of male homosexuality and a smaller amount of female homosexuality.'[3]

Although it is the Underground element of the Movement which most explicitly identifies sexual freedom with total freedom, everyone revels in the euphoria engendered by a 'revolutionary situation'. The Cohn-Bendits recall of the Paris May days: 'In such moments of collective enthusiasm, nothing could be more natural and simple than a warm relationship between the boys and girls. Everything was easy and uncomplicated.' One of my own friends put it more succinctly. When asked what he remembered most about his days behind the barricades, he replied: 'In one afternoon I fucked fifteen girls.'

Like Sweden, the Underground has no prostitutes, and like Denmark, it has abolished pornography.

[3] *Some of IT*, p. 158.

When the Boston subterranean newspaper *Avatar* was hounded by obscenity-hunting authorities, the paper retaliated with an imposingly calligraphed double spread of four-letter words. The New York Underground tabloid *Screw* visually rivals its Copenhagen counterparts and proclaims its determination to 'legitimise pornography.' *Screw* applied unsuccessfully for Press photographers' credentials to attend President Nixon's inauguration. 'We had planned to photograph the shit house in the White House and possibly even get a shot of President Nixon taking a leak, to determine whether he drips those last few drops like other mortal men.'[4] *Screw* was the first of a spate of much maligned, frequently busted New York sex tabloids inspired by the success of Underground newspapers. It possesses a crucial quality which excludes it from the generally accepted category of pornography, and indeed distinguishes it from all standard, sex-drenched fare — a boisterous, self-directed sense of humour. ('*Screw* is a two-bit whore,' boast their ads.) New insight into that metaphysical conundrum of how to objectify aesthetic judgments has been achieved with such games as the 'Female Fuckability Test' and *Screw*'s invention of the Peter Meter, a graph for the reviewer to record, in inches, the erection potential of pornographic films. ('It is a useful tool for those of you unable to read but sufficiently adroit to comprehend the numbers system.') Obviously the refreshing irresponsibility of such an approach will prompt a severe counter-reaction — as it did in the case of the play *Che*, by Lennox Raphael, another Underground press luminary.[5]

Along with mass demonstrations and cannabis smoking,

[4] 'How they stopped *Screw* from swinging at Dick's balls.' The United States' Senate Press Gallery wrote: 'This rejection does not reflect unfavourably either upon you or the organisation you represent.'
Screw No. 4, February 7, 1969.
[5] An off-off-Broadway play, *Che* was notable for containing the first official act of sexual intercourse performed on stage. This and the additional sight of members of the cast touching each other's genitals proved too much

77

'obscenity' provides a popular pretext for confrontations between Authority and the Movement. All over the world Underground papers are harassed and prosecuted for infringing sexual by-laws.[6] The international flow of such publications, and of Underground books and films is interfered with by crusading Customs men. Despite such celebrated victories in English courts as *Lady Chatterley's Lover* and *Last Exit to Brooklyn*, the proprietor of Brighton's only avant-garde bookshop is quietly convicted of selling obscene prose and poetry. In August 1968 he was fined £230 plus 180 guineas costs. When passing judgment, the Chief Magistrate, Mr (Laughing Jack) Ripper commented: 'May I say how appalled my colleagues and I have been at the filth produced in this court, and at the fact that responsible people, including members of this university faculty have come here to defend it. It is completely indefensible from our point of view.' The filth produced in court included the usual bulwarks of the sex literature battlefront, plus *OZ*, *IT*, *East Village Other*, *The Seed* from Chicago, *Evergreen Review* and Tuli Kupferberg's *Fucknam*.

Yet it is not readers of the Underground papers who are perturbed by linguistic frankness, but outsiders. It is only when journalists complain, 'But why print so many four-letter words?' that one notices that any have been printed at all. Consider the reaction of Mr Derek Jewell, jazz critic of the *Sunday Times*, to a rival columnist's recommendation of *Rolling Stone* magazine: 'He can't mean the recent and

---

for the New York police who arrested the entire cast and charged them with public lewdness and sodomy (April 1969). Kenneth Tynan's *Oh Calcutta* which opened shortly afterwards, depicts fucking and nudity on stage somewhat more satirically, has not run seriously foul of the law and is making a fortune for all concerned. 'Which isn't necessarily to put it down: it does present sex more honestly than previous commercial hits and it will free the theatre (and its predominantly middle-class audiences) that much more. But will *Oh Calcutta* ever see the debt that it owes to *Che*?' John Wilcock, *Other Scenes. OZ* 22.

[6] For more details, see chapter on the Underground Press.

not untypical issue can he, where most readers' letters on its first inside page contained one or both of the commonest four-letter words? Exhilarating? Creative? Well, maybe as energetic as writing on lavatory walls. Great gobs of prose elsewhere in the magazine heavily featured the same dreary words, and others similar ... '[7] This observation would astonish the young readers of *Rolling Stone*. Such 'dreary' words appear as randomly and validly as 'music' 'love' 'Elvis' and 'rock'—it is Mr Jewell who seems upset by their presence, not the readers. A new generation has emerged who find that such terms contain no suggestion of prurience. They can barely remember the grey days when Norman Mailer had to invent the euphemism 'fug' for his G.I.'s in *The Naked and the Dead*. Nowadays they buy magazines with titles such as *Fuck You—a Magazine of the Arts*, listen to the word shrieked out on pop records, or employ it with the utmost tenderness to invite their lovers to bed. The unequivocal use of language is not confined to the Underground literary scene; it is part of the everyday politics of the Movement. Obscenity is traditionally among the armoury of weapons employed by the alienated and frustrated. What is different about 'man fined for making obscene remarks about Premier', the *Book of Rugby Songs*, Jonathan Swift and the manic bawdiness of today's militants, is that the latter use it *en masse* intersexually, instinctively, not only to entertain their listeners but as a matter of policy to communicate animosity to their enemies *and* love for each other.

'Fuck', with its dual connotation of sex and violence, is used publicly as a prefix for any undesirable person or object. The 'One two three four—we don't want to go to war' of former days is now a simple 'Fuck Nixon'. As the crowd surged past the *Daily Express* building in Fleet Street during London's October '68 anti-Vietnam demonstration, a spontaneous mixed chorus of 'Fuck the bourgeoisie' aggravated the hostility of the onlooking staff. Most

[7] The *Sunday Times*, March 29, 1969.

79

of the Movement's street-actions, on whatever soil they occur, resound with a monosyllabic vocabulary that would have delighted Lenny Bruce had he not been sent to the grave in a fight for his own right to speak as plainly. Not that Father Bruce would always have been particularly impressed by the wit or originality of today's militants; an example of which is the song written by Eldridge Cleaver and taught to radical students as a finale to the first of his disputed lectures at Berkeley—three identical verses consisting of Fuck Reagan, Fuck Reagan, Fuck Reagan, an anthem which, even by Eurovision Song Contest standards, lacks inspiration. The incidence and intensity of this 'filthy' language will increase as the new revolutionaries become less concerned with immediate issues and more determined to create total social chaos. If anarchy is an essential precursor to the creation of an alternative society, so the deflowering of language, rendering it obscene and useless is merely part of the process of structuring a new one.

'Gillian Freeman's article on page 94 includes the use of a four-letter word. I am still slightly shocked.'
Paul Johnson, Editor of *New Statesman*. June 1967

Nudity has also become a popular and effective diversionary tactic. It instantly communicates a commitment to total rehabilitation of social values, it makes news, and surprisingly discourages arrest.

Albert
Hall,
London
1968.
The
Alchemical
Wedding.
An
'evening
of
silence'.
Underground
Christmas
freak-out.

Soft, fraternal, expectant atmosphere. A fair-haired girl in the audience disrobes. The management, already alerted by the whiff of incense, calls the police. Four eager young constables move in for the arrest. The crowd solidifies around the culprit, many beginning to remove their own clothes. Police retreat. The serene young nude watches the rest of the performance unhindered, along with the audience. Only the press continue to regard her as the centre of attraction. Meanwhile John Lennon and Yoko Ono move about under a sheet, to the accompaniment of a man playing the flute, while another gentleman, dressed in the grey of the politically conscientious, parades with a banner about Biafra, screaming: 'Do you care, John Lennon, do you care?' Over their coffee and marmalade next morning, readers of London's newspapers admired the same girl on the front pages, her tits titillatingly touched-up, and pondered the plaintive plea of the President of the Albert Hall, Sir Louis Gluckstein: 'But how do you *stop* a girl taking her clothes off?'

Innocent bystanders near the New York Stock Exchange have occasionally had their days brightened by packs of nude anti-war demonstrators. Last year seven German students stripped in Court to protest a decision by a Hamburg judge. No Central Park love-in or bust-out has ever been complete without the presence of Louis Abolafia, executive director of the East Village Foundation for Runaway Children, who campaigned for the Presidency of the US with the slogan: 'What have I got to hide?' Passers-by were invited to 'travel the world with the only nude presidential candidate and his cabinet of naked boys and girls'. There have been nude demonstrations in front of IBM offices ('to protest their de-humanizing influence'), at political rallies and at polling booths.

When a *Playboy* magazine executive turned up to 'public-relate' at Grinnell College in Iowa, he was confronted by a mixed group of naked students. The demonstration was sponsored by local Women's Liberation and guerrilla theatre organisations, who claimed '(While) pretending to appreciate and respect the beauty of the naked female form, *Playboy* is actually stereotyping the body and commercialises on it. *Playboy* substitutes fetishisms for honest appreciation of the endless variety of human forms.' Photos showed attractive unselfconscious unclad students displaying the placards: 'High salaries create inflated tits.'

One of the consequences of a communal lifestyle, as the Living Theatre's experiences confirm, is communal sex. Likewise, the diffused fraternalism of today's generation resolves itself into generalised sex experiences, such as the gang bang rituals, which extend from the well documented antics of the Hell's Angels (both in the US and the UK) to the lesser known tribal rites of Australian surfies.[8] Then

[8] The enviably pragmatic attitude of this 12–16-year-old pagan beach society is evidenced by the decision of some to confine their heterosexual activity to sodomy, 'because she won't get up the duff that way.' On festive occasions, such as a surf carnival, a generous girl will 'put on a queue' behind the sand dunes for a seemingly unlimited line-up of young men. The boy on the end is said to be 'stirring the porridge'.

there are the slightly more homely 'orgies' and 'multiples'.
The former, endemic these days, in 'swinger' land, is
group sex among strangers or minor acquaintances, of a
number greater than say, five. Orgies are planned, and
usually take place in comfortable locations. The latter term,
multiple, denotes a more intimate and spontaneous affair
among close friends and/or lovers, which can be, on several
levels, a joyous experience. Although the group-grope scene
is given-&-taken for granted among the Underground, it
infuriates paperback sociologists. G. Legman in his shrill
attack on radical society in *The Fake Revolt*, reviews the
entire movement through sperm-spattered spectacles:

'How does the sexual piggery of sharing your girl or your
wife with three to six other guys, at every end of her pink
little anatomy show your rebellion against your parents'
bad old world? How does it expose the backside of your
parents' ludicrous ideal of "togetherness" for you to stand
in line to gang-bang your own undergraduate wife, with
her ass baby-oiled and her teats tattoo-painted like Art
Nouveau easter eggs?'[9]

Such games are not considered a substitute for meaningful
relationships but manifestations of the frenzied curiosity
and lack of guilt of a new generation. Legman, incidentally,
is railing against the Movement's literal interpretation of a
slogan which he himself claims to have invented – 'make
love, not war'.

Heavy-handed attempts to cash in on this permissiveness
(artificial vaginas, orgy butter, etc.) are often ridiculed
in the Underground papers, whose common-sense attitude
to group sex is summed up in this paragraph from
Vancouver's *Georgia Straight*:[10]

'Chances are that you will attend three or four more parties.
You will feel more relaxed at the next ones and eventually
try most of the things you have heard, dreamed or read

[9] *The Fake Revolt*, G. Legman. Breaking Point/New York 1967. Pp. 18–19.
[10] *Georgia Straight*. December 13, 1968.

about. You will forget to ask names and may not even think twice about sleeping with someone you don't know anything about much less have any feeling for. You will find that you can still have sexual fantasies and that V.D. is easily taken care of. Chances of lasting friendships are rare. You will still have most of your sexual and emotional hang-ups and maybe a few new ones. The hang-ups of the people you will meet may be worse. You will be more sexually aware and you certainly will be jaded to a certain extent. With relief, you will go back to sex on a private basis, not sorry that you participated in the "scene" but feeling somewhat about "organised sex" as you do about "organised religion".'

If agony columns are any guide to a community's sexual mores, the letters received by Dr Schoenfeld in his Hippocrates feature (syndicated throughout the Underground press) reveal breathtaking breakthroughs in the fields of sexual candour and curiosity. Any complications connected with cunnilingus, fellatio, urolagnia, anal-intercourse, venereal warts, vaginal farting or bestiality are here discussed in a breezy, informed, healthy, helpful style.[11] The tone of this correspondence compared with the crass pseudo-clinical horror letters of the glossy mag 'serious' symposiums leaves little doubt as to which of the two schools are truly sexually liberated. The pastimes mentioned above provide a metaphorical staircase of virginities. As a girl progresses say from *soixante-neuf* to human sandwiches, she mentally ticks off another lost hymen.

As with other Underground trends, some inspiration for the sex practices of the Spock generation stems from the activities of pop personalities. The more bizarre anecdotes are probably wishful inventions, but veracity is irrelevant. *Beliefs* spur imitation—not truth or falsity. Occasionally rumours are confirmed and the public is vouchsafed a glimpse into the private sex lives of celebrities. Remember

[11] For some examples of letters and Dr Schoenfeld's replies, see pages 165 et al.

the Rolling Stones' house party? The raiding police professed themselves so shocked by the carefree nudity of a young lady that in court they cited her behaviour as evidence that everyone at the party must have been stoned out of their minds. The rumour which swept round a delighted London at the time (sworn as gospel by a variety of 'irrefutable sources', alluded to on the cover of *Private Eye* and printed in full in US Underground newspapers) was that when the police gate-crashed, a guest was sucking a chocolate bar out of the cunt of the girl in question.

Rock music has always been associated with controversy. Denmark Street impresarios still smirk over Elvis' habit of stuffing his Levis with a piece of hose pipe. Jimi Hendrix leaves little doubt as to which sensory organ his guitar is an extension of (forcing TV cameras to feign obsessive interest in his face), the Beatles, even during their *Woman's Weekly* pin-up stage, were happily uninhibited about premarital relationships. P. J. Proby split his trousers in a Rank cinema—a short-sighted choice of venue, as he was subsequently banned from all of them. A writ was issued against Jim Morrison of The Doors by Miami police for masturbating on stage, a rather unfair victimisation when one considers that members of his audience were certainly doing the same thing.

Not all pop fans are destined to enact their sexual fantasies in the oblivion of the back stalls. Some make it to the stars' dressing rooms and beyond. Known as groupies, these people are the sexological phenomenon of the sixties, as fascinating as anthropological specimens as were the Trobriand Islanders in their day.[12] Suffice here to point out that they are young, mostly female, plentiful, direct ('I'm over 18, I'm clean, let's fuck'), and everywhere that pop stars are (' ... we even found them in Singapore'— Jimmy Page). In Sydney during the 1966 tours of the

[12] See *Groupies* prepared by Bantam Books for *Rolling Stone*. 'The Groupies', a series of LP's. ALP Records Inc. *Groupie* by Jenny Fabian and Johnny Byrne. New English Library.

Beatles and the Rolling Stones, the hungry girls outside King's Cross hotels caused traffic jams. In pop centres like London and San Francisco, groupies pose for magazines, form pop groups, and become celebrities in their own right.

Most famous are The Plaster Casters of Chicago, a cheerful double act, who immortalise pop stars' penises in plaster of Paris. One of them procures the erection, the other prepares the alginate. 'I appreciate what they are doing,' says Frank Zappa, 'both artistically and sociologically. Sociologically it's really heavy.' Cynthia Plaster Caster concurs, 'I think every girl should be a plaster caster—try it at least once. It's going to be a significant element in the revolution.'[13]

An English starfucker who is a long-time friend of mine recalls how she suddenly got the call:

'It was evident that there was a pop conspiracy to blow the minds of my generation. I was interested but not involved. I only began to understand the group symbol when I met Simon Dupree and the Big Sound in a TV studio. The place was full of smoothies and groovers being cool and calculating every move. The sounds of sucking filled the air, when these little guys blasted off, singing what was already an old number, "Reservations", I remember, and his underpants showed. And he sweated a lot. And his sound blew out all the crap and BBC gumshoes and I knew I was on his side. You know what it is like; all the technicians regard rock stars as freaks, the management regards them as charming, grubby mental defectives. They do their thing and don't give a fuck. The message is sent. When I was being dressed for some change or other in some tight little thing that squeezed all my boobs up, I looked up and they were all looking at me ... with a kind of hot innocence and I suddenly realised that groupiedom was possible.'[14]

[13] *Ann Arbor Argus*, April 1969. From an interview recorded while she was in Ann Arbor, Michigan, to cast the MC 5.
[14] The Universal Tonguebath, A Groupie's Vision. *OZ* 19.

What's the difference? What is it about this generation's compulsively uninhibited sexuality that throws the contrived decadence of yesterday's famed botany teachers into such tragi-comic perspective? All that Hemingway stuff about 'cojones', Connie Chatterley's absurd 'blood and gut' lusts, Gide's constipated Immoralising, Sweeney Erect or de Beauvoir recumbent—all about as relevant today as a Victor Sylvester fox-trot. Marshall McLuhan detects the difference and ascribes it, of course, to television. He argues that as youth are becoming more tribalised: ' ... the electric media, by stimulating all senses simultaneously, also gives a new and richer sensual dimension to everyday sexuality that makes Henry Miller's style of randy rutting old-fashioned and obsolete.' (Interview in March 1969, in *Playboy*, a magazine which ought to be coupled with Miller, as that nude student demonstration at Grinnell indicated.)

It is not surprising that such a generation should find itself insulted by the synthetic rituals of a middle-aged Erotica Incorporated. The 'Ladies' Page' of one Underground newspaper, for instance, protested the 'degrading mindless-boob-girlie-symbol' of Miss America contests. 'The Pageant contestants epitomise the roles we are all forced to play as women. ... where the nervous animals are judged for teeth, fleece, etc., where the best "specimen" gets the blue ribbon. So are women in our society forced daily to compete for male approval, enslaved by ludicrous beauty standards we ourselves are conditioned to take seriously.' THE UNBEATABLE MADONNA-WHORE COMBINATION.[15] With such protests women are seeking an

[15] *Helix*, September 1968. Other objections to such contests included: RACISM WITH ROSES—Since its inception in 1921 the Pageant has not had one Black finalist, and this has not been for a lack of test-case contestants. There has never been a Puerto Rican, Alaskan, Hawaiian or Mexican-Indian winner. Nor has there ever been a *true* Miss America—an American Indian.
MISS AMERICA AS MILITARY DEATH MASCOT—The highlight of her reign each year is a cheer-leader tour of American troops abroad—last year she went

87

extension of that same equality that they have already achieved within the Movement. Or *partly* achieved. In a feature on The Sexual Revolution in *IT*,[16] Emmanuel Petrakis, President of the Sexual Freedom League exhorts women to 'learn to give yourselves a bit more ... even if you don't enjoy it at first, why not give pleasure to others? Given time, you might learn to enjoy the experience.' (Or indeed, if given Mr Petrakis.)

Such sad, senile condescension is no more appropriate to today's girls than the much publicised motion adopted at the 1968 Trades Union Congress (Brighton), acknowledging after 100 years, the PRINCIPLE of equal pay for equal work. The Labour Government's announcement a year later that it would enforce equal pay by the mid-70s, was considered 'revolutionary' by the press. While such controversies are irrelevant to the Movement, its own members are not blameless. By relegating their girlfriends to mimeograph machines and petty cash boxes, they have revealed the standard set of anti-female prejudices — to which the new women have rousingly retaliated. 'Liberated women don't cook,' warned the girls who occupied the halls of Columbia University, and these days it is less dangerous to suggest, 'Let's fuck,' to a militant companion than request she brew the Ovaltine. Several fiery and youthful Liberation Leagues have been established in the US and UK (a London chapter publishes a magazine called *Harpies Bizarre*) and an encounter

---

to Vietnam to pep-talk our fathers, husbands, sons and boyfriends into dying and killing with a better spirit. She personifies the 'unstained patriotic American womanhood our boys are fighting for.' The Living Bra and the Dead Soldier. We refuse to be mascots for murder.

THE WOMAN AS POP CULTURE OBSOLESCENT THEME — Spindle, mutilate, and then discard tomorrow. What is so ignored as last year's Miss America. This only reflects the gospel of our society according to Saint Male: women must be young, juicy, malleable — hence age discrimination and the cult of youth. And we women are brainwashed into believing this ourselves.

THE IRRELEVANT CROWN ON THE THRONE OF MEDIOCRITY.

NO MORE MISS AMERICA.

[16] *IT*, February 14-27, 1969.

with any of their recruits is rather like a US general's meeting with a member of the Viet Cong. During mass confrontations, girls are everywhere – at sit-ins, be-ins, loot-ins; 'equi-sexual with ease', although not above exploiting society's traditional conception of their roles. 'Chicks up front' is a common battle cry. The girls advance to form a disarming line of breasts against the brawn of police cordons and soldiers with fixed bayonets.

'Black women should be selective about their boyfriends and put off those who will not identify with the revolution.'
Eldridge Cleaver, *Berkeley Barb*, August '68.

An age-old female weapon has been revived with a new name: pussy-power. Some of its manifestations recall the aura of suffragette days, others are psychotically 20th century, like SCUM (The Society for Cutting Up Men) created by Valerie Solanas, who began by cutting up Andy Warhol. Her manifesto asserts what is hopefully a minority viewpoint:

'To call a man an animal is to flatter him; he's a machine, a walking dildoe ... Eaten up with shame, guilt, fears and insecurities and obtaining, if he's lucky, a barely perceptible feeling, the male is, nonetheless, obsessed with screwing; he'll swim in a river of snot, wade nostril deep through a pile of vomit if he thinks there's a friendly pussy waiting for him ... The male claim that females find fulfilment through motherhood and sexuality reflects what males think they'd find fulfilling if *they* were female. Women, in other words, don't have penis envy; men have pussy envy.'[17]

WITCH – Women's International Terrorist Conspiracy from Hell, has conducted several (black) mass demonstrations outside New York business institutions. Witches, it is pointed out, have been the original guerrillas and resistance

[17] This version is from a roneoed leaflet. A full, and slightly different version has been published by Olympia Press.

fighters against oppression down through the ages. Historically witches are seen as non-conformist, free, intelligent, joyous, aggressive, creative, scientific and actively rebellious (birth controllers, abortionists, herbalists, heads and pushers). On Hallowe'en Eve (1968) WITCH haunted the New York Stock Exchange. Nervous commissionaires barred the way while witches in black fairy tale cloaks claimed they had an appointment with the Chief Executor of Wall Street himself—Satan. ('With closed eyes and lowered heads the women incanted the Berber Yeall—sacred to Algerian witches—and proclaimed the coming demise of various stocks. A few hours later the market closed 1.5 points down, and the following day it dropped five points.' (*Rat*, November 6, 1968). On St Valentine's Day (1969) witches disrupted New York's first Bridal Fair at Madison Square Garden (a sample slogan: Love starts at Chase Manhattan) and were roughed up by uniformed bouncers who screamed: 'You're sick, you're sick, you're sick.'

'These witches knew not Marx or Engels,' goes part of their chant, 'but their conquerors knew Freud,' which is possibly an allusion to the Freudian vaginal ethic rejected by the Movement. One of the most significant conclusions of Human Sexual Response, that clinical, cinemascopic investigation into the physiology of sex, was that *anatomically* all female orgasms derive from the clitoris. Vaginal orgasms do not exist. This discovery is said to have liberated women from the Freudian concoction that vaginal orgasm is *superior* to clitoral orgasm—vaginal women being feminine, well-adjusted, maternal, while clitoral women are immature, neurotic, masculine. Whereas the achievement of the mythical vaginal orgasm depends on the penis, clitoral ecstasy is gaily independent of it. 'The definition of feminine sexuality as normally vaginal', writes Susan Lydon in *Ramparts*[18] 'was part of keeping them down, of making them sexually as well as economically, socially and

[18] To whom I'm indebted for this vaginal dissertation.

politically subservient.' While women may indeed be in the throes of freeing themselves from the vestiges of male dominance, there are as yet no widespread signs of boycott. Not at least, on the girls' part. But perhaps this female exclusiveness with its lesbian undertones, has had something to do with the surfacing of male homosexuality which in 1969 was being marketed everywhere like a new brand of petrol. ' ... the wonderful thing about it is', remarked Angelo d'Arcangelo, as he published a list of prominent living homosexuals, 'nobody really gives a damn anymore — even in print.'[19]

> 'Burroughs is getting to be a good lay.'
>> Allen Ginsberg. The *East Village Other*,
>>> March 14, 1969.

Not all the problems have been solved. Julian Beck admits that even for his liberated ensemble, 'sex is one of the most difficult areas.' This generation, which is learning to devalue property and revalue humanity, is still fettered by the concept of possession. Jealousy, while unfashionable, is not yet extinct. For all this swinging endorsement of the new ethic, young men are still caught drunkenly kissing Danish au pair girls in party bedrooms and dragged home by enraged lovers, *à la* Dick van Dyke TV comedy. And although sexual relationships flow more easily than ever before, the most that many young people ever communicate to each other is VD, which has not yet gone the way of moonlight and roses.

> 'Crabs are beautiful.'
>> Donovan

Question Do you have to be a homosexual, a woman's liberator, a witch, a Valerie Solanas, a plaster caster or an anonymous link in a copulative chain to be part of the

---

[19] Actually someone did — J. Edgar Hoover — who caused the book (The *Homosexual Handbook*) to be withdrawn and his name expunged.

Underground sex scene? No. Thousands of young people all over the world are quietly accomplishing an authentic sexual revolution without even knowing they are part of it.

When boy meets girl, within minutes of drifting off to a comfortable location, boy can be happily splashing about in girl's cunt, both of them up each other's arses, sucking and fucking with compassionate enthusiasm. No more tedious 'will she or won't she by Saturday?' but a total tactile information exchange, and an unambiguous foundation upon which to build a temporary or permanent relationship. The pot of gold at the end of the rainbow comes first; later one decides whether the rainbow is worth having for its own sake. If the attraction is only biological, nothing is lost except a few million spermatozoa and both parties continue their separate ways. If there is a deeper involvement, the relationship becomes richer, and so does the sexual experience. One way to a girl's mind is through her cunt.

AND
GOD
CHOSE
POP

'Pop is the perfect religious vehicle. It's as if God had come down to earth and seen all the ugliness that was being created and chosen pop to be the great force for love and beauty.'

Donovan, Queen

'Jimi Hendrix plays the "Star Spangled Banner" as the introduction to "Purple Haze". He does not do it as Jose Feliciano sang it at the World Series. He does it screwing the guitar and it is, I submit, a revolutionary act surely as important as getting arrested at a Humbert Humbert rally.'

Ralph J. Gleason, Rolling Stone

'Columbia Records' 'Revolutionaries' program ... is being extended through April by field demand. The program's astounding success to date has forced the label to continue the campaign, which has been one of the most successful in Columbia's history and is even exceeding the success of Columbia's 'Rock Machine' promotion of last year.

The 'Revolutionaries' campaign is an all-out merchandising program on Columbia's rock album product and has served as the launching pad for a number of outstanding contemporary artists who had debuted on Columbia in the past three months ...

The 'Revolutionaries' campaign itself has been receiving tremendous retailer and rack-jobber response. The airplay on the product has been fabulous, and the sales have been pushing the albums up the charts ... There have been special 'Revolutionaries' display racks, window streamers and posters.'

Columbia Records Press Release

'Comrade
 ... In your Vietnam issue you devote space to some doggerel by Mick Jagger, an unfortunate nothing whom the world could do well without, and more disgusting still, you couple his name on your front page, alongside Marx and Engels; something which will surely make any sincere Socialist want to vomit.'

Letter to The Black Dwarf

Some people keep photo albums, but my life is measured out with dusty 45s. 1954: First of the new unbreakable plastic mini-discs. Pop historians stress Bill Haley's ephemerality and genealogical unimportance, but the professionals know either too much about pop or too little. For millions, this record began it all. It pushed the award winning 'Volare' off the hit parades. It wooed us to see the film for which it was written, *Blackboard Jungle*, which, despite middle class insularity, subliminally planted the notion that the future really belonged to those classroom rowdies, not Glenn Ford.

At school in Sydney there was a cadet brass band, Traditionally on the last day before summer holidays, it played for the whole assembly. One year, 'Colonel Bogey' was replaced with 'Rock Around the Clock'. Everyone beamed and moved their heads in time to the music. Amid thunderous applause, the headmaster glowered and forbade an encore. Suddenly it was apparent that even over music you had to take sides (school song :'*Do not think that we'll forget/Lessons that we treasure yet*').

And those destined to grow rich from pop, hated it. Radio stations—soon literally to rock around the clock 24 hours a day, 7 days a week—desperately plugged Mr Stan Freeberg's version of 'Heartbreak Hotel' in preference to Presley's. New Zealand banned rock outright. Frank Sinatra ran with the Rat Pack and recommended wheat germ for extra potency—but when Jerry Lee Lewis married his 13-year-old cousin, he was force-fed hemlock. (Not that you can keep a good rocker down; he bounced back years later with 'High Heel Sneakers'.) Within a few months, Australia had its first home-grown rock hit. I can remember the lyrics more clearly than any trigonometry exercise:

I'm just outa school / Like I'm real real cool / Gotta shake, gotta jive / Got the message that I gotta be alive / I'm a wild one / Oh yeah ... I'm a wild one./

96

No one had their first kiss beneath the June moon. It was playing spin-the-bottle in a friend's living room to the sound of the Platters (*Oh yes! I'm the great pretender*). The first time I ever won a prize was on a TV pop show for guessing the Big Bopper's age. To celebrate the passing of final exams, I queued up to see Elvis looking for trouble in *King Creole*. The first time the Other Man beat me up, the Chiffons were No. 7 on the top 100 with 'My Boyfriend's Back'. (*You're gonna be sorry you ever were born/Cause he's kind of big and he's awful strong/My Boyfriend's Back/He's gonna save my reputation/If I were you I'd take a permanent vacation*'.) I discovered the cultural gap with a girl called Robin who—would you believe it—preferred Italian castrati and medieval Latin masses to Gene Vincent and 'Be Bop-a-Lula' (maybe she was on to something).

My pleasure dome was 'Surf City' (*Here I come: Two girls for every boy.*); 'The Mona Lisa', a song by Conway Twitty. The first time I ever met and mingled with the working class ('rockers') was at a precarious corrugated iron and timber stadium built 'temporarily' in the thirties which housed the greatest rock shows on that sunburnt earth: Little Richard, Gene Vincent, Freddie Bell and the Bell Boys, the Platters, Fabian, Bobby Darin, Fats Domino, the Everley Brothers, Dell Shannon, Bobby Rydell, Jerry Lee Lewis, Bill Haley and the Comets and Crash Craddock. Crash Craddock? Yes, a mythical figure, billed as a Nashville sensation, but actually invented by genius local promoters. *The stadium rock shows*: outside, notices warned that no one over 25 would be admitted—suspicious parents complained and it was amended to 'no one over 25 *at heart*'. All this before rock and roll became respectable; when apologies were necessary. (Ho ho, er, I'm tone deaf actually.) Despite earnest forays into Eliot, Yeats, Wordsworth and Browning and the brainwash of intellectual guilt and snobbery, my emotions were still most accurately articulated by the doggerel of Chuck Berry's 'School Days' (*Soon as three o'clock rolls around/You finally lay your burden down*), Eddie Cochran's 'Summertime Blues' (*I'd like to help you son but you're too young to vote*), and the Coaster's 'Yakkety Yak' (*Take out the papers and the trash/ Or you don't get no spending cash*) ... all panoramic in their banality, cheaply sentimental, profoundly shallow, providing asylum for emotional imbeciles, but that's the way we are; like most people in the phone book. Not Greek heroes or Renaissance scholars. For us, the coolest translation of Catullus comes nowhere near the Drifters' 'Save the Last Dance for Me'.

When the Beatles happened, the man on the beach who was forever having sand thrown in his face by the muscular bully, became a star. John Wayne mounted his mare (not without effort) and cantered off into the sunset. From then on, the pigeon-chested weaklings always got to fuck the best girls. The pop symbols mounted their guitars and rocked to the centre of the stage. To account for the tough poignant cynicism of their early music, critics have observed that the Beatles grew up in the shadow of the Bomb. To account for the manners of the sixties generation, it should be remembered that we all grew up in the shadow of the Beatles ... the Rolling Stones, Animals, Manfred Mann, Kinks, The Who and a score of other now forgotten sounds, which finally buried those panic attempts to revive skiffle, jazz, the big band, white sports coats, pink carnations and community singalongs.

Even today, people who should know better believe that 'pop and thought do not go together' (to quote a BBC producer). The Beatles proved patently that they did. As much as one forgave Conway Twitty and Tommy Steele, the notorious Peter Sellers parody ('Twit — when the carpet starts, you stop') was not an inaccurate reflection of the prevailing pop IQ level at the time. All groaned at the overdose of anecdotes about Beatle wit, precocity and irreverence, squirmed at the 'even-mum-likes-them' euphoria,

98

but thankful at the same time to have the correlation between pop and idiocy finally dispelled. Now, *The Times* music critic welcomes a new album as the 'most important musical event of the year'. Their art is intelligently evaluated, even by the unintelligent, a man from the *Sunday Times* publishes their *official* biography, and every morning, 50,000,000 kids change their minds about them.

If Mersey was pop's puberty, Bob Dylan was its political coming of age. There were previous protesters, the Seegers and the Baezs who taught us that the world outside was weeping, but it was Dylan who taught us to weep inside ourselves. You don't have to be a Liverpudlian to know Eleanor Rigby, or American to know Medger Evers, Hattie Carrol, or that South Dakota farm where *seven shots ring out* ... and ... *there's seven new people born.* Dylan's ... *mothers and fathers throughout the land ... don't criticise what you can't understand* meant *your* mothers and fathers, and that girl in 'Ballad in Plain D' with her back to your face, was a recent one-night stand. And if in his later albums his message was ambiguous, and he was quoted as saying that he only wrote protest songs because that's what everyone in New York was doing at the time, and we saw films of him harassing a party drunk like a temperance league heavy, and his lawyers threatened legal action against Underground newspapers, and he teamed up with Johnny Cash, not exactly a musical yippie, and made lofty announcements that no one was to make excess profit from his personal appearances, as he pocketed his £35,000 fee, it didn't matter. He had helped open the eyes of a generation. Nothing would close them now.

Dylan had led us to 'Desolation Row', and in 1967 a new sort of music showed us 'Strawberry Fields forever' — it was nicknamed acid rock, after the famous Monterey Pop Festival, and then instantly internationalised with the release of The Beatles' 'Sergeant Pepper'. Acid rock was flower power's jingle. A generation took to LSD, having discovered that the spiritual values of the world they inherited were bankrupt. (Later, some took to the Maharishi, having discovered that it was not the world which was spiritually bankrupt, but themselves.) Pop musicians reflected their lives and those of the people around them in their art. Groups became gurus. All the relevant sounds seemed somehow associated with acid and universal love. The Beatles, Donovan, Cream, Jefferson Airplane, Quicksilver Messenger Service, Grateful Dead, Doors, Country Joe and the Fish all celebrated the LSD experience and revived our faith in each other. In these hardened times of charred barricades, Mace and free karate classes, it seems ludicrously sentimental, but even one's most criminally misanthropic friends were somehow mellowed by mass-cult's aura of benevolence.

An entertaining example of the media's desperate attempts to come to grips with rock's mystic period is this BBC television interview with one of the Procul Harum, whose hit 'A Whiter Shade of Pale' must have orchestrated a million trips. From memory, it went like this.

Sound over suitable psychedelic slides:

> *We skipped the light fandango,*
> *And turned cartwheels cross the floor,*
> *I was feeling kind of seasick,*
> *But the crowd called out for more ...*

INTERVIEWER: Your record, 'A Whiter Shade of Pale', has shot to the top of the charts in three days. What do the rather obscure lyrics mean?

GARY BOOKER: Nothing in particular, man.

INTERVIEWER: Come now. You must have had something in mind when you wrote it.

GARY BOOKER: No ... (mumble mumble)

INTERVIEWER: You mean it was a random selection of made-up phrases?

GARY BOOKER: Yeah ... sort of ... mumble, mumble.

INTERVIEWER: But there is one line which is made to

	stand out, isn't there? The line about vestal virgins going to the coast.
GARY BOOKER:	(expression of surprise) It just happened that way, during the arranging. It could have been any line.
INTERVIEWER:	(archly) Do you regard what you wrote as good music?
GARY BOOKER:	It's just a song.
INTERVIEWER:	I suppose everyone will have forgotten about it in two weeks.
GARY BOOKER:	Sure, man.
INTERVIEWER:	Doesn't that worry you?
GARY BOOKER:	No.

Does it worry you? Rock by its very nature defies encap-sulation in words, or at least my words. You hear, see, sway to the Stones, momentarily sharing their egotistic fantasies, smelling their armpits, while the cerebrum quivers and hypothalmus shivers. 'Rock appeals to the intelligence', Chester Anderson once said, 'without interference from the intellect.'

Some
Pop
Pensées

— Unlike established culture, pop is classless, international, alive.
— Most people who write about pop have never bought a pair of high heel sneakers in their lives.
— Rock music and avant-garde electronic music are already rubbing decibels. Watch out when they meet head on.
— What England needs most is six all-night pop music stations.
— To dig rock, the less you know about jazz the better.
— Billie Holliday was great too.

— Most significant contemporary cultural experiments are associated with pop.
— Banal lyrics or a repetitive melody do not spoil rock. They can make it.
— Addicts will endure incredible deprivations to hear sub-standard rock sounds. Would Mantovani enthusiasts queue all night, sit in the sun all day, pay 30% extra for any refreshments, be bullied by bouncers, searched by police, jostled continually because the proprietor has over-filled the venue, sit through seven bad groups, endure totally inadequate toilet facilities, and be satisfied even though the view throughout has been obscured.
— There has never been a great rock movie (*The Girl Can't Help It*, *Gather No Moss*, *A Hard Day's Night*, *Help*, *Jailhouse Rock*, *King Creole*, etc., contain fascinating historical moments, but the music is still subservient to the celluloid.) *Easy Rider* points the way.
— From how a girl reacts to pop, you can tell how she feels about fucking.
— Sir Arthur Bliss, Master of the Queen's Music, once described the BBC's pop programme as aural hashish, but it's not *that* good.
— Rock groups were the first of the new nomad communes.
— If you're embarking on any contemporary subversive project, you'll have more chance of getting finance from the pop world than a bank.
— People in discotheques sipping martinis and requesting Buddy Holly medleys from guest performers know nothing about rock.
— Buddy Holly was great too.
— The lesson of Tiny Tim is that every age has its own music, much of it great, including what grandmother used to dance to, and instead of getting so generationally aggressive and self-conscious (as we all do at times) we should be getting into it. Sing it again, Tiny.
— Beethoven was great, but ...

102

- Some obsessive rock addicts have so abandoned their basic literate skills that they can't even read the labels of the records they play.
- Rock stars are like people — shits or saints.
- Simon and Garfunkel produce beautiful antique poetry.
- Jimi Hendrix is not an intellectual, but a great rock musician. (Once when shown a poster of Van Gogh, he cried, 'Wow, man! What group does he sing for?') But he once half emptied London's Queen Elizabeth Hall with incredible speed. The Young Liberals had organised a guitar-in. Everyone sat politely through the classical and folk guitar. When Hendrix came on at the end, the middle-aged arose, rattled their jewellery and stalked noisily out; demonstrating yet again that educated elders can be as intolerant and ill-mannered as their children.
- Ugly but soulful man-eating female superstars can rock the Albert Hall, and receive tumultuous applause when they warn over-possessive boys that they're not fucking their girlfriends properly. Impossible two years ago.
- The opera with the most relevance for anyone alive today is *Tommy* by The Who.
- So you know all about rock. Think again. What is the following about?

'Obviously Heraclitus contains Anaxagoras but crystallisation out of flux in music or sub-way car stability assertions might also be a different scene.

from Richard Meltzer's dissertation on
The Rolling Stones. (*Crawdaddy*)

- Rock is revolutionary. Usually the performers and promoters are not, at least consciously.
- Rock is radio's only validity. However, the medium is technically too backward to transmit it on anything but the most primitive electronic level. It's like trying to listen to the surf with a conch.
- Bankers and brigadiers hate long hair. Rock stars grew

theirs; encouraging everyone to do the same, including tomorrow's brigadiers and bankers, who will flunk bayonet practice and blot their ledgers. (According to a *Wall Street Journal* report, miniskirts are permitted by 52% of the business community as acceptable for office wear. Moustaches are accepted by 73%, sideburns by 46%, beards 26%, *and long hair is accepted by only 5% of the business surveyed.* From *East Village Other*, July 19, 1968.)

— The days of rock hysteria have gone. Phew! but not forever.

— Rock is fun; sometimes heavy; mostly playful.

— Rockaphiles can be fascists. (Hell's Angels, Teddy Boys, Skinheads, Rockers, Maoists.)

— You can judge a rock star by his groupies and vice-versa.

— Rock could become the newspapers of a cybernated future. David Bowie's record 'Space Oddity' more successfully captured the mood of the first moon landing than Norman Mailer's turgid world-serialisations.

— The rock/TV marriage *can* work. Eg: *All My Loving* by Tony Palmer, *Around the Beatles*, *Master of Pop*, by Jack Good, *Shindig*, (sometimes), *Ready Steady Go*. Beatles and Stones inserts (only!) on *Top of the Pops*.

— Don't draw conclusions from what's in yesterday's papers. When press and rock talk, it's in two different languages, with no interpreter (cf. Dylan and *Time* man in *Don't Look Back*). Their correspondents generally report pop festivals from the press bar.

— Jazz has become middle-aged, middle-brow, middle of the road; alcoholic, cool, moneyed and aren't we intelligent.

— Rock began as a series of grunts, got hung up with language, and may yet evolve into a new poetry of laughter, chants and howls.

104

Praise Marx and Pass the Stereo Headphones

—At the close of the decade the great debate raged: is rock music revolutionary?

The Paradox: The behaviour of rock stars, the mode of the music and the attitudes of many of its fans are unequivocally subversive, but the product is packaged and marketed by the establishment, at dizzy profits for all involved, and at the time of writing has failed to transform the world into a Battleship Potemkin. The controversy was further convoluted when groups waxed lyrical. The Beatles sought to be excluded from the revolutionary vanguard (*'don't you know you can count me out'*); The Rolling Stones betrayed more enthusiasm but regretted that in sleepy London Town a poor boy was restricted to vocalising upon the subject. In *The Black Dwarf*, John Hoyland, a British radical, exchanged letters with John Lennon. It was a classic New Left/psychedelic Left dialogue, and was syndicated throughout the world's Underground press. Mr Hoyland explained that the *system* is inhuman and immoral, not people, therefore all relationships within it are poisoned; it must be ruthlessly destroyed; and incidentally Lennon's music was losing its bite, unlike that of the Stones. In reply John Lennon asked what system would replace the one currently in use, and argued that what was wrong with the world was people — were they to be ruthlessly destroyed? P.S. Mr Hoyland could smash it and the Beatle would build around it. John Hoyland had the final say: 'What makes you so sure that a lot of us haven't changed our heads in something like the way you recommend — and then found out it wasn't enough, because you simply cannot be turned on and happy when you know that kids are being roasted to death in Vietnam, when all around you, you see peoples' individuality being stunted by the system.'

—While Beatle lyrics were compared unfavourably to those of the Stones (and both unfavourably to the Thoughts of Mao) the street fighting man himself was overpowered by Decca record executives, who prevented Jagger releasing 'Beggars Banquet' in the sleeve originally designed. This time-bomb album was promoted in the UK with an appalling feast at a Ye Olde Englande tourist restaurant, where waitresses dressed as yeomen's daughters encouraged tipsy men to drink mead and pinch their bottoms. During dessert, The Stones and West End magnates threw custard pies at each other amidst grovelling pressmen.

—Although pop music's claim that: *The time has come for violent revolution* echoes contemporary political events, a tradition of conscious cultural subversion had been long established by the Fugs—a group which emerged from the beat/literary New York scene. In the publishing activities of Tuli Kupferberg and Ed Sanders, in their private lives and in their music, the Fugs have always been identified with marijuana, pacifism, satire and sexual adventure. They were the fathers of the Mothers of Invention, who with Frank Zappa extended the possibilities of rock way beyond its logical inconclusions.

—In July 1969 the Underground Press received the most definitive pop pin-up since Elvis was first photographed in gold lamé. In the sunlight, four sexy young men walk across a field towards camera. One carries a guitar, three hold machine guns. Eons away from waitress-pinching business men, it was the graphical culmination of a proclamation issued earlier by John Sinclair, founder of the MC5, co-ordinator of the Trans-Love commune and Minister of Information of the White Panther Party:

'The MC5 is totally committed to the revolution. With our music and our economic genius we plunder the

106

unsuspecting straight world for money and the means to carry out our program, and revolutionise its children at the same time. And with our entrance into the straight media we have demonstrated to the honkies that anything they do to fuck with us will be exposed to their children. You don't need to get rid of all the honkies, you just rob them of their replacements and let their breed atrophy and die out, with its heirs cheering triumphantly around it. We don't have guns yet—not all of us anyway—because we have more powerful weapons—direct access to millions of teenagers is one of our most potent, and their belief in us is another. But we will use guns if we have to—we will do anything—if we have to. We have no illusions.'

The Ann Arbor judge who gaoled John Sinclair for ten years had no illusions either, at least about rock politics. Sinclair's crime was to give two free marijuana cigarettes to undercover narcotic agents. Before passing sentence, Judge Colombo said of Sinclair: 'He represents a person who has deliberately flaunted and scoffed at the law,' a conclusion he may well have derived from listening to the defendant's *alter ego*, 'Kick Out the Jams, Mother-fuckers', by the MC5. Children who took the advice of their Underground music critics, and listened fully stoned, with stereo headphones, 'volume on full ... bass three-quarters round to full, treble neutral', would have had their minds blown to anarchy and learned more about the state of American rebellion in 1969 than a thirsty scrutiny of twenty miles of paperbacks. A typical irony is that 'Kick Out the Jams, Motherfuckers', was voluntarily modified to 'Kick Out the Jams, Brothers and Sisters', for the 45 version—a 'compromise solution' said those who regard lyrics as the essence of rock.

—In Prague, pop stands for the resistance, claims a sober *Observer* correspondent, baffled by his own discovery. He saw the same kids who had thrown petrol bombs at Russian tanks score cannabis off touring British rock groups a year later. Nearly all planned pop concerts by visiting groups are cancelled by the Government for 'political reasons'. He reported:

'The Blossom Toes were in the Czechoslovak Socialist Republic to preach revolution. They preach it in their music, which is a strange hybrid of beat and electric guitar Asian jazz. "I'm a peace-loving man — but haven't you ever wanted to shout NO," they screamed, and the crowd whistles back its approval.'

Observer, 14.9.69

A
Final
Comment
on
the
Revolutionary
Controversy

Good rock stars take drugs, put their penises in plaster of Paris, collectivise their sex, molest policemen, promote self-curiosity, unlock myriad spirits, epitomise fun, freedom and bullshit. Can the busiest Anarchist on your block match THAT?

'Rock is out, dynamite is coming in — let's see what Madison Avenue does to that —'

Jim Morrison

Pop
on
a
Summer's
Day

Rolling Stones Concert. Hyde Park, London, July. 1969. The plump girl with a straw hat and freckled midriff, her eyes assaulted by bottle-green mascara, her hips as wide as a Texan's smile, sat in the very front row. She must have established her beach-head the previous morning. Now there was no one to block her view, except those, like me, in the press section. It was a minor personal triumph that on that Saturday afternoon in Hyde Park I had double-talked my way into that privileged enclosure, past two sets of heavily guarded gates, without possessing the imperative blue or red card. When I arrived King Crimson were disgorging their particular brand of fury. The odour from our collectively perspiring bodies, intensified by the hot sun, recalled less blissful moments within the school gymnasium. On the right of the stage, Suzy Creamcheese clambered up a ladder to an elevated platform which supported several loudspeakers, her ascents and descents throughout the afternoon providing a pleasant bonus for us uncomplaining Portnoys below. King Crimson climaxed with sledge-hammer crescendo and Sam Cutler, the master of ceremonies, assuming that air of strained tolerance and paternal cameraderie which was to characterise his performance throughout, gripped the microphone. He told us when to stretch our legs and when to sit down. He told us to be grateful for the great Marshall amplification team who had done such a great job with the sound, and for the Hyawatt ('that's what the Stones will be using') amplification boys—who were also doing a great job. Sam told us what to do if we fainted and how to hold on if we happened to be watching from a tree top. He read a roll call of lost children and parents and suggested they should all meet up at the boatshed. The Screw came on stage and performed as though they were disappearing through a meat grinder.

Between the front row of the press barrier and the stage, a wooden path had been constructed to enable a wheeled camera to catch the full panoramic excitement of the occasion. It was between this path and the stage that the Hell's Angels, hired as stewards, assembled themselves like a line-up of veteran chorus girls—a role they must have sensed,

because with their hands on hips, they pivoted rhythmic-
ally backwards and forwards in time to the music, in
formal, ritualistic dance. 'Hey, Sam', shouted Miss Creamcheese, 'get some Angels over this side, there's a whole
lotta crushin' 'n shov'n and man, someone's gonna get
awful hurt ... ' and for a moment the macabre line-up
would be interrupted, while in arrow formation, these
harbingers of civilised order, swept in to subdue the dissident natives, like UN troops dispatched to an international
trouble spot, though with more effect. Another smaller
group of Angels, led by Wild Child, a perpendicular,
gesticulative figure in a gruesomely ornate leather dress,
adorned by a Nazi helmet—the Auntie Mame of the pack—
made frequent forays through the swelling numbers of
pressmen, ruthlessly inspecting blue and red cards.

The wooden camera-path became an inanimate *agent
provocateur*. Profuse abuse would descend upon anyone
who trod upon it. In fairness to the Angels, their belli-
gerence was mainly skin-deep, as a later incident was to
prove, and in countless other ways, their courtesy was as
plentiful as it was surprising.

The Screw finished. Their black vocalist, someone the
Chicago plaster casters should immortalise in alginate—
leaned backwards with exaggerated lasciviousness, while
the harmonica player collapsed to the floor, coughing up
blood (it was the first time the Angels had taken any real
interest in the events on stage). He arose, the scarlet liquid
gleaming from his Ariel-white shirt. The faint look of
incredulity of the audience contrasted with disdained
detachment from the rest of the group. Was the blood real
or fake? Only his launderer would know for sure.

It was getting hotter and uncomfortably cramped. Marsha
Hunt, late of *Hair*, arrived in white buckskin, with a
flurry of attendant drones. Sam resumed announcing the
estimated attendance figures, presuming listeners shared
his excitement with each new increase. 'Wow', he said,
'some people guess the crowd's reached over half a million

... I hope those of you who can't see the bandstand heard that.' More assignations were arranged at the boathouse between lost children and parents. There were more fainting warnings. Sam then cast an exasperated eye over the press section and proclaimed that all women should be removed. 'There isn't enough room for everyone', he said, 'so chicks will have to leave ... Angels, get rid of them.' The girls protested vehemently and the Angels withdrew their implements of persuasion; chain belts and iron levers. 'You too, Marsha', called out Sam familiarly, 'give the girls a lead.' Marsha arose with a resigned smile, unmatched by the fierce gleam in her eye, and led the way. But not all the girls followed. 'Get them out,' yelled an Angel lieutenant. 'But how?' replied a younger member, miserably, 'do you want me to use force or something?' 'I don't care how you do it,' replied the former, as he himself hurried off urgently in the opposite direction. So the stubborn girls stayed, which proves either that British Hell's Angels are about as circumspect as British policemen or that the age of chivalry is alive and well, mounted on a Harley Davidson. Meanwhile Sam was busily escorting drably dressed middle-aged men with expensive cameras to plum vantage points, and Marsha safely ascended the Cream-cheese ladder, thus assuring herself of a perfect, uninterrupted view for the rest of the day.

The Family came on in brilliant form. The lead singer, with his stoned, haunted Trotskyite eyes, smashed his tambourine mid-way through the second number and then set upon the microphone, hurling it about the stage. The man in the white shirt who had supplied all the great equipment from his great factory, called for extra screwdrivers, and the scattered stage hands donned that look of extra deep concern which they save for a situation such as this. A lone, semi-naked, black tribesman, enscarved around the forehead and elbow, danced with frenzied majesty. The Granada camera lumbered around to catch a medium-close-up-of-colourful-West-Indian-being-spontaneous.

The heavy calibre celebrities began to arrive. Groupies scrambled up behind Marsha Hunt, again revealing that worm's eye view of beckoning rump. The director of the Granada team ('let's thank them for being so groovy,') clung tightly to his shooting script and histrionically paced the wooden path. A Nordic blonde in a tight Ibizan T-shirt draped in telephoto lenses, did a brilliant impersonation of Linda Eastman. Geoffrey Cannon made his entrance (no doubt on the scent of those magnetic forces he once divined so eloquently for *Rolling Stone*), closely followed by the gnomes of the Club dell'Aretusa; those expensively dressed young men, with faintly familiar faces, who follow the money like most of us follow the sun. To make way for the newcomers, the Angels joined hands and crushed us against the back of the enclosure, some of them threading their way to the barrier to administer rebuke to the girl in the straw hat, whose unbridled excitement was threatening to destroy the crowd's civilised but tense restraint. The Family went off, leaving our nerves exposed and numb. I cannot say more about their music. Those of us who are tone deaf and musically illiterate, who know nothing of contrapuntal sequences or modulated recursive riffs, have to rely on a gut response to pop – a breath-taking handicap, of course, but it simplifies judgment, which becomes as automatic as litmus paper – we either dig it, or we don't.

Sam reigned again. The crowd to the left of him was giving trouble. The crowd to the right of him was giving trouble. Would everyone stand up and move backwards one pace. No? Would the Angels mind helping away those girls in front who are jammed against the barrier. The Battered Ornaments were introduced 'at this most difficult spot' and turned out to be most appropriately named. It wasn't fair. The crowd had waited long enough. The saxophonist played like a frightened man whistling in the dark. 'Louder! Louder!' he commanded the softly clapping crowd at the end of the first number. 'No. Don't worry. Don't worry,' countered the guitarist, who rightly guessed that modesty was the only strategy available for them. Somewhere along the line, I've omitted Alexis Korner, who gave the most varied and, in a sense, the freshest performance of the day, as he let the depth and warmth of his musical past flow out into the audience.

The Ornaments made a battered exit, and the 500,000 children of summer in the Park, now squashed and impatient, calmed themselves to an expectant hush. Even the most trivial announcements contributed to the tension; there were hordes of lost Scandinavian little boys—'who can't speak a word of English'. The Angels plucked a man in a wheel chair out from the midst of the press gang and manoeuvred him to a (safer?) position near the exit. Large colour photos of Brian Jones were nailed up. Unpleasant men in tight blue suits and square-cuts inspected the stage arrangements. A safari queue deposited little brown boxes on the left hand side, from which a solitary white butterfly would occasionally flitter away. The stage had become awash with celebrities. Children frolicked, and they had that special look of belonging to someone important— for they are to the pop fraternity, what Corgis are to the Palace.

The murmurs from behind the stage escalated to a roar. Suddenly, it was Mick. In a white, bow-buttoned billowing frock over tight white pants, a gold-studded leather collar, 'NOOooo,' he shouted as the crowd began to applaud —(Sam had asked us to respect the Stones' wishes and prepare ourselves for a minute of silence for Brian Jones)—but Jagger relented, screaming, 'Yeah. We're gonna have a good time.' But first a word from Shelley. 'Cool it for a minute', he said, 'I would really like to say something about Brian.' And he began: *Peace, peace, he is not dead, he does not sleep: he has awakened from the dreams of life* ... And the girl in the straw hat, along with many others in that front row of groundlings, wept unashamedly. Pabbooooomscreech da da da aaahhhhh! Shelley was now dancing in his grave, as Mick whipped himself into a lathering frenzy, pumping, pouting, the veins running up and down his body like cables. Pabbooooooom screech yeah dadadada ahhhhhhh! jumping Jack Jagger. The camera men went berserk, the Granada heavies trundled their cumbersome machine along the wooden path, an Underground television man craned excitedly with a portable Sony video and the *Time-Life* bores flashed incessantly. The butterflies fluttered forth and Jagger began to disrobe.

The group seemed a musical mess – all awkward endings and misplaced cues. But it didn't matter; only Mick Taylor, Brian Jones' replacement, appeared uncomfortable, hiding behind his hair, solemn, remote, over-concentrating, with less stage presence than a road manager. Jagger removed his gold-studded antique leather belt and the hands of the Angels shot up like starving Biafrans. 'No', admonished Jagger under his breath, 'it's the only one I have.' He thumped the stage with it. 'Wow, we'll get it together for you ... we're not finished yet ... Are you having a good time?' Sam was crouching at one end of the stage, pointing at a spot behind me, whispering urgently to the Angel lieutenants, who ploughed through the crowd ... their quarry turned out to be luckless Miss Straw Hat, who was banging two Pepsi cans together in harmless percussion accompaniment ('bring some drums,' Mick had said in the *Evening Standard*). The cans were confiscated, just as 'Satisfaction' was overtured; 'This is the only oldie we're doing this afternoon,' and soon everyone was on their feet, reliving their earlier fucks, thrills and despair; dancing, clapping; each person an island within his own nostalgia, *I-can't-get-no ... satisfaction ...* 1969, the year that the street fighting man meets black power – a black drumming combo emerged from the wings, one in full jungle regalia, war-painted and performing religiously to camera, like a hand-picked extra from *Sanders of the River*. Jagger sparred with him awhile and then had him herded safely to a bass drum.

As 'Sympathy for the Devil' shuddered to a climax, some of the girl groundlings broke into the press barrier, and tried to claw their way onto the stage. Guardian Angels rushed forward, hurling them, like garbage, back into the crowds. Jagger was kissing us all goodbye, just as Straw Hat managed to reach the stage; 'Mick', she called up to him, 'Mick, Mick,' but she was turned back by an elegant young man with ginger hair, who knew that the likes of her were not to mingle with the likes of him. She had missed her chance; the object of her 30-hour vigil was now being escorted to a military green armoured car. 'That's the Rolling Stones. Wow! The greatest rock-'n-roll group in the world,' said Sam, who was asking the 'clever people' to put out the bonfires and inviting us to collect the rubbish—well, not us exactly; we in the special enclosure had to rush home to process our infra-red footage, pen trendy essays for hip underground media and prepare ourselves for the final night at the Albert Hall pop proms ... The luckless young lady in the straw hat set off home to Nottingham, where she packs tobacco, £7/15/- a week, including compulsory overtime.

Pop on a Summer's Night. Chuck Berry/The Who, Albert Hall, London. July 1969. The Stones had their usual amphetamine effect, and from Hyde Park I ran all the way home. Ice-cold Foster's lager greedily interspersed with chunks of magic fudge, then, with no time to wash off the afternoon sweat, set off with several friends for the final night of the Pop Proms at the Albert Hall—Chuck Berry and The Who. At that time, with The Who's pop opera, *Tommy*, every critic's rave, the night promised Stone Age to stoned age. Then and now, 1066 to the moonshot. The Albert Hall was fully booked, so for the second time that day, ticketless again, I was among off-duty pop stars and friends of friends backstage. After the warm-up group, I floated into the 'performers' bar' on a cloud of fudge.

Groupies, over-conscious of their identity since the publicity boom, sat guarding the doors, clutching bright red patent leather handbags and eyeing all suspiciously, lest they be up-and-coming bass guitarists. Mick Jagger drifted casually about, with scarcely a nod of recognition from anyone, still in his afternoon party frock. The Who knitted tightly around a circle of pale ales, their drummer, Keith Moon, laughing and clowning extravagantly. The word flashed around the bar that Chuck Berry had gone home, refusing to perform and the promoters, quivering with anxiety, were afraid to tell the crowd. Everyone savoured the panic. Keith Moon eclipsed his antics and we donned CAN *I* SAVE THE DAY? expressions. Chuck Berry expected top billing. The Who insisted on closing the show. Both refused to give way.

Rushing back to my seat, bursting with the news, I was overcome with a sound that conjured up the smell of ink, chalk, and blackboards, football dressing sheds, jiving, driving, the first kiss, parties, new phone numbers, masturbation, pimples, sports coats and arguments about staying out late ... it was Chuck Berry, already on stage, with his shiny, finely chiselled face, grinning in profile, thump, thump, thumping on that truly unique guitar, *Rolling over Beethoven ... Reeling and Rocking ... deep-down-in-Louisiana ... all-that-night-he-held-a-grudge/against-Peter-Townshend-who-wouldn't-budge ... Oh-what-a-sight-to-see-somebody-steal-the-show ... rocking and reeling* Chuck Berry, holding a guitar up to nature, thump, thump, thumping, when CRASH! from behind the stage to our left, a line of marching, charging, leathered figures, punching and kneeing their way through the few elderly commissionaires quixotic enought to stand in their way. The leaders of the line jumped the balustrade into the front of the hall, the others pouring menacingly after them like a flood of oil, to the accompaniment of the crowd's screams, the blowing of whistles ... Chuck Berry, continuing to churn it out with the determination of an eternal merry-go-round. 'Rockers' moaned the audience. A few policemen trailed through the hall only to be lost in the mêlée of leather-jacketed ecstasy.

Their disruption of the Albert Hall enraptured Mr Berry, who had energised foaming packs of humans before, but never in such a plush, sacrosanct monument to establishment culture. The rockers surged forth, reaching out to touch the shoes of the man who they had listened and grooved to for the past 15 years—pantechnicons or motorbikes outside roadside cafés, while inside they endlessly fed juke boxes. *Up in the morning and off to school*, sang Chuck, providing guitar only for the next line, while the rockers answered him, *Teacher's teaching the golden rule*, and Chuck smiled to his non-existent friends backstage, seeking someone who would share his triumph. Both he and the rockers joined in the chorus—*Hail, Hail, Rock 'n Roll, It's been going since days of old.* Chuck smiled again, the same expression of candid joy that Janis Joplin had shared with the audience some months before, when she too had conquered the invincible Albert Hall public. The rockers were climbing onto each others' backs now, dancing cock-fighters, tumbling onto the stage, troubled by the glare of the spotlight, retreating to their fellows' backs, oblivious to their surroundings, rocking backwards and forwards like steam pistons. Some of them were relics from another generation, ageing Teddy Boys in jackets with green velvet facings, comic sideburns, puffing at the pace, their faces agonies of supplication before Chuck, the Master, now singing 'Johnny B. Good', jerking across stage with that famous crab-like locomotion, sending them berserk, sucking them up onto the platform, like dandruff in the wind ...

The Who were backstage now, digging the music in the manner of Mayfair gallery owners contemplating slum art. Chuck moved rearwards, calm and unfazed by the crowding stage, rockers grinning inches away as he socked them 'Memphis', letting them singalong, ignoring the house lights turned on as an obvious signal to desist. The entire Hall was rocking now, groups in the gods, in private boxes, in pockets scattered all about the multi-tiered arena. The stage was so crowded that Chuck was forced behind the drum kit. With the finale of 'Memphis', the house lights glared brighter than summer daylight, the flower child compère was softly urging calm, 'enjoy yourself, but don't fight, that doesn't get you anywhere' (it had got the rockers past the commissionaires) and suddenly everyone noticed that Chuck Berry had vanished. The compère played records, apologising to those in the front section who had had their view blocked by the rockers. A greasy youth in a long draped jacket commandeered the microphone to deliver a message to 'all the Teds', which to the untrained ear was indecipherable, but elicited applause from the Teds and relieved smiles from hovering attendants.

I went for another drink, but England being what it is, the bar was shut. On my way back, I passed Chuck Berry, glistening heroically, bound for the exit. 'You were fantastic,' I frothed, and he responded with a rousing thank you as though it were the most unexpected and original compliment ever to come his way. 'Wait a minute, Chuck,' came a female voice, and through the swing doors emerged a predatory, middle-aged platinum blonde; gathering her coat and handbag about her, she paraded away in Chuck's wake.

It was inexplicably melancholic, she and Chuck Berry darting off alone, while inside the rockers waited desperately for an after-interval encore; 'We want Chuck, we want Chuck.'

Inside a friend said: 'That was fun, but rubbish. Now you'll hear some real music,' on which cue The Who emerged, with Townshend in white overalls hoping to dispose of any lingering nostalgia by promising: 'We'll be reliving our past too.' Accompanied by an overdose of decibels, megacycles and multi-kilowatts, The Who screamed into action, but I was mesmerised by the rockers, lounging in the aisles or dotted throughout the hall, being goaded by The Who into such expressions of acute hate that I shivered with unease. They began hurling beer cans and pennies, not lobbing them symbolically, but with the full thrust of their bodies behind them, intending to silence The Who forever. 'Up your arse', they gestured towards Roger Daltrey, loathing his freak-out frizzled hair, the Beau Brummel elegance of his hand-fringed white suède jacket, as he swirled his microphone like a lasso, responding to their jeers by casting it further towards them, like an angry fisherman aiming to crown his quarry with the sinker. Loathing him as he turned the musical clock forward before their very ears.

Having exhausted their supply of missiles, the rockers surged even closer to the stage, intent surely on hand-to-hand combat. The whistles again. The cavalry. A squad of London bobbies flanked each side of the hall, moved in and subdued the more physical declarations of detestation. 'Listen,' said Peter Townshend, 'we dig Chuck Berry too. Yeah, we dig Chuck. Now you dig us!' The vast, less vociferous majority of the crowd, culled from Chelsea, Kensington, Notting Hill, Knightsbridge and Hampstead, cheered in acknowledgement, and The Who with a flourish of naked diplomacy, went straight into 'Summertime Blues'. ... *I'm gonna raise a fuss/I'm gonna raise a holler/Been working all day/Just to earn a dollar* ... A pause, then a frenzied drive into a medley from *Tommy*. Keith Moon wallowing in his own hilariously infectious sense of burlesque, playing the drums with the same astonishing mixture of exhibitionism and realism with which he stage-manages a glass of water — hurling the contents high in the air so that it splashes down refreshingly over his face — chucking the glass over his shoulder to be caught, like his drumsticks, by an accomplice. Townshend swirling his right arm around stiffly like a windmill. Daltrey with his microphone lariat, aiming for the people in the gods. A man in ear phones at side stage, astride a complex of knobs, attempting with frantic skill to eliminate the difference between the live *Tommy* and the studio brainchild of the same name. But he could unbend now as The Who went flashing back to their origins. *P-P-P-People try to put us down/Just because we get around* stammered Townshend, careering across the stage in a parody of Berry's crablike momentum, to the amusement of the crowd, and the derision of some unconverted rockers.

And so too did Townshend, Daltrey & Moon sweep the audience from their seats, stomping and cheering, screaming for an encore, with even one or two rockers jumping up to exchange handshakes. In genuine rage, Townshend smashed his guitar, pummelled the giant amplifiers, and finally stormed off stage. Immediately the soft, silken tones of the DJ began soothing the crowd, pouring balm on agitated waters, thanking them for being such a good audience, thanking the organisation for the great series of Pop Proms, anticipating an even greater event next year ...

An unforgettable night of rock. Or was it? Doubts nagged. It was like having consumed a meal which looked, tasted sensational, but left one clogged and not content. Chuck Berry should have closed the show, of course. The primitive, organic, pile-driving jungle rhythms of rock should have – despite rock chronology – climaxed the pop proms. The evening began with a riot and ended with cerebral bedazzlement. It should have been the other way round.

Townshend's hippie summers, the rich exotic labyrinths of acid and rock – the message of his own opera:

> *We don't have to take it.*
> *Gonna break it!*
> *Gonna shake it!*
> *Let's forget it better still!*

His general 'sensitivity' ('If you're concerned with meditation ... or just grooving ... or if you're hung up on life, or just living, if you're lucky enough to have that, then pot is a way of digging it more easily.' DID IT ALL MEAN NOTHING? Chuck Berry, without whom The Who would still be panel-beating tractors, slinking out at interval, trailed by a solo middle-aged groupie. The grand plans for Berry and Townshend to jam jointly, buried in a squalid show biz tussle over—for Christ's sake—which one tops the bill. Herman's Hermits versus Engelbert Humperdinck, yes! But Townshend? M-m-m-m-m-my generation?

And looking back over that day of pop '69, that summer's day of liberated rhythms, unchained energies; the new geology, the restless, wild, electric warnings of a change in lifestyle; half a million at the Hyde Park concert—free, courtesy of Blackhill Enterprises, Granada's groovy camera team, Marshall's great amplification system and triple-priced Lyons ice-cream ... recalling the death of Brian Jones a few days before, a corpse at the bottom of his swimming pool, like a hundred other glittering Hollywood exits of the thirties and forties; the supra-élite of Hyde Park protected from the masses by wire-mesh, the fawning hipster journalists in spotted ties and ragamuffin silks ...

Pop's swing-swing version of Prince Charles' Investiture which had dazzled a different generation a few days earlier; similar solemn pageantry and shallow circumstance at a Welsh castle, the same prostrate media and indoctrinated crowds, the medieval-bedecked flunkeys matching the Hell's Angels; Prince Charles' over-praised eloquence with a useless dialect no less a gilded sham than Jagger stumbling over Shelley in the sun. Pop's own institutions become like Buckingham Palace without the efficiency, like Apple, collapsing in a confusion of crooked accountants, straw-clutching stunts, snivelling celebrity fuckers. For what? A neo-aristocracy to roam Chelsea in black windowed Minis while the pop proletariat hum doggerel and giggle derisively at their mother's Investiture porcelain. Tonight I rest my head on Jefferson Airplane's Surrealistic Pillow, praying it weaves its magic warmth, for if not ...

They're changing the guard at Buckingham Palace,
I might even go down with Alice

It's free *every*day.

> *We forsake you*
> *Gonna rape you*
> *Let's forget you ... better still!*
>
> Peter Townshend

JOHNNY
POT
WEARS
GOLD
SANDALS
AND
A
BLACK
DERBY
HAT

'Come to the edge.
We might fall.
Come to the edge.
It's too high!

COME TO THE EDGE

And they came
and he pushed
and they flew ... '
Christopher Logue *New Numbers*

'There is as much chance of repealing the 18th Amendment as there is for a humming bird to fly to the planet Mars with the Washington Monument tied to its tail.'
Senator Morris Sheppard of Texas, author of the amendment which banned booze and ushered in the Prohibition era.

'I refer to a drug which was known early in Chinese history and was then recommended as:
highly prized for possessing the virtues of relieving fatigue, delighting the soul, strengthening the will and repairing the eyesight.
... at the beginning of this century ... the same drug was referred to ... by the then Regius Professor of Medicine in the University of Cambridge ... :
'It is especially efficient in producing nightmares with hallucinations which may be alarming in their intensity. Another peculiar quality of this drug is to produce a strange and extreme degree of physical depression. An hour or two after it has been taken, a grievous sinking may seize upon the sufferer so that to speak is an effort. Speech may become weak and vague. By miseries such as these the best years of life may be spoilt."

My Lords, I regret to say that this is a drug to which all

the evidence shows your Lordships' House is seriously addicted; and the drug in question is tea.'
  Baroness Wootton of Abinger, House of Lords, Debate on Drug Dependence. March 1969

'The marijuana problem is a cultural civil war in which the traditional moral, ethical and religious conservative conforming way of thinking clashes with the new dynamic global expanded planetary awareness.'
  The Marijuana Review, June–August 1969

'Clang! Honk! Tweet! OOOoooOOOoooOOO! EEEEEeeeeEEEEEE! Zow! Pow! Sproing! Zonk! FLASH! ... pretty good stuff we have there, brother!'
  The Fabulous Freak Brothers, *Georgia Straight*

Who
smokes
marijuana?

The question is as meaningless as who drinks beer. I do. Most people I know do. Public servants, politicians, school teachers, social workers, bus drivers, night watchmen, lawyers, Indian chiefs, police officers and schoolboys do. It is easier to say who doesn't: Enoch Powell, Ronald Reagan, and pep-pilled astronauts ... make your own list. 'Pot is becoming as American as H. Rap Brown and apple pie,' notes *Esquire*. And it's as British as muffins and West Indian bus drivers, as international as a pop song.

  'So many students smoke grass today it is already unofficially legal.' Bard Grosse, director of US National Students' Association studies on drugs (1969).

What
is
cannabis?

The correct name is cannabis sativa, or Indian hemp. It

is a tall, annual, weedy herb; the male and female flowers are on separate plants. Stems of the male plant yield hemp. The resinous exudation from the female flower clusters and from the top of the female plants yields the following products:

Bhang A smoking mixture derived from the cut tops of uncultivated female plants. The resin content is usually low.
Marijuana A Mexican-Spanish name for bhang.
Ganja A specially cultivated and harvested grade of the female plants of cannabis sativa. The tops are cut and used in making smoking mixtures, beverages, sweets and cakes without extraction of the resin.
Charas The pure, unadulterated resin from the tops of the finest female plants of cannabis sativa, usually those grown for ganja. It is known to us as *hashish*.

> Adapted from *The Marijuana Papers*, edited by David Solomon. Signet Books, 1968.

What
will
marijuana
do
to
me?

Like Spearmint, it aids concentration and helps you do almost anything a little bit better. It grows hair on the palm of your hands, introduces you to a nice type black man, overcomes impotence, improves the appetite, banishes excess fat, constipation and headaches, relieves rheumatism, lumbago, backache, fibrositis, unpleasant body odours and work. In short, it's a miracle drug. A pot nation is a powerful nation. You think Zambia's moon project is a joke? Watch them reach Mars first.

Possible side effects: A feeling of dreamy nonchalance, heightened sense of awareness, bursts of introspection, mellowing attitude towards one's fellow man (especially if he's stoned beside you) and a formidable sense of contemporaneity.

'Marijuana has a corroding effect on the body and mind, weakening the entire physical system and often leading to insanity after prolonged use.'
      Harry J. Anslinger, former Commissioner of the Federal Bureau of Narcotics, USA

'I think we can now say that marijuana does not lead to degeneration, does not affect the brain cells, is not habit forming, and does not lead to heroin addiction.'
      Dr James H. Fox, Director of the Bureau of Drug Abuse Control, US Food and Drug Administration

'Marijuana tends to cause greater and more vivid imagery, shift of time orientations from past or future to present, increased free associative quality and intimacy and decreased awareness of a listener.'
      Dr Norman Zinberg, *Nature*, May 1969

Why
didn't
my
parents
smoke
pot?

They were too busy getting blind on bootleg whisky.

Samples from the *Daily Mirror* (1939):
    Marijuana drives its victims into society, forcing them to violence, often murder.
    It is easily the most sinister menace to our young people today.
    Marijuana can turn happy lives into hell.

In extreme cases marijuana can so destroy a man's character that he mixes freely with persons of another race.
South African textbook on Criminology
(quoted in *Sunday Telegraph*, 27th November 1966)

When
will
pot
be
made
legal?

Never, if the World Health Organization has anything to do with it. ('Cannabis is a drug of dependence, producing public and social problems and these controls must be continued.') 1969.
Never, if the International Narcotic Control Board has anything to do with it. ('The severity of penalties creates a social atmosphere. If they are reduced too far, and an abuse, such as cannabis becomes socially acceptable, then it soon becomes impossible not to legalise it.') 1969.
Never, if the present British Home Secretary, Mr Callaghan, has anything to do with it. In January 1969, he rejected the recommendations of the Advisory Committee on Drug Dependence (The Wootton Report), as being excessively influenced by the 'pot lobby'. Mr Callaghan is said to have not been inexcessively influenced by brewery and cigarette lobbies.
Never, if the US National Institute of Mental Health has anything to do with it. In 1969, they spent one hundred thousand dollars on a TV advertising campaign against drugs, including marijuana. Films featured the voice of Rod Sterling over a background of tense teenagers recounting sordid marijuana experiences.
Never, if President Nixon has anything to do with it, which he has. When introducing his administration's omnibus drug bill in July 1969, he claimed that dope had been 'the

primary cause of street crimes over the last decade'. Nixon proposed increased penalties all round.

'The law against marijuana is immoral in principle and unworkable in practice.'
>From a full page advertisement taken in *The Times* by SOMA (The Society of Mental Awareness), July 24th, 1967

What was the Wootton Report?
It was a comprehensive report on cannabis by the Advisory Committee on Drug Dependence, which was prepared by an expert sub-committee headed by Baroness Wootton of Abinger, a distinguished social scientist and magistrate of forty years' standing. The Report was published by the British Government Home Office in January 1969.

What were the Wootton Report's main recommendations?
That penalties for various marijuana offences should be reduced. The Report summarised the arguments for legalization as:

(i) So long as cannabis is a prohibited substance, anyone who consumes it breaks the law, and by necessity associates with law breakers; and he may associate with persons whose interest in this is far more sinister than his own. So long as cannabis is illegal there may be social pressures which lead those who are taking cannabis into forming acquaintance and experimenting with more dangerous drugs.
(ii) Adult men and women should be allowed to decide for themselves what substances they will consume and that the State has no right to interfere except when it can clearly demonstrate that damage is done to other people.

130

The Report advanced three main arguments against legalization:

(i) Cannabis is a very tricky drug, in some respects like alcohol, with very variable effects upon different individuals. Unless and until it can be shown that cannabis is less dangerous than alcohol and would be an effective substitute, it is far better that it remain prohibited.
(ii) It is likely that since the consumption of cannabis distorts the senses of space and time it is extremely dangerous if taken by someone who is going to drive a motor car. Unfortunately it is not possible to detect cannabis in body fluids yet.
(iii) Very little is known about the really long-term effects. — From Baroness Wootton's Address to the House of Lords, Wednesday, 26th March 1969.

While the press treated the Report like a bombshell from Babylon, perusal of the Indian Hemp Drugs Commission places it in a more subdued perspective. In 1894, this Commission concluded 'that the moderate use of hemp drugs is practically attended by no evil results at all'. On the question of driving while stoned, as we shall see, the report may well be incorrect. To say nothing is known of the long-term effects is an insult to the peoples of Africa, Asia and the Middle East.

'Relaxing the penalties on cannabis would be a perilous experiment. Why run the risk?'
Daily Mirror editorial, 13.1.69

A game: repeat the above two sentences, substituting for 'cannabis' words like homosexuality, reading *Ulysses*, abortion, demonstrations, etc.

'The report, one would gather from the Press, was the diseased brainchild of my own disordered mind.'
Baroness Wootton (March 1969)

131

Has Baroness Wootton ever smoked pot?

Whenever I am asked that question, I refuse to answer.
Baroness Wootton, *Sunday Mirror*, 12 Jan, 1969

*What
will
legalisation
mean?*

Government control, taxation, adulteration. Less anxiety.
An end to the lurking sense of conspiracy. Good bye to
your local pusher and the lovely Caroline Coon of Release.
Hello to high pressure campaigns from the tobacco giants
who are already reliably rumoured to have registered such
names as Nepalese Blue, Acapulco Gold and Panama Red
... the kind of joint one smokes will become a status symbol.
There'll be TV jingles, flip-top boxes, cool as a mountain
stream mentholateds ... English joints will be the smallest
and most expensive in the world and the only kick left will
be to dip them in heroin, or maybe they'll go and legalise
that as well.

'The danger in illegalising marijuana ... is that you make
criminals out of the most intelligent and sensitive people in
the country.'
Allen Ginsberg

*What
is
the
'pot
lobby'?*

It exists not as a single, identifiable, unified body dedicated
to legalising marijuana, but rather as a loose propaganda

network. In the UK there is SOMA (Society of Mental Awareness) which calls for law *reform* and is currently researching the isolated active ingredient of cannabis. LEMAR INTERNATIONAL is a similar organization in the US which publishes the *Marijuana Review*.[1] Release, established to assist people arrested for alleged drug offences, has published a report on its activities, and has built up a panel of lawyers who are skilled in the problems of drug cases.[2] The Underground Press provides the most accessible, up-to-date progress reports on marijuana and psychedelic drugs, with recipes, market trends, general advice and information on arrests. In New York on St Valentine's Day 1969, 30,000 freshly rolled joints were posted out to surprised householders with a disarming manifesto and a reminder that 'Marijuana has been used for over 2,500 years throughout the world'. It was promised that on Mother's Day, 10 joints would be sent to people randomly selected from the phone book. One lucky recipient, Jeff Shero, the editor of *Rat*, noted: 'The enclosed cigarette was lit-up, passed around, it was the real stuff, but of average quality.' In October 1968, Federal authorities were hunting a hippie who was scattering marijuana seeds on land throughout the Midwest. He wears gold sandals and a black derby hat, hitch-hiking around areas early in the morning and sowing his seeds on abandoned farms. He hides in the woods and posts a regular map showing the latest pot planting to fellow smokers.

[1] SOMA, 4 Camden High Street, London N.W.1.
LEMAR INTERNATIONAL, Box 71, Norton Hall, S.U.N.Y. at Buffalo, New York 14214, USA.
[2] RELEASE, 50A Princedale Road, London W.11. *The Release Report on Drug Offenders and the Law* by Caroline Coon & Rufus Harris. Sphere Books 1969.

Why
are
so
many
of
my
friends
boring
when
they're
stoned?

(i) Because they're boring anyway.
(ii) Because they're being brilliantly witty, intelligent and charming, or dreamy and poetic, and you are too tiresomely unstoned to understand.

If
I
smoke,
will
I
get
caught?

Only if you're stupid, unlucky or a pop super-star. There were 3,071 people convicted in Great Britain in 1968 for possession of cannabis. In the US in 1968, customs officers confiscated 30 tons of it, nationwide drug arrests in 1968 were up to 60%, while in California, they were up 324%. These figures represent only a tiny proportion of offenders. Smoke in the comfort and safety of your own home (especially if it's in the Himalayas). Buy from a friend or make sure your dealer hasn't got your address in a little black book. You are unlikely to be busted at large outdoor hip gatherings where police are forced to ignore the pot fog—they can't arrest 10,000 at once.

'In Indiana, an elderly farmer has let a field grow up in marijuana. He sits in his farmhouse with field glasses waiting for youths to come and pick the crop. Then he calls the police and collects an informer's fee.'

The Times, November 8, 1969.

'Eventually the US hopes to encourage Mexican agents to use planes equipped with electronic sniffers to detect where marijuana is being grown and then spray the plants with a *still experimental* (my italics) compound that will nauseate users who later smoke the products.'

Time, September 26, 1969, quoting the US Attorney General, Richard Kleindeinst, on Operation Intercept.

'Remember what the dormouse said:
"Feed your head.
Feed your head.
Feed your head".'

Grace Slick, The Jefferson Airplane.
White Rabbit. Copper Penny Music Publishing Co.

If
I
take
too
much
hashish,
what
should
I
do?

Enjoy yourself. Otherwise, drink something soothing, preferably containing Vitamin C, such as lemon or orange juice. Lie down and have sweet dreams. You will wake in the morning newborn, without a hangover (unless it's that deadly Congolese).

Smoking
hash
mixed
with
tobacco
makes
me
sick.
What
other
ways
can
I
get
stoned?

Eat it. Melt it into your coffee (over the gas in a tablespoon of water), bake it into a cake, flavour your omelette, make fudge or puff a pipe. Some recipes are so complicated you have to be stoned to prepare them. Try this:

Chili
Pot

2 lbs Pinto beans
½ clove garlic
1 lb bacon, cut into 2-inch sections
2 cups red wine
½ cup mushrooms
1 cup chopped grass
4 tablespoons chili powder

Soak beans overnight in a large pot. Pour boiling water over beans and simmer for at least an hour, adding more water to keep the beans covered. Now add all other ingredients and continue to simmer for another three hours. Salt to taste. Stones about 10.

Dallas Notes

Is
marijuana
an aphrodisiac?

It depends on who you're with when you're high.

'Marijuana inflames the erotic impulses and leads to revolting sex crimes ... one girl, known for her quietness and
modesty, suddenly threw all caution to the winds. She
began staying out late at nights.'

Daily Mirror, 1924

Should
I
smoke
and
drive?

Why waste good grass? Marijuana in moderate quantities
does not impair driving ability; although driving will
probably impair the high. Simulated driving tests conducted
over a period of six weeks at the University of Washington
Pharmacology Department early in 1969, with thirty-six
young regular users of both pot and alcohol resulted in the
following conclusions: Marijuana smokers can operate a
driving simulator just as well when they are high as when
they are normal. Under the influence of alcohol, however,
their simulated driving performance dropped by 15%. The
only difference noted in performance when high on marijuana was that the guinea pigs tended to watch the speedo-
meter more than usual, resulting in slower driving. Tests
with real vehicles rather than simulators are now being
undertaken. Personally, driving stoned is enjoyable, although the highway feels like a giant rubber band and
one's efforts to compensate are disquieting for other
passengers. At night the lights make it feel like flying.

137

'I personally would rather drive in a car where the chauffeur is high on pot than drive in a car where the chauffeur is high on alcohol.'

Alfred Crancer, Chief Research Assistant, Washington State Motor Vehicle Department

'I'd like to encourage the cops to keep a little of the next stash they confiscate and try it. It really is great shit. Maybe they'll understand if you say it's like pouring your best bourbon down the sink.'

Sergeant Richard Bergess
(Sergeant Sunshine)

Is
it
true
that
the
great
majority
of
heroin
addicts
start
with
marijuana?

Yes. Even more of them begin with milk. Admittedly in the process of establishing a regular supply of cannabis, one can more easily come into contact with people who supply hard drugs. Also, when one discovers that cannabis is harmless, exposing society's lie, heroin by analogy may seem tempting. Moral: Tell the truth about pot and there will be fewer junkies.

'I'll die young, but it's like kissing God.'

Lenny Bruce

Is
there
any
connection
between
drugs
and
pop
music?

'Name me one rock group that doesn't have in its repertoire, hymns to LSD and marijuana.'

Timothy Leary

'Pop stars should be subjected to a system of tests — like horses and greyhounds — before they go on stage.'
Mrs D. Baylis, Noss Mayo, near Plymouth, Devon.
News of the World, February 26, 1967

Is
marijuana
addictive?

Yes, in the sense that most of the really pleasant things in life are worth endlessly repeating.

Should
I
carry
pot
through
customs?

It's better to be stoned and clean than to be straight and holding. In Israel, trained 'hash-puppies' will sniff you out (they had them as early as 1954). In Tashkent a beautiful redhead picks up the scent. She has uncanny olfaction, acutely sensitive to cannabis, and on a hot day, with the

139

wind in the right direction, her nostrils will flare as you walk across the tarmac. In Turkey, you could be buried in gaol for thirty years. In Iraq you risk the death penalty. In England you might even get away with it. In August 1969, a friend of mine was passing through London's Heathrow Airport, 10.30 p.m. Friday. His flowing blond hair, Garbo hat, and mauve jacket predictably attracted two polite Customs officials. The usual questions. Bag searched, and among the toothpaste and talc a silver-balled lump of hash is discovered. He is amazed. He remembered mislaying it a month before and its rediscovery is an embarrassing surprise. A group of customs officials laughed good-naturedly at his 'stupidity'. He was then thoroughly searched and painstakingly interrogated. When it became apparent that he was not the member of a flourishing smuggling ring, and that he had merely been careless, customs apologized for their inability to free him, explaining that it was already a police matter. A young detective arrived, escorted him to a brightly lit room, and over an amicable conversation implied the matter was trivial and unfortunate. The airport police had gone home, so the detective telephoned the nearest station, which did not have any car to send for the arrest. It was a smallish lump, customs were not pressing charges ... OK yawned the detective and segeant in harmony, let him go. Customs reappeared to help him catch another plane, and the journey was resumed minus the hash, which no doubt made its way into a late night cup of airport coffee.

I'm
scared.
What
if
my
supply
is
suddenly
cut
off?

Grow your own. If you can tell grass from other birdseed, try your local pet shop. You could be lucky. Otherwise next time you see good grass, save some of the fattest seeds for an emergency. When it comes, fold seeds between two Kleenex, place in a shallow dish and saturate. Three or four days later, the seeds should have sprouted at least $\frac{1}{2}$ inch. Place each one in an individual flower pot. In natural sunlight they will grow fifteen hard-to-hide feet. There's not enough 'natural sunlight' in Britain to worry anyone. Instead mature them in a cupboard with artificial light placed a foot above the tops of the plants. Light continuously with blue bulb for the first month, then change to red, reducing the time to 16 hours the first week, 14 the second, and then 12 until the plants bloom. Only female plants (which can be identified by their larger more luxuriant flowers) are worth harvesting. The whole female plant can be used for smoking, but the flowers and top leaves provide the most potent grass and the root and stems the least. Dry the plant in the sun for at least two weeks until the leaves are crumbly. Cut flowers and leaves finely with a sharp knife, separating them carefully from seeds and pieces of stem.[3]

Plant any spare seeds in a Kew Gardens hot house.

[3] Extracted from an international chain letter circulated in 1969.

Is
pot
helping
to
change
the
world?

Meaning the Western world. Yes, as long as it remains illegal. Essentially, marijuana smoking is a fashionable affectation with ambiguous implications. Although the contribution of marijuana to the evolvement of the New Man is marginal, it is not irrelevant:

— It teaches us to relax again, drains competitive zeal and encourages laziness — which is going to be important in the future.

— It warms man to his fellow man — in the same way that sit-ins and poetry readings sometimes do, and gymnasiums and prize-givings don't.

— It tends to nourish man's creative instinct — rather than endorse his capacity for drudgery.

— It has broken down cultural/racial prejudice. Instead of being denigrated, African and Oriental lifestyles are now romanticised.

— It turns men into stoned Houdinis, who can escape the strait-jacket of Aristotelian logic. Lateral thinking, mystical drifters rarely maim other people.

— Sceptical about the last point? Why do you think America lost the Vietnam War? The pilots are alcoholics but the GIs are stoned. John Steinbeck IV estimated that 75% of the 'young soldiers smoke it, for all sorts of reasons, all the time'.[4] Actually, the fact that soldiers smoke pot is an indication of the drug's indifferent effect.

The sociological implications of drugs, like rock music, sex and long hair, cannot be examined in isolation. Pot is

[4] 'The Politics of Pot,' *Esquire*, August, 1968.

part of a sub-cultural pattern and its effect is ultimately contingent upon the environment it's smoked in.

'All commanders are unanimous in their considered judgment that the smoking of marijuana is not a problem of major proportions among the US forces in Vietnam. All agree there has been no discernible impact on morale, health welfare, or efficiency or combat effectiveness that can be attributed to the use of this drug.'
   Ambiguous statement from Pentagon in reply to John Steinbeck IV

'We need dialogue—on how to make this a marijuana nation, not the same old US with a new kick.'
   Los Angeles Free Press, 1968

'Partly I think the younger generation like to take cannabis for very much the same reasons as the younger women now use eye shadow instead of lipstick—because their mothers use lipstick, they have to use eye shadow and no lipstick.'
   Baroness Wootton of Abinger, 1969

'Grass is the gift of the black culture to the white middle class. It was the blacks and the Mexicans who were turning on to grass long long decades before the white man discovered it. Psychedelic drugs blacken the white man.'
   Timothy Leary, *Berkeley Barb*, Feb. 1969

'It can also make a difference whether one is a chronic or moderate marijuana user. The first category have been shown to differ from the latter in their negative attitude towards society, their nonconformist appearance and their display of paranoia and acute anxiety.'
   Zinber & Weil / *Nature*.

   *What
   about
   psychedelic
   drugs?*

Properly supervised, you will almost certainly come down

143

safely from a psychedelic flight, but not necessarily in the same spot you took off from. Old favourites are mescalin (Huxley's door-jamb), peyote and psilocybin. Man-made LSD, an entirely synthetic product, is generally rated 100 times as powerful as psilocybin (extracted from Mexican mushrooms) and 7,000 times as powerful as mescalin (derived from peyote). STP is considerably stronger than LSD but the latter remains the most widely used and easiest to get.

Non-acid takers regard the LSD trip as a remarkable flight from reality, whereas cautious devotees feel they've flown *into* reality. Many feel about acid the same as Victorians would have felt about Instant tea – it's too easy, and prefer to work hard for mystical experiences. Try Yoga, meditation or Meher Babaism (as did Dr Allen Cohen, a former colleague of Timothy Leary's, who became disillusioned with chemicals). After an acid trip, you can reject everything you have ever been taught. If Pavlov's dogs had taken LSD, they would have danced to the sound of the bell, not salivated. LSD has profoundly affected the lives of thousands of people. Indirectly it has also had far-ranging effects because of the influence of acid on key Underground personalities, and pop culture. LSD transforms the mundane into the sensational. This applies to sounds, smells, colours, tastes, touch, everyday experiences. The corollary is that exciting events become unbearably so. The world becomes a circus, with the emphasis on parody and our roles within it confirmed as clowns.

'Acid has had a very big effect on my life. I consider the yippies to be an acid movement, in that the attempt is to wipe out a person's total frame of reference, and to establish a new frame of reference. We are trying to put the country on an acid trip.'

Jerry Rubin, *Liberation*, February 1969

'LSD demands more than marijuana. You can keep your

plastic job and then come home at night and turn on and make love better and enjoy music better and enjoy your dinner better and enjoy your friends better. That's good, that moves the whole middle class up a notch. But LSD is still the only challenge of the really intelligent person, because LSD requires a change of mind. Marijuana is the perfect drug to make you feel better which is obviously necessary now, but there is no great spiritual challenge.'

Timothy Leary, *The God Game, Berkeley Barb*, February 1969

'Every time you take LSD you put all your chips on the table.'

Timothy Leary

*What
can
I
do
if
I'm
having
a
bad
trip?*

Keep cool. No bad trip lasts forever. Breathe slowly and deeply until you feel calmer. Convince yourself there's nothing to be frightened of. Try to find out what has gone wrong and correct it.

The presence of a trusted friend can help. A sympathetic guide should be able to talk you off a bad trip. Orange juice and sugar works well if you take lots. A cup of sugar to a quart of orange juice. Niacinimide is beneficial. You need 1,000 milligrams for every 100 micrograms of acid. If you don't know the acid dosage, assume 500 micrograms and use 50 tablets of niacinimide. Too much niacinimide cannot hurt you. Landing time for both the orange juice + sugar method and the niacinimide is between 30 and 40 minutes. As a last resort, a doctor could be called to administer a tranquiliser such as thorazine. Mental hospitalization is the worst trip of all. Don't drop acid again until you have worked out what misfired.[5]

Try to check the source of your acid. LSD is often mixed with methedrine, sometimes with deadlier drugs. At a party I once attended, the acid stirred clandestinely into the punch had previously been mixed with strychnine and those innocent alcoholics who downed three or four glasses wound up in hospital for a day or two. Have all your trips been complete nothings? Are you sure they weren't aspirins?

Is
LSD
dangerous?

Is electricity? Like everything else, danger lies not so much in the drug itself as in how it is used. Newspaper horror reports – suicides, murders, deformed LSD babies – can be so far ignored. In January 1968, the following story appeared in the *Sunday Times*:

'Six undergraduates at a Western Pennsylvania college were totally and permanently blinded by staring at the sun while they were 'high' on LSD. The students have been under rehabilitation at the Pennsylvania Welfare Department. They had gone to a grassy clearing in the woods near the college for their LSD session. After taking it they lay on their backs on the grass and gazed at the sun. Six hours later, friends found them blinded.'

[5] Adapted from *Project Free London*.

146

The story turned out to be a total fabrication, invented by one Dr Yoder of the Pennsylvania Institute for the Blind, who said: 'I invented this story because of my concern about the illegal use of LSD and other drugs.'

The fact that it was a hoax received scant publicity.

*What
about
amphetamines?*

Deadly. If you must, use them to pass exams or to make that deadline. Otherwise, don't.

'Speed kills. It really does. Methedrine and amphetamine, etc., can and will rot your teeth, freeze your mind, and kill your body. The life expectancy of the average speed freak, from first shot to the morgue, is about five years. What a drag.'

Communications Company, 1967

*What
about
heroin?*

Being a junkie is a full-time occupation and has little to do with being alive. It is one of many ways to destroy yourself, if that's what you want.

*

'There are three groups who are bringing about the great evolution of the new age that we are going through now. They are the DOPE DEALERS, the ROCK MUSICIANS and the Underground ARTISTS AND WRITERS.'

Timothy Leary
East Village Other, Sept. '69

147

SUNSHINE IS PURE ACID. A SMALL PIECE WILL GET YOU SPACED. IN NEW YORK ONLY A DOZEN VERY HIGH PEOPLE HANDLE SUNSHINE. YOU WILL RECOGNIZE THEM WHEN YOU MEET THEM, THEY ARE VERY TOGETHER PEOPLE, DOING A GOOD THING. IF YOU ARE DEALING WITH SUNSHINE, YOU KNOW THAT YOU HAVE A LOT OF POWER IN YOUR HANDS WITH AN ENORMOUS RESPONSIBILITY FOR MANY HEADS. IT'S NOT DEALING IN THE SENSE OF MAKING MONEY. IT'S MUCH CLOSER TO DISTRIBUTING SUNSHINE.

YOU ARE AWARE THAT YOU ARE NOT JUST DISTRIBUTING DRUGS BUT MAKING SURE TO KEEP UP THE FLOW OF AN IMPORTANT PART OF OUR BEING AND OF OUR GREATEST EXPERIENCE. THE EXPANDING OF OUR CONSCIOUSNESS THE SENSING OF DIVINITY, BY TAKING SUNSHINE ACID. THE AIM OF ALL EASTERN RELIGION, LIKE THE AIM OF LSD IS BASICALLY TO GET HIGH, THAT IS, TO EXPAND THE CONSCIOUSNESS AND FIND ECSTASY AND REVELATION WITHIN.

INTERGALACTIC UNION
Extracted from/DOPOGRAM, EVO,
March 24, 1970.

148

THE
GUERRILLA
PRESS

'*Gandalf's Garden* is a soulflow from the pens of creators—
mystics, writers, artists, delvers and poets. A wellspring
of love and anguish that those with searching thirsts may
drink thereof.'
>   Muz Murray, Editor, *Gandalf's Garden*, London

'My personal aim is to destroy. To fuck up my readers for
25 cents.'
>   Steve Jones, Editor, *Loving Couch Press*,
>   Manitoba, Canada.

Dear Mr Wilcock,
Thank you for your card. Although it has been good of
you to send me a regular copy of *Other Scenes* it may very
well be that it would be more appreciated by another
recipient. So, grateful as I am to have had this experience
of the new journalism, I shall not expect to receive it in the
future.
>   Yours sincerely,
>   Alastair Burnet, Editor
>   *The Economist*, London

If you don't read Underground papers you don't know
what's going on in the world. If you do, don't judge them
by the standards of yesterday's *Times*. Underground
publications are not launched as vehicles for advertising.
They are not thinly disguised party organs, disseminating
'news analysis' as a pretext for perpetrating a rigid, mori-
bund ideology. Usually, they are begun for fun, attracting a
pool of underemployed creators bent on inventing a new
language to communicate new ideas in a new style. They
are not used like a cheer leader's megaphone, to amplify
last season's jingo-chants, but are free-for-all forums for a
fresh kind of debate. They are a generation's call—sometimes a whisper—to arms, not glorified memos from the
bored-rooms of power. Their aim is not so much to dissent
as to disrupt, and their editorial policies—either explicitly
or implicitly—seek an overthrow of society as we know it.

151

The term Underground Press denotes a great variety of publications, each unusually sensitive to the collective personality of its editorial staff. Some are blazing filigree tabloids, intoxicated by their own compassion for their readers, others are crudely mimeographed hate sheets — yet they are all, somehow, instantly identifiable as products of the new journalism. Just as the *New York Times* and the *News of the World*, which represent antithetical editorial approaches, are agents of an identical *status quo* philosophy, so too publications such as *Horseshit* and *Superlove*, for all their stylistic disparity, are incontrovertibly Underground.

In 1969, ninety-nine publications were officially listed as members of the Underground Press Syndicate (UPS). Seven are published in New York, thirteen in California and eleven in London. American Underground papers flourish in such unlikely places as Dallas, Texas; Atlanta, Georgia; Jackson, Mississippi; Omaha, Nebraska; Bloomington, Indiana; and Taos, New Mexico. One is published from a roving 1948 Chevrolet school bus. Others survive in Italy, Holland, Belgium, Denmark, Sweden, Yugoslavia, Columbia, Curaçao and Japan. Most of these newspapers and hundreds more, are subscribers to Liberation News Service (LNS), the Reuters of the Underground. Based in New York it mails twice-weekly bulletins of news, poetry, gossip, essays, interviews, photographs and cartoons to over 300 papers, and the estimated total readership of member publications is five million (sceptical? See Appendix ii). From LNS' New York office, a High School Independent Press Service (HIPS) dispatches several hundred weekly newspackets to school papers. There are other Underground organisations such as APM (Anarchist Press Movement), AUM (Alliance of Underground Media), COSMIC (a loosely woven world-wide fabric of small press magazines and newspapers to promote the 'Awakening of True Consciousness towards the Brotherhood of Planetary Man).

While both the Underground Press Syndicate and Liberation News Service ensure that important stories get world-wide exposure, many of the big-city Underground papers circulate internationally.

An analysis of the content of the Underground Press reveals much about the pre-occupations of the Youth Movement in general and its fluctuating areas of emphasis over the last few years.

Vietnam

The first of the US media to tell its burgeoning public such facts of death as the Dow chemistry of napalm. First to support and publicise the burning of draft cards. The Underground Press emphasised the gains to be made by corporations from prolonging the war and, by publishing 'Confidential' documents, exposed the links between University Research Departments and the requirements of the Pentagon. As mass-media awoke from its moral slumber, UPS papers have concentrated on targets nearer home. The accompanying statistical chart (Fig. I) shows the decline of the *East Village Other*'s content on Vietnam from 6.6% in 1966 to .7% in 1969. For the Underground Press the war is over.

Pot

Another won cause. Now, even the Post-Underground glossies, e.g. the late *New York Scenes*, offer glowing A to Zs of marijuana, growing your own, how to roll a joint, how to score, market reports on prices and quality, why it should be legal. The dangers and delights of LSD and other drugs are also fully documented. The *East Village Other*'s 11.4% drug content in 1966 dropped to 5.6% a year later, and by 1969 it was down to .9%. *IT*'s drug coverage dropped from 6.6% to 2.2% between 1968 and 1969. Now it is news of synthetic dope discoveries, someone's favourite hash recipe or a particularly outrageous police plant story. The days of 'Hey man, let me tell you about my trip last night', have been replaced by small, regular, common-sense reports from local drug-bust organisations, advice on avoiding arrest, current cannabis prices and analyses of the wider political implications of drug taking.

Police

Obsession with police brutality is so far restricted to the US and the Continent (see Fig. 1). *Los Angeles Free Press* has pioneered exposure of 1984 police techniques (from lead-filled gloves to militaristically equipped 'super-fuzz' tank cars), and some papers have managed to manœuvre corrupt policemen from office. Youth confrontations with police are remorselessly photographed by Movement photographers and the horrifying results reproduced on front pages. Policemen read the Underground Press. Occasionally a 'turned on cop' writes to the letters column, and others, less friendly, are regular visitors to editorial offices—a courtesy once returned by London's *Black Dwarf*, which sent a spy to explore top security areas of New Scotland Yard, then published his findings.

'But officer, I'm an anti-communist.'
'I don't give a fuck what kind of communist you are. Wham!'

Tuli Kupferberg

Black Power

The Underground Press is sometimes smitten by the please-Stokeley-rape-my-sister syndrome—which partly compensates for the attitude of the overground press over the past few hundred years. Underground papers wept aloud for Malcolm X and Martin Luther King, enthusiastically endorsed Dick Gregory's Presidential bid, and they

154

ANALYSIS OF CONTENT—*Los Angeles Free Press, East Village Other, IT, Berkeley Barb, Good Times**

SUBJECT	1966 EVO %	1967 LAFP %	1967 EVO %	1967 IT %	1968 LAFP %	1968 EVO %	1968 IT %	1968 BARB %	1968 GT %	1969 LAFP %	1969 EVO %	1969 IT %	1969 BARB %	1969 GT %
VIETNAM + the DRAFT	6.6	6.9	5.5	1.9	.5	1.8	nil	4.1	4.0	1.2	.7	nil	5.5	6.5
BLACK POWER	4.1	1.7	1.2	4.6	3.0	2.9	3.3	4.0	4.7	1.9	1.0	nil	5.9	1.3
NEW POLITICS (from White Panthers to Gay Power)	3.3	1.2	4.0	.75	9.4	8.2	4.2	11.5	15.4	5.1	13.6	.8	5.4	8.6
POLICE BRUTALITY	nil	1.3	3.6	.25	2.0	4.6	nil	2.2	.6	1.2	1.3	1.5	4.7	2.6
STUDENT UNREST + activities re University admin.	nil	1.8	nil	nil	4.2	2.2	3.8	2.6	5.8	2.6	.3	.2	4.5	6.2
HIPPIES + the revolution in life-style	5.5	5.7	7.0	13.3	2.7	2.9	2.3	4.4	2.8	5.2	3.0	10.3	9.7	22.8
DRUGS	11.4	.8	5.6	4.4	1.6	3.0	6.6	1.2	.7	.3	.9	2.2	.2	.5
POP MUSIC	.5	3.9	1.0	7.8	4.0	4.9	7.0	.5	2.9	5.0	5.4	31.9	.3	nil
NEW SOCIETY IDEOLOGY	14.7	3.3	4.6	8.3	1.7	3.5	7.4	1.8	3.6	3.8	5.6	11.3	.9	8.7
CINEMA, theatre, books, etc.	8.0	12.9	3.1	3.4	10.2	6.6	6.0	2.4	6.8	6.2	7.7	1.6	2.1	7.7
COMIC STRIPS, cartoons, visual satire, etc.	3.3	1.0	6.8	1.6	1.2	11.1	2.8	2.6	8.8	1.8	7.9	8.8	2.5	6.3
ADVERTISING	22.9	45.5	46.0	37.5	59.2	37.8	38.6	51.2	23.2	60.0	39.0	22.9	49.5	11.2

*Formerly *San Francisco Express Times.*

FIG. I

continually chorus support for persecuted Black Panther leaders.

'Dick Gregory is a black man who is running for President, but if someone shot *him*, they'd put it on the entertainment page.'

Dallas Notes

Pop

The papers are caught up in its culture, and sustained by its advertising revenue.

Students

Not interested, until the 1968 resurrection of insurrection on the campus. When the police moved in, so did the Underground Press, subsequently publishing captured administration documents. Fig. 1 shows that *EVO* and *IT* had nothing on students in 1967, whereas by 1968 there was 2.2% and 3.8% respectively. In the same period, *LA Free Press* coverage rose from 1.8% to 4.2%.

'A new generation is finally getting an education, though the college may have to be destroyed in the process.'

Mayday

The contemporary explosion of anti-society, *mass circulation* newspapers and magazines was detonated, if belatedly, by the success of the Greenwich Village newspaper, *The Village Voice*. This was first published in October 1955, at a time when, according to publisher/editor Daniel Wolf, 'the best minds in America ... were repeating themselves.' *The Village Voice* showed that a newspaper could be run by amateurs, and that a relatively permissive editorial policy did not necessarily precipitate commercial suicide. *The Voice* is now the grand old man of the Underground, often shocked by its own progeny. Its columns acknowledge the existence of the new breed of publications, but its advertising manager is disinclined to accept their revenue.[1]

John Wilcock, that strange mixture of Gulliver, Randolph Hearst and Elsa Maxwell, arrived in Greenwich Village a year before *The Voice*. When he discovered that the famous artistic community lacked its own newspaper, he placed a sign in a nearby bookshop inviting 'like minded creative types' to help start one. Edwin Fancher and Daniel Wolf, co-founders of *The Village Voice*, asked Wilcock to join them, which he did, contributing his celebrated column, 'The Village Square', for the next ten years. Wilcock recalls fighting with Norman Mailer (who named the paper) over 'Whether his copy should be cut to fit like everybody else's'. Among small landmarks while working with *The Village Voice*, Wilcock lists (1) his discovery of Timothy Leary, (2) his decision to write about marijuana repeatedly, and (3) getting 'fuck' into a family newspaper.

The Underground press is a goldmine (or gravel pit) of news and opinion that can never find its way into straight media because it transcends the self-imposed bounds of good taste or infringes covenants of libel, blasphemy, obscenity, sedition or veracity. The two people who, more than any others, defied all such precedents and who turned editorial irresponsibility into a therapeutic art-form, were John Wilcock and Paul Krassner, the Katzenjammer kids of Underground publishing.

Paul Krassner's *Realist*, begun in July 1958 with a print run of 600 expanding to over 100,000 within ten years, trail-blazed the virgin territories of journalistic anarchy. The *Realist* was originally concerned with the classic

[1] Issue No. 3 of New York's *Screw*, reports that, '*The Village Voice* refused our ad, acting as Village censor. Its publisher, Ed Fancher, is a gentleman, but his brittle and rude advertising girl is an old warhorse of another colour who would probably have fallen in love with Anthony Comstock and at the age of 86 is still a virgin.' (January 4th, 1969)—a further example of disregard for the Queensberry Rules of Publishing.

radical issues of Separation of Church and State, Civil Liberties, Political Freedom, Obscenity and Authoritarianism until Krassner took LSD in 1964 and became an outrageous prankster editor. He published Lenny Bruce's obituary two years before he died, 'so Lenny would know what I thought of him', invited Boris Karloff to write about heart transplants, and published a plaster-casted array of pop stars' pricks. By the summer of 1968 Krassner's thirty-six trips and his ringmastering of the yippie circus put paid to the petulant angst of earlier days. (A former contributor, Madelaine Murray O'Hare, has remarked: 'Krassner would not take my last two articles. He said the first one indicated that I was full of hate.') Not that the *Realist* ever lost its bite. At the height of the scandal over William Manchester's book *Death of a President*, the *Realist* published what was claimed to be the censored excerpts from the original manuscript. These excerpts revealed an incident on the plane carrying the body of the assassinated President from Dallas to Washington—a celebrant and intoxicated LBJ staggered to the rear of the plane where the corpse of JFK lay, pulled out his penis, inserted it in the neck bullet wound and began fucking. That so many readers found this appalling anecdote credible is an indication of the esteem in which the President of the United States was held at the time, and a justification of Paul Krassner's idiosyncratic editorial judgment.

Such was the example for Underground editors. Pseudo 'objectivity' is a liberal shibboleth discarded by new-style journalists. The tone of Underground papers is pugnaciously partisan and each reporter is, in a sense, his own editorialist—which is why so few of these papers carry distinct 'opinion' sections. The feeling that each contributor sees himself as a sort of psychic guerrilla, produces some lively and original propaganda as well as garbled and sub-literate war cries. Much depends on the talents of the editor. Good Underground papers analyse key issues and unlike everyday papers, attempt to relate and interweave them into a coherent critique of society. The violence in Vietnam is not seen in isolation—it is related to the violence inherent in corporate bureaucracy: the violence of poverty, the violence of Chicago and the ghettoes, the unconscious violence of the conveyor belt.

When John Wilcock spied what he calls 'the first radical alternative to the rapidly ageing *Voice*'—the *East Village Other*, he offered to write a column for it. The first issue of the *East Village Other* was a broadsheet, with a ragged, parochial effusion of pataphysics, and diffuse 'anti-civilisation' vibrations. It exhibited a square concern for its physical environment, the East Side, and passionately propagated 'renovation instead of urban renewal, and a sane policy of rent control, slumlord routing, better business and safer streets'. It was not so much anti-*Vietnam* as anti-*West Village*. However, the narrow, Junior Chamber of Commerce tone, had, by the second issue, been restrained to the point of silence. There was still a worry about the streets being 'a breeding place for crime' (something it would be rejoicing over three years later), but John Wilcock's column 'Other Scenes' made its first appearance, and there was a story on the first prosecution of a draft card burner.[2]

Miles began writing from London, Simon Vinkenoog from Amsterdam, Jean-Jacques Lebel from Paris. Timothy Leary sermonised from Millbrook, and Simon Watson Taylor weighed in with a report from a Bangkok massage parlour. It was all presented in a rollicking, raunchy anti-literate, semi-satirical style, with panoramic collages, display front pages and a 72-point bold-typed, crusading zeal. Ideas were lifted from conventional media and re-modelled. Playmates became, in the *East Village Other*, Slum Goddesses, candid, and spottily lifelike. New hip cartoonists,

[2] Twenty-two-year-old David Miller was arrested on October 18, 1965, by six FBI officials, and became the first person charged with a violation of a law signed by President Johnson on August 30 of that year, against destroying Selective Service System cards. The President's press secretary commented, unprophetically, that David Miller was 'giving our adversaries a false picture of what the people actually feel in this country'.

which until then had begun and ended with Jules Feiffer, decorated the pages with Breughellian savagery.

By issue 12, John Wilcock had become editor, Tuli Kupferberg, one of The Fugs, co-editor, and the paper had begun to peek beyond the environs of 42nd St and Eighth Avenue. When Leary was arrested *EVO* sent its reporter to interview the county sheriff, 'disguised as a straight man from *Look* ... in the hope that the sheriff would talk more freely to someone that he would assume was on his side.' He did. In August 1966 there was a front page interview with Mark Lane, author of *Rush to Judgment*, who outlined his dissatisfaction with the Warren Commission's report on the assassination of President Kennedy. This was months before anyone had heard of Lane or questioned the Commission's conclusions. In the same column three years later Lane was dropping even bigger bombshells. (*EVO*, July 9, 1969).

John Wilcock edited the *East Village Other* for four months, doubling its circulation from 10,000 to 20,000, and along with Walter Bowart founded the *Underground Press Syndicate*, 'to facilitate the transmission of news, features and advertising between anti-establishment, avant garde, new left, youth orientated periodicals which share common aims and interests. Its members are free to pick up each other's features without remuneration' (*EVO*, July, 1966).[3]

The present editor of the *East Village Other*, Allan Katzman, says that his paper is dedicated to the belief that the Devil is God as he is misunderstood by others, and he aims to 'bridge this psychic gap by word, graphic and revolution'. Katzman goes on, 'We were extremely effective in making madmen laugh and convincing those who thought they were crazy and alone that they were not.' When the overground press submit their seasonal feature on the

---

[3] A more recently formed rough equivalent is the Cosmic Circuit which is a loosely-woven worldwide fabric of small press magazines and newspapers to promote the 'Awakening of True Consciousness towards the Brotherhood of Planetary Man.'

Underground, the angle is pivotal on the *EVO* 'porno advertisements'. Certainly the Wheel & Deal sections are wild by *Exchange and Mart* standards:

'Great Ray, cunnilinguist, desires clean attractive nympho type woman for oral genital stimulating Frenching times. Private, discreet, serious.'[4]

But sex is not the soul of the alternative press. Personal ads are a valid community service, profitable, and proportionately no more intrusive than the morning paper's TV guide. A word of caution: it is said that the CIA and the FBI are stockpiling files on the Underground from them.

When Brooklyn magistrates prosecuted *EVO* for obscenity the paper front-paged an enlargement of the contested picture, depicting it as a series of numbered dots, with the headline YOU CAN BE ARRESTED IF YOU DRAW THIS[5]. The accompanying caption, 'The Last Supper' and a series of onomatopoeic 'SLURGUL, SHLOSH, and SLURPS' left little doubt as to the nature of the activity which would be animated by artistically inclined readers, who were invited to forward their efforts to the District Attorney.

Like most UPS papers, the *East Village Other* is not only an instrument of the Underground but a mirror of its complexion, and is thus highly sensitive to the Movement's changing moods. It hailed the hippies,[6] preaching a dropped-out detachment, and later, threw itself, somewhat diffidently, into the more violent antics of confrontation.

[4] The talents of Great Ray have been scrutinised by *Screw* in a lengthy interview (March 7, 1969).

[5] One copy of this rare edition found its way to a Brighton (UK) magistrates court in August 1968, during the prosecution of bookshop owner Bill Butler (see p. 78). In this exhibit the dots had been connected. In answer to a question from the Bench, a plain-clothesman sheepishly confessed to wielding the exploratory pencil. He was not arrested.

[6] Although *EVO*'s publisher, Walter Bowart, firmly maintained before the US Senate sub-committee investigating juvenile delinquency: 'If God can be found through the medium of any drug, God is not worthy of being God.'

Today, *EVO* is more obviously political, professional and predictable. A pig appears on the cover under the banner: 'George Wallace for President'. Technological visions of the new society are elaborated and an astropsychologist pontificates regularly. At a time when 31 Iranian towns were devastated by an earthquake, *EVO*'s seer saw: 'FBI investigations into civil rights violations in Chicago were based on injury to—well, 31 reporters. Remember: 31 in Hebrew is EL or the Godhead and its opposite is LE or 'not' or negation and has the numerical value of 13. 13 is the number of years Mayor Daley has been in office ... '. The onetime concern for community growth has now metamorphosed into the solution, 'piss on it'. *EVO*'s own discovery is A. J. Weberman, 'the world's only living Dylanologist', who lectures on Dylan at the Free School, and typically begins his columns: 'After listening to Dylan's new LP ten times a day for ten months, I have finally gotten some insight into it'—an affirmation often belied by his conclusions.

Another Underground newspaper based in New York, but produced from anywhere he happens to be, is John Wilcock's *Other Scenes*. Wilcock travels 30,000 miles a year, writing travel books to earn the money he spends on the paper. He has published *Other Scenes* in New York, London, Athens, Amsterdam, Hong Kong, even in Tokyo, where he merged with Japan's first Underground newspaper, *Shinjuku Sutra*, launched by a pair of teenagers at a local college. *Other Scenes* complies with Wilcock's own formula for the perfect newspaper—'pop, art, religion, politics, sex, sociology and revolution'—although on a more intelligent level than such deadpan chronicling of categories would indicate. The first entirely self-contained issue of *Other Scenes*—the name was derived from his world-wide syndicated column and previous merger-papers—appeared in March 1968, and contained an intense, wierdly prophetic discussion with Wilcock and the yippie triumvirate, Paul Krassner, Abbie Hoffman and Jerry

162

Rubin, which predicted the Chicago violence and consequent polarisation of the participants, five months before it happened. Edward de Bono thought laterally, Leary mystically. Horror conditions in Arkansas gaols were exposed via the unlikely source of a BBC documentary transcript. Wilcock's advantage over 'rival' Underground editors, and the reason for *Other Scenes* being one of the most quoted UPS documents, is his international source of contacts, and his professional indifference to the archaic legal and professional niceties of publishing. He not only invades people's privacy—he eliminates it. Addresses, phone numbers and personal correspondence of friends and celebrities throughout the world are publicly indexed. Even write-ups of himself, favourable or otherwise, are reprinted in *Other Scenes* without compunction. After fifteen years of commitment to the Underground, Wilcock's publishing flair is as fresh and unpredictable as tomorrow. In June 1969 *Other Scenes* began to appear every two weeks, with more humour, more sex and more colour. One issue appeared with sixteen blank pages, announcing a unique design-it-yourself newspaper competition. Anyone could enter no matter what their political views—and they did. Home-made newspapers flowed in from all over the world, many to be later published as part of *Other Scenes*. Six months later, Wilcock announced that in future his paper would be available on subscription only—forced to retreat from the newsstands by the overpowering sexpapers for which he had helped to create the climate.

Wherever Wilcock walks—New York, Rome, Calcutta, anywhere,[7] he lugs scores of *Other Scenes* to drop into accessible vehicles, bus seats, and the unwary arms of passing strangers. This peripatetic Santa Clausing unloads more copies than are ever sold. His instinct is by now so ingrained that on the rare occasions Wilcock runs out of his own supplies he will load up with the nearest novelty (balloons, toys, a friend's newspaper). He is a real life, mini-

[7] Except Moscow, where *Other Scenes* was impounded at the airport.

Magic Christian, surreptitiously hotting-up the air conditioning in an already sweltering restaurant, gluing Heinz soup labels on vacant tins of 'pure mountain air', blasting masculine passers-by with bursts of aerosol Woolworth's perfume, playing games with friends and strangers alike.

The *Los Angeles Free Press* was founded in July 1964, with a fifteen-dollar initial investment, to be 'a platform for debate among writers of differing controversial points of view', and is now a fat weekly tabloid of some 48 pages, five of which are of classified advertisements. Within a few years of its launching, *Free Press* had spawned three book shops and was incurring a weekly payroll of 3,000 dollars for thirty full-time editorial and clerical employees, for whom it has allegedly installed a time clock. The *Free Press* is not one of the 72% of Underground publications which lose money.[8]

In spirit, the *Los Angeles Free Press* rests somewhere between *The Village Voice* and the *East Village Other*. Its lack of kinky hysteria is compensated for by hard news and detailed information. It offers its readers a variety of useful advice, from 'how, when and where to get food stamps' to 'how to tell if your phone is bugged' and 'whether Mexican abortions are dangerous'. Marcuse's speeches at nearby San Diego campus are faithfully reproduced, slabs of 'soon to be published fiction' are serialised, and in their monthly culture supplement, there are convoluted exegeses of Underground art forms.

In August 1969 it published the names, addresses and phone numbers of all narcotics agents in Los Angeles, San Diego, Santa Ana and San Francisco. 'There should be no secret police' announced the *Free Press*, justifying its action, but finding itself being sued for 25 million dollars.

The *Los Angeles Free Press* provides a more comprehensive coverage of its local radical scene than any other Underground newspaper — local strikes, pickets, student rallies, minor legal battles, and indeed every permutation

[8] Survey by *Orpheus Magazine*, August 1968.

of anti-authoritarian activity is delineated, dissected and digested for its 300,000 readers.

Efficient as it is, the *Free Press* lacks the tough hysteria of Max Scherr's *Berkeley Barb*, which, until the entire staff went on strike in July 1969, threw itself recklessly each week into the contemporary political holocausts of black power, student strikes and civil rights ... PICKETS WILL BE NEEDED FOR THE GRAPE BOYCOTT THIS SATURDAY ... STATE WIDE SUPPORT FORESEEN FOR CONS' FIGHTS FOR RIGHTS ... OVER 240 JOIN HUNGER STRIKE TO BACK CLEAVER ... PIGS SHOOT TO KILL—BYSTANDERS GUNNED DOWN—PEOPLE'S WAR ON ... and eventually ... MAX IS A PIG ...

The *Barb* dispute stemmed from disagreement about the low wages Scherr gave his staff and the high profits he took for himself. A raise was unacceptable unless Scherr made a contribution to the community as well. His offer to sell *Barb* to the staff fell through, and two weeks later they came out with their own paper, *Berkeley Tribe*. Max Scherr then sold the *Barb* to Dr Allan Coult. A move he regretted when the first issue was widely regarded as 'a police blotter'.

The *Barb* has always been ugly, angry, and anti-sentimental. The Beatles' *Revolution* was said to sound 'like the hawk plank adopted this week in the Chicago convention of the national Democratic Death Party'. While most underground newspapers were running semi-obituaries for Andy Warhol after Valerie Solanas' attempted assassination, the *Barb* reprinted the manifesto of her Society for Cutting Up Men (SCUM). The *Barb* introduced the Underground's first agony column, Hip-pocrates, by Dr Eugene Schoenfeld, who offers intelligent, informed answers to Underground press readers on any aspect of the human condition. 'What are the physical dangers, if any, for the passive partner in anal intercourse? ... After a recent session with acid I noticed severe pain in the joints of my knees. Is this common? ... I recently at the advice

165

of my friends, drank a bottle of Romilar CF cough syrup. What possible damage did I do to myself?' Hip-pocrates differs from other Dear Dorothys in that one reacts not with a sympathy for his correspondents, but with numb incredulity.

'Dear Dr Schoenfeld,
A couple of weeks ago my girlfriend and I got loaded and were making love. She told me she wanted to show me something new that would be a real thrill to me ...

What she did was to stretch my scrotum out tightly, then she took a pair of finger nail scissors and cut a small hole in the sac. I began to get scared but she said not to worry, it was fun and didn't hurt much. Next she stuck a small plastic straw into the hole in my sac and started blowing air into it.

My sac got bigger than a baseball, but surprisingly didn't hurt much and felt kind of good. I began to worry that it might burst so she stopped blowing and removed the straw. Then she quickly put a piece of adhesive tape over the hole to keep the air in. Then we continued with intercourse and I had a climax that was out of this world.

Afterwards she removed the tape from my scrotum and squeezed the air out with her hand. Then she dabbed my scrotum with rubbing alcohol (to prevent infection she said) and retaped the hole ... the next day my penis was swollen to about double its size and it itched like hell, but two days later it was O.K. again. What I want to know is could this practice cause me any harm?'

Before you reach for your nail scissors. Here is Hippocrates' reply:

' ... if any readers doubt that the practices mentioned are harmful, I should point out firstly that more bacteria exist in the mouth than in any other body orifice. Our skin is a natural barrier to bacteria and other micro-organisms which are not normally found in the ... scrotum. Infections of the scrotum? Not a pleasant prospect. Even more dangerous

166

is the possibility of an air embolism. Air forced into a closed tissue space may enter the blood stream, go to the heart, lungs or brain, and cause sudden death or a stroke.'[9]

Some Underground papers explore transcendental worlds, lyrical with love, beauty and technicoloured truth, far removed from the painful realities of a ballooning scrotum, black demagogues, Ronald Reagan, and grape pickets. Such a paper is *The San Francisco Oracle*, described by its editors as a 'visionary journal that relates social repression and reaction to the ecstatic intelligence of man ... a rainbow report from the inner eye'. Each issue is a unique work of art, individually coloured and typeset, difficult to read because it is so beautiful to look at. It is the paper which, more than any other, mirrored the true intensity of spiritual and aesthetic upheaval accompanying the hippie phase of Underground evolution. For many, these were the hallowed doors of psychedelic perception, sculptured on an electric typewriter, and splashed with colours most printers didn't know existed. This was the paper that sat Alan Watts, Timothy Leary, Allen Ginsberg and Gary Snyder on a ferry boat and turned on the tape-recorder:

[9] It is well known that Britishers are more fond of their pets than each other, and for them, the following extracts from Hip-pocrates' column might prove illuminating:

Q: My wife and I think it might be interesting for her to have intercourse, perhaps regularly, with a German Shepherd dog. We have not experimented however because we are afraid of weird diseases we might get. What's the deal?

The answer, among more detailed advice, recommended caution when displaying affection for furred or feathered friends, and said to beware of intestinal worms.

Q: I have fantasies of balling a female gorilla or other large ape. What's happening? I don't desire this to the exclusion of human females though. I now enjoy all varieties of sexual experience with females from 14 to 63. I am 28. This is not a put on.

A: You didn't give your sex or the ages of the apes you desire. Since your letter was postmarked New York City I would advise you to go to the Central Park or Bronx Zoos, to observe at first hand the wooing of apes. Gorillas are quite affectionate, but are also very exuberant. Bestiality is prohibited by law. Besides, what would you do about those fangs and claws?

the summit symposium on hippiedom, the great philosophic scrutiny of Leary's 'drop out' manifesto—how can you drop out *and* qualify as an astronomer or engineer? The answer, twenty three thousand, four hundred and eighty five words later—find a guru. The *Oracle*, as its name implies is preoccupied with prophecy, and appears whenever it feels like it. In these days, when Molotov cocktails are more literal than figurative, the rather occasional appearance of the *Oracle* comes as a nostalgic relic of bygone euphoria and its editors

simply
   sit   THE
      undisturbing   PEACE
  LETTING it   flow
    (as they put it)

The East Coast equivalent was *Avatar*, devoted to the genius of its own editor Mel Lyman (Aries): 'To those of you who are unfamiliar with me, let me introduce myself by saying that ... I am truth and I speak the truth ... In all humility I tell you I am the greatest man in the world and it doesn't trouble me in the least ... ' a theme which is further expounded in the letters column: 'Mel is the most gifted person in the universe—love Bill' ... 'Mel, I love you! I need you so bad! Kathy.' The front page shouts: 'We've been building a wall around Mel's house out of heavy heavy stone' and the subsequent twenty-seven pages depict people doing just that. The Spring 1969 issue consisted solely of large glossy photographs of Mel Lyman accompanied by his thoughts ('I'm Christ, I swear to God in PERSON, and I'm about to turn this foolish world upside down ... love Christ'). When not dominated by the greatest man in the world, *Avatar*, now re-titled *American Avatar* offers highly original, introspective explorations of the future, which are a relief from some of the more strident trumpetings of allied media.

This mystical mish-mash of madness and megalomania – associated with the Underground – is represented in the UK by *Gandalf's Garden*, which, like London's Middle Earth organisation takes its name from Professor Tolkien's Ring trilogy, in the belief that Gandalf, the White Wizard, 'is fast becoming absorbed in the youthful world spirit as the mythological hero of the age'. The cover picture of the first issue (November 1967) depicted its editor, Muzz Murray, cracking the shell of an egg from the inside, happily hatching. 'Gandalf's Garden seeks the sun in you' is the slogan, and in return it offers moonshine. Although the magazine is scheduled as a monthly it seems more in harmony with the natural seasons ('humble apologies for the lateness of the hour but someone dropped the seeds of issue Two in the undergrowth and we had a hard time finding them until they began to sprout'). A shop in Chelsea has also sprouted, which helps finance the magazine, sells home-made ties, candles, pottery, jewellery and homeopathic bath salts.

IT – formerly *International Times* until Lord Thomson's *Times* instigated breach of copyright proceedings – is the British Underground's first and only regular newspaper. For a journal dedicated to propagating an alternative theology, the recurring intrigues and machinations of its proprietors would elicit cries of admiration from hardened city speculators. Launched originally by Love Books Ltd. in October 1966, it was taken over by its staff two years later – in a fit of revolutionary fervour inspired by Paris and Hornsey (as everyone was in those days) – and re-registered as a workers' co-operative in the name of Knullar Ltd. ('fuck' in Swedish). At this time (August 1968) their offices in Betterton Street exuded a remarkably un-Underground atmosphere of rancour, paranoia and contortionistic back-stabbing. History repeated itself in October 1969, when staff rebels took over the offices, recruiting the squatting services of the London Street Commune fresh from their debacle at 144 Piccadilly. After another round of unsavoury squabbles a new tabloid, International Free Press, surfaced to compete with *IT*, then promptly sank.

The drably typographed first issue of *IT* contained a sad little editorial about how London didn't really swing. The 'International' in its title was interpreted with vehement literalism—reports flowed in from Stockholm, Warsaw, New York, Amsterdam (Simon Vinkenoog) and Paris (Jean-Jacques Lebel). Miles, one of the original co-owners, boosted the sales of early *IT*s with his eccentric un-edited interviews with Paul McCartney, Peter Townshend and John Lennon (who, believe it or not, once played hard-to-get). Other contributors included Allen Ginsberg, Yoko Ono, John Wilcock, Adrian Mitchell, Ray Durgnat, William Burroughs and Bertrand Russell. Harvey Matusow, a tireless infiltrator of all establishments, filed a grinning account of his attempts to telephone the CIA at the US Embassy. *IT*'s first significant manifesto was the front page reprint of Paolo Lionni's 'A Message to the Queen':[10] 'That every man, woman and child alive is an actual or potential poet ... That the reign of usury still standing between man and his desire to do a good job must finally come to an end ... that love need not remain a banal cliché but is and must be a constantly original and divine verb.' *IT* scoffed at journalists ('autonomous, advertising-supported uncreative writers') and journalists scoffed back— early subscription ads featured their welcoming raves: 'American anti-socialist beatnikery' (*New Statesman*), 'A flower children's comic' (*Sunday Telegraph*), 'Anti-white' (*People*), 'Completely destructive' (*Morning Star*), 'Slovenly and amateurish' (*Encounter*).

Euphoric freak-outs in Tottenham Court Road (UFO) were organised to bolster *IT* but 90% of the gate money was stolen; the police raided *IT*'s offices, John 'Hoppy' Hopkins, co-founder of UFO and *IT*'s production engineer was gaoled and Miles was rejected by the Arts Council committee because of his association with the paper. No

[10] *International Times*, No. 5, December 12–25, 1966.

wonder the editor at that time, J. Henry Moore, felt compelled to 'scream ... it seems that one is going to have to sever relationships with these bastards once and for all so as to have no involvement in their inhumanity (which is costing us a fortune). Don't buy things from them you can buy from your friends. Don't tell them anything ... If you can't turn your parents on, turn on them.'

By *IT*'s second birthday the tone had mellowed. The rage, paranoia and cultism had been replaced by languid lengthy theses on the Workless Society, Marcuse, Miseducation and an Alternative World, From Rock to Acid Rock, The Sexual Revolution, Arts in Society. *IT* 10 hinted that 'The world of the future may have no clocks.' Two years later *IT* lamented, in a new-found circumloquacity 'disappointing progress preconceptualising time. Humanity still experiencing itself in a clockwise direction, based on a deeply embedded assumption that time is a runaway vehicle hurtling through the universe to a destination called death.' In its own way, the paper had become influential. A small paragraph appealing for spectacles for the Albert Bailey Mission ensnared 1,575 pairs within two weeks. A month later they were being counted in ton loads.

IT's begging has given way to nervous apologies for making a profit. Their international link lines are as multifarious and informative as ever, but the paper now and again loses its local news sense and suffers from a lack of solid articulate reporters who could be less concerned with the metaphysics of time and more determined to probe the vagaries of their own community. In its fifty-second issue, the editor admits, ' ... we've become a little static, a little stale and whiskered, breathtaken by the fact that we have consolidated our economic standing and enchanted by our continually increasing circulation'.[11] *IT*'s most important contribution to England's Underground has

[11] 45,000 by December 1969.

been its own existence. The 'information sheet' approach has wet-nursed hundreds of Underground ventures and with editorial impartiality *IT* has integrated all kinds of Underground phenomena within its pages.

OZ began in Australia on April Fool's Day, 1963, as a monthly magazine of satire and opinion. A London *OZ* was launched in February 1967 and it has outlived its colonial predecessor. The magazine's success as an irritant (and the necessity of its existence) can be gauged from the reaction of a Sydney magistrate who found: 'the publication would deprave young people or unhealthy minded adults so injudicious as to fancy it as literature and so misguided as to cultivate the habit of reading it.' He disregarded the testimony of seventeen qualified witnesses who were so injudicious as to fancy the magazine had literary merit and so misguided as to deny its tendency to deprave and corrupt. He sentenced the editors to six months' hard labour. The next two years were spent in and out of courtrooms and TV studios protesting purity of motives and quality of character until eventual acquittal.

Australian *OZ* was never strictly an Underground publication, although it ran John Wilcock's *Village Voice* column, some sulphurous scandals from Paul Krassner's *Realist*, a sparkling endorsement of marijuana and a splendidly obscene fragment from Lenny Bruce. Australian *OZ* provided a desperate alternative to that country's puritan hang-over and monopolistic media structure. Since Australian *OZ*'s demise in February 1969[12] the burden of subterranean communication has fallen upon *Ubu News*, which is free, purple and angry, and getting better all the time, despite heavy-handed harassment from local police.

The genesis of London *OZ* was due more to the enthusiasm of a Fleet Street newspaper than the determination of its founder. Shortly after arriving in the UK from

[12] An inside confidential news sheet continues, as acidic and lonely as ever.

Australia I was interviewed by the *Evening Standard*. The idea of launching a London *OZ*, at that time barely a passing fancy, somehow ended up a headline: 'Rebel Aussie whizz-kid to publish here.' Telephones began buzzing with eager contributors, printers extended lunch invitations (where are they now?), and what was once merely my exhibitionistic impulse to impress a friendly gossip columnist soon gathered its own momentum and hit the streets a few months later with a resounding thud. The early *OZ*'s were an uncomfortable hybrid of satire, Sunday journalism and pirated Underground tit-bits. The art work of Martin Sharp and the excellence of some early contributors saved the magazine from total calamity. In Australia one was responding satirically to the daily diet of pomposity, intolerance and suicidal idiocy, employing like most satirists, a frame of reference obvious and acceptable to all. In London, not only did satirical intention seem redundant—other people were doing it better—but as a critical reaction to society it seemed inadequate and ultimately reactionary.

OZ went Underground with the help of John Wilcock who guest-edited the sixth issue, but stoutly maintained its self-cynicism: 'Hippies in England', wrote David Widgery, 'represent about as powerful a challenge to the power structure of the state as people who put foreign coins in their gas meters.'

Every *OZ* looks different and occasional guest editors are given full freedom to experiment. *OZ* intends to surprise. Often it contains posters, games, coloured comic supplements and always—psst—dirty pictures.

The first British paper to join the Underground Press Syndicate was *Peace News*, established in 1936 and respectable enough to qualify for distribution by W. H. Smith & Sons.[13] Neither its staff—nor presumably its readers—consider 'Underground' a felicitous description despite its membership of UPS.

[13] Except in times of war, when distribution is automatically suspended.

The Hustler, an angry, bitchy voice of British black power, shrieks out from the ghettoes of Notting Hill and North Kensington. It rails as much against the complacency of its black brethren as against white racism—or white sympathy, of which it is furiously suspicious: 'It is claimed that black men go dizzy when a woman takes her clothes off, so more than the usual amount of nymphomaniacs start knocking on black men's doors or inviting them for coffee or dinner, etc. ...' Maybe they are knocking on the door of Courtney Tulloch, head Hustler, a vibrantly eloquent local spokesman who has guest-edited *IT* and is a regular contributor, a one-time colleague of Michael (X) Abdul Malik. It is an honest community newspaper, crude, committed and direct as a slamming door.

A white man's answer to *The Hustler* is *The Black Dwarf*, which makes up in rhetoric what it lacks in jocularity. For its staff, *The Black Dwarf* is not so much a newspaper as a way of life—as it is too for the police who not only tumble in and out of the offices with highly publicised regularity, but make clumsy attempts to persuade overlooking residents to photograph every visitor. The Scotland Yard men must forever bump into the assorted drunks and sailors who also grope their way up the stairs in the belief that the mysterious 'Black Dwarf' is a particularly exotic species of prostitute.

The language of *The Black Dwarf* alternates between the academic (Marx, Engels and Ernest Mandel are regular contributors) and the colloquial ('We piss on you.') Unquestionably conscientious (the layout is said to be purposely dull so it can be sold successfully outside factories), *The Black Dwarf* with its heavy-handed applied Trotskyism and monosyllabic punch-up lingo seems outside the mainstream of Underground journalism, although if ever the barricades are erected across Trafalgar Square, it will be this newspaper that the rolled-neck sweater brigade will stuff in the backs of their jeans—or each other, for the British Left is nothing if not fratricidal. Already *The Red*

Mole has split from the *Dwarf* and a third publication, *The Idiot*, oscillates uneasily between the two.

One of the Underground's most sensationally successful media adventures is *Rolling Stone*. It was launched in San Francisco in November 1967 by 22-year-old Jan Wenner, who by April 1969 was air-freighting the negatives to London for a local edition produced in shaky partnership with Mick Jagger.[13a] While Wenner himself is lucidly contemptuous of the standards of the US Underground press, *Rolling Stone* is strictly a product of the phenomenon — not only by virtue of its subject matter (rock music) but by the uncompromising flair of its presentation. It was the only magazine circulating in England which reproduced *both* covers of John Lennon and Yoko Ono's *Two Virgins* LP, which showed the pair entirely nude, front and back.

With a West Coast circulation of 130,000, Wenner draws two hundred dollars a week on top of international travelling expenses. None of the staff receives less than one hundred dollars a week — an unusual prosperity in the annals of Underground publishing. Such resources enable *Rolling Stone* to analyse a selected subject with a breadth and depth not dissimilar to a *Sunday Times* Insight investigation, at the same time packaging it with considerably more wit and imagination.[14] What differentiates *Rolling Stone* from every other commercially orientated music publication (apart from its inherent libertarianism) is that its young staff actually *like* rock music — breathe it, feel it, understand it and even perform it.

There is now also *Earth Times*, which deals in the same comprehensive long-winded way with ecology and Rags,

---

[13a] Shaky indeed. By November 1969, Jan Wenner had disassociated himself from his progeny, and had persuaded Mick Jagger to do the same. Changing the paper's name to *Friends* the U.K. staff persevered with a modified version.

[14] See their reports on Groupies, American Revolutionaries, 1969, The Dope Story and The Underground Press, the Altamont Disaster and the Chicago Conspiracy Trial.

which uncovers what the kids are wearing to the latest rock festival.

Hapt is a free roneoed digger paper published in Colchester, linked with diggers in Europe. *Fire* is a luscious art-poetry event produced by Joe Berke of the elusive Anti-University, and occurs occasionally at 10/- a time. The breathtakingly futuristic *Image* was rescued from some bureaucratic scrap heap by John Esam who moulded it to his personal vision, organised 'Christmas on Earth Continued', a pop freak-out, in December 1967 to support it, swathed it in square career advertisements for Her Majesty's armed services and sent it bankrupt. The Notting Hill situationists unleash their Dada-Molotov cocktails wrapped in *King Mob Echo*, a plagiarised anarchistic batter. Associated with it is *The Oxford Wall*, published by 'the Oxford motherfuckers' as a counter to tradition-bound *Cherwell*. *Synic*, closely bound up with Black Power and hard core left-wing political activity in London seems determined to keep its circulation small by being deadly serious.

In June 1969, *Grass Eye*, a fortnightly Underground newspaper, appeared in Manchester and immediately encountered trouble with printers for using the word 'fuck'. In April 1969 came *The Catonsville Road Runner*, 'a revolutionary Christian monthly' which grew out of a radical Christian movement and disenchantment with the Establishment Church. Che Guevara, left-wing student activity, yippie philosophy and religious protest ('St Pauls is a liberated zone. We shall defend it') rest in its pages as uncomfortable bedfellows.

In America, the Underground Press has provoked substantial overhauls in media as disparate as Hearst glossies and high school newspapers, but in the UK overground media have proved typically resilient — even student papers, which (with rare exceptions) resemble trade journals for the asbestos industry, and read like unconscious panegyrics to Fleet Street.

In Europe there are dozens of Underground papers,

some of which double as clearing houses for the distribution of English and American hip-media. In Milan, middleaged Fernanda Sottsass Pivano and her husband Ettore produce the beautiful 168-page, 10 coloured *Pianeta Fresco*, which is passionately non-violent and benignly embroiled with hallucinogenic exploration. *Pianeta Fresco* is as about as Underground as you can get under Italian law, which stipulates that only a professional (i.e. belonging to the Press Association) can edit a magazine, and despite its pacifist intentions, Fernanda says that many of her friends are in gaol. Fernanda and Ettore are the Italian translators of Allen Ginsberg (who named their paper) and with their hippie bells and euphoric generosity are probably the youngest oldest Underground paper editors in the world.

The Dutch Underground press began with the first issue of *Provo*, published in Amsterdam in July 1965 and given away free (often wrapped in the morning papers). '*Provo* is a monthly for anarchists, provos, beatniks, layaabouts, tinkers, jailbirds, saints, sorcerers, pacifists, charlatans, philosophers, germ carriers, happeners, vegetarians, syndicalists, hustlers, incendiarists ... and of course we must not forget the men of the Internal Security Service. *Provo* opposes capitalism, communism, fascism, bureaucracy, militarism, snobbism, professionalism, dogmatism and authoritarianism.' For the first issue, 500 pamphlets were published, for the last, in April 1967, 20,000. A month after *Provo*'s demise came *Witte Krant* which lasted until February of the following year. A few days after the first issue, one of the principals, R. Olaf Stoop, was gaoled for possessing cannabis. Now Olaf Stoop is the organiser of *The Real Free Press* which, for a while, he operated from Belgium to avoid arrest by Dutch authorities who were anxious that he complete two more months of his prison sentence. The innocuous, Carnaby coloured *Aloha* (originally a music paper, *Hitweek*, founded in 1965 by Willem de Ridder who is credited with launching Amsterdam's hippie movement) has humorous nudes, comics, articles

177

of general interest, and a *Rolling Stone* format. In September 1969, Europe's first sex paper, *Suck* (printed in Amsterdam), was launched by veterans of the English *IT*/Arts Lab scene. *Suck* styles itself as an alternative to 'the kind of mind which could create obscenity laws'. They might have included 'libel laws' as well, considering the content of Earth Rose's 'Sucky Fucky' gossip column. *Suck* is an unabashed imitation of its New York prototypes with a bit of home grown culture thrown in – e.g. W. H. Auden's 'Gobble Poem', and Germaine Green's 'Lady, Haul Your Cunt!'

De Anders Krant, one of Europe's most regular and committed Underground papers, maintains fervent contact with all European Underground organisations and promotes brother magazines *Moksha* and *Om*. Belgium's *Eindelijk* from Ghent survived seven issues before being seized for publishing an allegedly obscene cartoon of one of the Belgian Royal family. Bernhard Willem Holtrop, Dutch Underground cartoonist and publisher of *God Nederland and Oranje* was likewise prosecuted for a cartoon offensive to a Royal person. Willem is the envy of Underground cartoonists on account of his prosecution for 'cruelty to the police'.[15]

Copenhagen's music orientated *Superlove* began in 1967 (circulation 10,000) and resembles *Rolling Stone* in style and content. George Streeton, a young Australian, launched *Superlove* to 'test whether a paper had to be bad in order to exist', and also operates as a base for distributing a complete range of Underground artifacts. Early in 1970, *Rotten*, more radical, less musically orientated but relying heavily on American material, appeared, taking a hard political line and making full use of the absence of pornography laws in Denmark.

From Berlin, *Linkeck* and *Radikalinski*, which produced communally by militant students, both take a tough line: for fighting against live targets, *Linkeck* recommends 'stones and bits of old iron, screws, nails, etc., which can be

178

mixed with explosives to add to the fragmentation effect ... '
and their graphics come straight from Swedish pornography
magazines. *Peng* from Wuppertal, *Po Po Po* from Cologne,
but the most dynamic German language Underground
paper, *Hotcha*, comes from Zurich in Switzerland, which
started in March 1968. It is the only example in the country,
says its founder, Urban Gwerder, of 'the celebrated Swiss
Press liberty'.

From Sweden comes the exhilaratingly obscene *Puss*
which is a vicious mixture of photomontage, cartoon and
copy which juxtaposes pornography and satire with a
freedom unequalled anywhere else in the world.

From Zagreb, Yugoslavia, comes *Paradoks*, graphically
superior, and exotically coloured.

Finland's *International Organ*—harassed by police for
organising an eight-day Sperm Festival, which, as a local
poet understated, 'made the cops notice that something
was happening'—changed its name to *Ultra* in late 1968,
and is the major Finnish underground paper. For a time
in 1969, a magazine called *Aamurusko* (The Dawn) was
published in Turku, and there is now a non-profit record
company called Love Records.

Several Underground papers (in the more immediately
militant sense) sprang up during the French crisis of May
1968, although there do not yet appear to be any regular,
widely circulated newspapers linked with the world's
Underground Press, in France. One of the products of the
May revolution, *Action*, announced excitedly a year later
that it had become 'the first daily underground newspaper'
but after a week, it died of exhaustion. European student
papers have produced special Underground editions and
occasional one-shot publications appear, scattered liberally
with extracts from Marcuse, R. D. Laing, Bakunin and
Situationist manifestos.

Eco Contemporaneo, a member of the Underground Press
Syndicate from Argentina, appeared in November 1961
as an 'interAmerican' magazine, which aimed to contact

young and rebellious poets from the Americas (North, Central and South). Within two years, along with the Mexican magazines, *The Plumed Horn* and *Pajaro Cascabel*, *Eco Contemporaneo* had helped create the New Solidarity Movement, which brought together poets from fifteen American republics for the 'first encounter of American poets', in Mexico.

In 1965 the editor of *Eco Contemporaneo*, Miguel Grinberg, altered the pre-occupation of his paper, recalling, 'when I stopped printing poems the solidarity of many poets stopped'. He further modified his aims to the imperative: 'create an alternative', thus bringing him more directly in line with other UPS members. A 31-year-old 'white Indian' son of Polish immigrants, he believes that UPS publications '*must* point routes and/or ideas for the development of human and creative ways of living in a poisoned world. In fact, for each marginal being who has done his "inner revolution" and points towards knowledge, there are thousands more citizens pointing towards darkness and angst. We – I call ourselves *psychenauts* – must become a creative tribe ... our Life must become an Art.' *Eco Contemporaneo*'s freedom to print has been interfered with in a desultory bewildered way by local police, who detained 500 copies at the printers and then forgot all about it. 'We are not the thing the Man considers dangerous,' says Miguel. 'Workers do not read us. At the Department of Police, my card reads "Leftist but Pacifist". Amen.'

Perhaps the bravest Underground newspaper is *Vito* from the tiny Caribbean island of Curaçao. In 1968, at Christmas, they published a special English edition for American tourists, beautifully designed and illustrated with woodcuts. Tourists were told that 10,000 of the 140,000 people had no toilets and that for those in the black ghettoes there was 'no tap, no house, no work, no future ... ' A unique 'tourist guide' invited them to: 'smell the polluted air which Shell spits over half of Curaçao ... notice how all the public beaches are owned by foreign hotels and the natives have no place for recreation ... notice the big palaces of churches next to the houses built for seven children families with no more than two bedrooms ... ' These observations were not unheeded. In May 1969, after days of violent rioting, the Dutch government flew 700 marines to the island to restore order. *Vito*, a ready-made scapegoat, was banned and the editor arrested.

In Jamaica, there is an underground/left newspaper, *Abeng* which supports the Rastafari, a wild-haired organisation of revolutionary militants, and advocates pot as a political weapon. *Abeng* circulates openly in Kingston, while across the water, an underground newspaper, *Lambi*, circulates clandestinely in Duvalier's Haiti. The editor of *Por Que?* the only radical newspaper in Mexico, was arrested in February 1970 and charged with instigating bomb explosions in Mexico City. One of the explosions destroyed his own magazine office.

Other papers deserving of a special merit badge for managing to navigate their way into existence, include Bombay's *Anti/Pro*, and Wellington's *Cock* (both assisted by the indefatigible John Wilcock) and *Olvidate*, an aggressive, brightly coloured tabloid from Bogota, which is sprinkled with Dada graphics, and looks like a sophisticated *IT*.

Canada has several UPS papers, of which the most beautiful is Montreal's *Logos*, and the most adventurous is the *Georgia Straight*—alias the *Vancouver Free Press*. The *Georgia Straight* achieved notoriety in the Underground when it published eight short instalments of Bob Dylan's unreleased novel *Tarantula*, and followed it up with the letter from Dylan's solicitors threatening prosecution if they persisted. Much concerned with victimisation of drug users, it issues each week a list of 'heads busted' and in June 1969, published a double page manifesto to the Canadian Government calling for legalisation of marijuana. From Ottawa there's the *Canadian Free Press*, better known as *Octopus*, which began in January 1967 ('The crucible of purifying experience'). From Winnipeg, Manitoba, came Steve Jones, *The Loving Couch Press* about which Jones once said: 'I throw in liberal trickies like little stories and sometimes even NEWS but mainly I try through graphics and anything else to destroy peoples' one-sided concept of reality.' In June 1969, the *Loving Couch Press* died and gave birth to *Omphalos*, which is devoted to Indian lore and presentation of the case of the Canadian Indian for racial and social equality.

It is in the United States that the Underground press predominates – some papers collapse, but at a much faster rate, others spring up to take their place. One of the most important UPS papers is New York's *Rat*, which was launched early in 1968 by Jeff Shero, former Vice-President of SDS and founder of *The Rag* from Austin, Texas. 'There's now a real underground paper, *Rat*, giving us the information we need to stay alive – even though Gems Spa pushes the *East Village Other* on its outside stand and hides *Rat* indoors on the back,' writes Kenneth Pitchford in *The Village Voice* (November 28, 1968) during the course of a savage manifesto from the Lower East Side Community.

Rat is the East Coast equivalent of the *Berkeley Barb* but with the fuse alight. In the pre-Chicago issue (August 23, 1968) the paper devoted 58.5% of its total content to preparations for the onslaught. This included a city map of Chicago, advice on how to cope with cops and Mace where to sleep, where to get first aid, how to survive. It listed the addresses of major hotels and which delegations would be staying in them, and published the phone numbers and addresses of the CIA and Armed Forces Induction Centres.[16] *Rat*'s report from Chicago – terse snippets of factual information and mini-interviews gathered by two staffmen with a tape recorder – provided a profoundly moving document from the American political furnace.

In their issue prior to the November Presidential

[16] This issue of *Rat* was cited by Mayor Daley as evidence of an organised plot to 'disrupt the National Democratic Convention and paralyse the city of Chicago'.

elections, *Rat* led off with an electoral bedtime story (from *Liberation News Service*) putting the contradictions of the Liberal ('a sad lizard named Lesser Evil') and the urgency of youthful revolt in neat perspective. Youth, imbued with a genuine vision, historical necessity and a good deal of grass, were not fooled. The *Rat* doesn't waste space with porridgey theoretical essays or because-it's-there news. Its raison d'être is uncomplicated: GET PEOPLE INTO THE STREETS. 'Direct action takes us into the streets, where we are visible, make contact with many different kinds of people and affect the life of a city. In the future, after we win, the streets won't just be another way to go from one office to another. They'll be meeting places, discussing places, communal gathering places: that's the significance of the cries "the streets belong to the people". ' In its famous 'How to Make it in the Jungle' series, *Rat* offered detailed instructions on how to steal from supermarkets ('If you can steal on the Lower East Side you can steal anywhere'), and how to plunge through turnstiles on the New York subway without paying. In 'Community Disservice' *Rat* offers advice on such schemes as how to close the local draft board office—with a phony letter-writing campaign. Dope availability, crash pads, cheap hotels, hustling free medicine—*Rat* gives its readers plenty of advice. It has an arrangement with the street guèrrilla group, the Motherfuckers, to let them have a page in an issue any time they want.

The integrity of *Rat* lies in its refusal to be swept along with fashionable rhetoric and in its dogged expositions of the stultifying mechanisms in force in society. Not many Underground newspapers have bothered to remind readers that: 'The cop's role is impossible in society. He's got to sit on top of all the legitimate anger that's a direct result of the failure of politicians' programmes to do any good. And at the same time he's getting fucked up himself—just another tool ... endless false consciousness.' A similar breadth of understanding is apparent in *Rat*'s report on

National GI Week, an effort by the Movement to link up with disgruntled GIs and to fight for their right to come home. This is a politics which is growing out of the Underground, not a hysterical manœuvre to contort contemporary dissent into the strait-jacket of Victorian economics. *Rat*'s world view permeates even its theatre and film reviews (sometimes riddled with soporific quotes from Marcuse) and their obsessive pop music coverage. *Rat* was quickly into the Underground pornzine scene, and following upon the success of *Screw*, unleashed *Pleasure* on uptown New Yorkers, who, unable to cope with *Rat*'s rabid politics, found themselves fascinated by its sexual equivalent. Early in 1970 *Rat* was taken over by a group of women liberators, who have proved a point because the paper remains just as aggressive and radical as it was under Jeff Shero's editorship.

It's one thing to call readers into the streets in New York, but in Dallas, an Underground editor is lucky if he can stop them burning down his office, to say nothing of police who have twice demolished the premises of *Dallas Notes*, and keep the office under constant surveillance. Although small and friendless (circulation 5,000) this newspaper dispatches its reporters to events of national significance and probes local news ignored or misrepresented by the Dallas press. It offers a lucid coverage of contemporary cultural trends and, like *Rat*, contains so much rock you can almost dance to it. Some humour too—from a record review of Gene Autrey's 'Back in the Saddle Again': 'The lyrics seem to be heavily dope orientated but in a magnificently subtle way. The astute listener will catch such gems as ... "where the longhorn cattle feed on the lowly Jimson weed, I'm back in the saddle again" ... Jimson weed indeed. We all know what he means, don't we gang?'

The Rag from Austin, Texas, *The Spectator* from Bloomington, Alabama, *The Great Speckled Bird* from Atlanta, Georgia, *News from Nowhere* from Dekalb,

Illinois, *Buffalo Chip* from Omaha, Nebraska and *Kudsu* from Jackson, Mississippi, share the same responsibilities of solitude — if they don't tell it how it is, no one else would. Who but *The Rag* could have reported for the people of Texas the very first performance of Mother Grit's Austin Anarcho-Terrorist New Left Beatnik Evangelical Travelling Troupe? And when George Wallace held his Omaha convention (March 5, 1958) the *Buffalo Chip* was on hand to record the police brutalities. Link-ups with *Liberation News Service* and the other UPS papers enable these outpost organs to provide their communities with world-wide coverage of radical-student-youth affairs.

Good Times was founded at the beginning of 1968 by the since departed Marvin Garson (his wife wrote *Macbird*) and until its incorporation as a member of the Universal Life Church was called *San Francisco Express Times*. It combines the intelligence of the London *Times* with the fire-breathing radicalism of *Rat*. Elegantly written, seductively designed, it is a strong contender for the leader of the pack.

To the north, in Seattle, *Helix* behind its indecipherable, highly original covers, is a good community newspaper, supporting local strikes, student demonstrations, sit-ins and monitoring police activities with almost as much fervour as the *Berkeley Tribe*. Benefit rock concerts every few months keep the paper financially afloat.

The American Underground continues to expand with profligate speed. Every month a new paper seems to make its appearance — lightweights such as *Miami Free Press*, *Long Beach Free Press*, *Space City News* (Houston), *Quicksilver Times* (Washington, DC) and *Astral Projection* (Albuquerque) follow, in varying permutations and combinations, the John Wilcock dope sex music politics formula. Others such as *Leviathan*, a heavy left-wing monthly from San Francisco and New York, follow a less successful tradition, and are likely to sink through their own political weight. As one dope freak at the '69 Woodstock Music and

Arts Festival shouted to a peddler of the *SDS New Left Notes*: 'Why don't you stop selling papers and join the revolution?'[17]

There have been at least two anthologies of material from UPS papers,[18] and some newspapers exist solely on reprints from UPS. *The Underground Digest* began in October 1967 ostensibly to 'feature the best of the underground press', but actually to make money. *Orpheus Magazine* was launched a month later to re-publish articles of importance and has since re-organised the entire structure of the Underground press.

'Due to the fact that the US is sick and is going to get sicker, we are going to make an all out effort to create a truly liberated zone ... *Orpheus Magazine* herewith announces its intention of moving its offices to a Free Zone located on the delta of the Colorado River, midway between California, Arizona and Mexico. Since the status of these deltas is ambiguous we will declare it a Free Liberated Zone and inhabitants will not be obliged to follow any of the irrational laws now in force in unliberated zones.'

Orpheus Press release, December 1968

In between relieving from bondage parts of the United States and taking care of UPS business, *Orpheus* still manages to publish a self-mutilated[19] multi-coloured bi-monthly collection of underground writing.

The brazen fecundity of the world's Underground — or 'alternative' or 'resistance' — Press, is the most significant

[17] Not that the heavies find it impossible to survive — *Washington Free Press*, and the White Panther orientated *Fifth Estate*, both long-established UPS members manage to combine steady circulations with dense political coverage and a total lack of humour.

[18] Jerry Hopkins, editor. *The Hippie Papers*. New American Library (Signet Book), 1968.

Jesse Kornbluth, editor. *Notes from the New Underground*. Viking Press, 1968.

[19] 'This magazine has been shot with a colt 45 automatic. Ugly, isn't it?'

publishing phenomenon of the decade, superseding the little magazines of the '50s and threatening the relevance of conventional mass media. It has demonstrated to scattered, isolated, psychic insurrectionists that they are not alone, that they are part of a swelling community and that their methodical internationalism is backed up, in practical terms, by the *Liberation News Service* and the *Underground Press Syndicate*, which have drawn these communities spiritually together into a global guerrilla camp.

In times of emergency, Underground newspapers are distributed free. *The Los Angeles Free Press* once gave away 75,000 copies to counteract an inflammatory and malicious demonstration report by downtown papers. Bundles of *Rat* were tossed to the crowds at Chicago. During the May revolution in Paris, *OZ* co-operated with the Vietnam Solidarity Campaign in printing leaflets of support and circulating them to Parisian students. *Outcry*, a free newspaper, sprang up during the Berkeley People's Park crisis. A copy reached London, where another 30,000 copies were printed and given away.

Readers write to Underground papers with the same intimacy and conviction that retired Colonels write to *The Times*—and sometimes with parallel results. Last year, a gentle Oxford Englishman, Robert Pontin, wrote to *IT* from a Turkish gaol, warning readers of the dangers of carrying cannabis in that country. At the time of writing Pontin had already served 2½ years of an eight-year sentence, and he revealed that some of the other 'foreign' inmates were serving terms of up to 30 years. An Underground committee to put pressure on the Turkish Government and publicise the issue, was immediately formed. The story was eventually picked up by the *Sunday Times*, the *Guardian* and BBC radio.[20] The prisoners, whose morale

[20] The Underground media's effect in cases such as these is contingent upon the story being taken up by the national press. Unless this happens, nothing else will. John Kois, editor of *Kaleidoscope* wrote to me: 'We detailed highly questionable finances on the part of the local District Attorney. A few months later, he was elected to judgeship with 80% of the vote.'

had already been boosted by the sudden attention, were moved to a less primitive central gaol. Sympathetic members of the public began corresponding with them, passing travellers visited them, and intending hikers were warned of the dangers of carrying drugs in Turkey. Finally, a special organisation was established in London to press for the release of, and to offer comfort and aid to, all travellers in overseas gaols for drugs and related offences.

The overground press operates with massive in-puts of capital and a poverty of imagination. The Underground's poverty is purely financial. This fact, coupled with a rabid, proselytising instinct and creative flair, determines the unique nature of Underground media. A dearth of type-setting facilities led to the discovery that simple, unjustified (ragged right-edged) columns are a pleasant alternative to rigid newspaper style. This led further in some cases to the abandonment of columns altogether, and the blending of typography with content. Underground publishers were the first to realise that if the paper is printed by a visual process, then it should be conceived of as a painting, not a child's set of picture blocks. Sections of Underground papers have often been magnified into posters. When did you last frame a page from *The Times*? Black inks were drained from rotary presses, and replaced by gold, turquoise, cyan blue, sienna, saffron, heliotrope, magenta and even white. A photographic process enables sweeping visual versatility, so the whole world can be plundered for decoration – from food labels, Oriental comic books, Tibetan scrolls and *Encyclopaedia Britannica*. Copyright is ignored. Underground designers enthusiastically inherited the graphic freedoms pioneered by Dadaist periodicals, but exceeded these horizons by clever exploitation of mass production techniques. It was the publisher of a 'hippie paper' who invented rainbow-inking on web offset machines by dislocating the automatic 'ink-mixing' roller.

The newspaper renaissance has produced a new race of graphic and comic strip artists, who assail the readers with an increasingly wild and outrageous synthesis of dope violence, sex and abstract fantasy. In the UK the work of artists like Martin Sharp, Mike McInnerney, John Hurford and Michael English, and the graphic ingenuity of Jon Goodchild have been decisive factors in the creation of the unique Underground visual style. In the US, it is the post-Feiffer comic strip artists who have predominated, introducing their readers to a world far removed from parent-approved Walt Disney's and his neuter ducks. Robert Crumb, the creator of Mr Natural, The Phonus Balonus Blues, Joe Blow and Angelfood McSpade, is perhaps the most famous of these. Angelfood is the archetypal white man's ideal animal fuck, 'with de biggest tits in town, fahn big laigs, an yo' awt to trah some o' mah sweet jelly roll.' She is rescued from her lazy dreamy jungle life by crew-cut civilisation, and put to work licking out lavatory bowls, while her captors shit upon her; an allegory which contradicts Crumb's earnest proclamation: 'No, I'm not political.' His works and those of other underground cartoonists (e.g. R. Cobb, Gilbert Sheldon, S. Clay Wilson, Spain Rodriguez, Kim Deitch, Vaughan Bode) appear regularly in the Underground press and in *Snatch*, *Yellow Dog*, *Zap Comix* and *The Gothic Blimp Works*, which is a comic monthly produced by the *East Village Other*. It has been said that Crumb 'kicks the American scene in the stomach', but with the akimbo-legged Angelfood, and the cunnilingering Mr Natural, the boot seems to be aimed more at the balls. Asked whether his work was intended to arouse the prurient interest of his readers, Crumb replied: 'I don't know about that ... but I'm aroused.'

'When a nation like America which holds its parliamentary 'democracy' so dear, which swears by its alienable rights, will blatantly abridge 'freedom of speech', somebody must be pretty fucking uptight.'

Liberation News Service

'Freedom of the press' is the gaudy armband of Western Democracy and compared with just about anywhere in the world it is a significant and precious adornment. Yet it is a freedom considerably constrained by discreet legal safeguards, and which discriminate against the poor, against minorities and against the Underground press. An international survey of subterranean newspapers conducted by *Orpheus Magazine* revealed that 60% of them had been harassed by police.[21] The tactics vary. Fourteen staff members of Mississippi's *Kudsu* were beaten up by deputy sheriffs who also confiscated equipment; the offices of *Dallas Notes* were sabotaged—the paper published a photo of the destruction entitled 'after the pigs left'; and both the office and the editor's car have been damaged by fire bombs.

In March 1969 the *Berkeley Barb* was busted for publishing a photograph of members of MC5 apparently fucking and sucking a female member of the White Panther party. Max Scherr, then still editor, claimed that the picture was designed to illustrate the White Panther demand for fucking in the streets.

The FBI intimidated *Rat*'s landlord and a friendly postal clerk warned the editor that the mail was being checked; Milwaukee adjusted its obscenity law to restrict *Kaleidoscope* and their street sellers are constantly, according to the editor, 'busted on unconstitutional permit ordinances'; in one day fifty young vendors of *Avatar* were arrested; the Parents' League for Decency conducted a smear/leaflet campaign against Atlanta's *Great Speckled Bird*; the editor of Los Angeles' *Open City* (now defunct) was sentenced to six months' gaol and fined one thousand dollars. *Space City News*, *Washington Free Press*, Philadelphia's *Distant Drummer*, St Louis' *Xanadu*, West Lafayette's *Bauls of the Brickyard* ('the only source of radical information for over 100 miles') and dozens of other Underground papers have

[21] Technical Supplement on Publishing. *Orpheus*, 1968. This survey completed before the post-Chicago wave of harassment.

suffered Government harassment of varying degrees of sophistication.[22]

Georgia Straight from Vancouver has perhaps suffered more than any other Underground newspaper—in September 1967 it had its business licence revoked and although this was eventually restored, the paper suffers continual police harassment and printing difficulties.[23] The editor has been indicted on charges of obscenity, police obstruction and incitement to commit an indictable offence (for publishing 'Plant Your Seeds'—advice on how to cultivate marijuana).

European Underground papers provoke a parallel official reaction, as we have seen in the case of Ghent's *Eindelijk* and Helsinki's *International Organ*. During the French May crisis, student papers were banned outright; issue 1 of Berlin's first Underground paper was confiscated for obscenity, and in January 1969, the editor of Zagreb's *Paradoks* wrote to his English readers:

'It is with a sad heart that I have to inform you that in the final round the dirty politics won over us—and PARADOKS, accused publically of anti-Sovietism and anti-communism, has ceased existing for the time being. Hopefully you will get our last condemned issue. We are, in spite of everything, fighting on, and I hope to start a new thing very soon.'

English Underground newspapers usually only have to contend with the occasional arrest of a street seller, dramatic office raids (*Black Dwarf*, *IT* and *OZ*) and 'friendly' police

[22] e.g. the editor of *Xanadu* was busted by a plain-clothes policeman masquerading as a hippie; the only two advertisers in the 1st issue of *Buffalo Chip* were threatened with violence. They didn't advertise again. The *East Village Other* has been charged approximately *twenty* times for obscenity.

[23] 'For almost two years, the forces of the law, order, power and the status quo have been trying to smash the *Straight*. They have used every legal, quasi-legal and blatantly illegal method at their disposal—short of coming down to the office with a goon squad and axes—to stop this paper from publishing. If they succeed it is certain that they will never again allow Underground paper to be started in this city' (*Georgia Straight*, March 6, '69).

visits—not necessarily because the politics of the papers is more subdued in this country or the authorities more merciful, but, because, unlike America, printers participate in legal responsibility along with the publisher, editor and distributor; acting as a censorial sieve. It is a stupid, reactionary and obsolete law which is as unfair to printers as it is to publishers. Complicated technical side-steps can be taken to immunise the printer (subcontracting, indemnification, libel insurance) but in practice the very existence of the law proves sufficient deterrent. London's *OZ*, *Black Dwarf* and *IT* have all experienced extreme difficulty in obtaining printers—despite the attractiveness of the job from a production and financial viewpoint.

Opponents of Underground publishing are quick to exploit this vulnerability. For some time in 1968 *OZ* was printed by a firm in Middlesbrough in which Woodrow Wyatt, Labour MP for Bosworth, had an interest. This was pointed out with some glee by *Private Eye* and with more effect by *News of the World*: ' ... he can hardly have been unaware of the true nature of *OZ*. How can he fail to be shocked by advertisements which offer do-it-yourself formulas for the drug LSD? Can he approve of the obscene poem or of the dirty pictures? Or of the advice to pot smokers? Clearly not.' A few days after this news item *OZ* was told to look for another printer, an arduous and depressing task. Even when assured that legal obstacles could be overcome printers raise other objections to Underground publications; it will upset other clients ('we print lots of religious material')—It will upset the unions ('too revolutionary')—It will upset the tealady. One printer once refused *OZ* because he was situated near Windsor Castle ('*They* mightn't like it'). If a publisher is able to withstand police harassment and is lucky enough to find a sympathetic printer, the last major obstacle is distribution.

In Great Britain two distributors virtually dictate what the majority of people in this country can select from their local bookshops and news-stands. Despite constant applications from Underground publications with tempting circulations and, in some cases, a willingness to vet material to taste, neither of them will consent to handle such publications.

The sense of camaraderie engendered by shared tribulations, overflows into the editorial pages. Most pages sympathetically headline their rivals' prosecutions and publicise each other's benefit functions. This picture caption to a full page illustration in the *Los Angeles Free Press* is typical. 'This is the first page of the current issue of *La Raza*, an Underground newspaper published in East Los Angeles by and for the Chicano community. Because of the harassment and gaoling of its editors, the FREE PRESS is printing this and a related story by FP reporter Jim Osborne on the next page as an act of fellowship with another Underground paper.' (June 7–13, 1968). There are dozens of other minority papers similar to *La Raza* which are wildly militant and spiritually linked with the Underground Press from Indian Reservation magazines (Rolling Thunder, an emissary from the Shoshone and Hopi nations attended the first UPS conference) to the famous *Bond*, the first anti-war newspaper for GIs, edited by Andrew Dean Stapp, founder of the American Serviceman's Union.[24]

The success of the Underground press has stimulated expansion in associated media. Film co-operatives mushroom everywhere. The US group, Newsreel, had made over 30 films by the beginning of 1969, the most famous being the hour-long revolt at Columbia, which has been shown on the Underground circuit throughout Western Europe. In

[24] An Underground paper was started in June 1968 by a group of 5 GIs at Fort Knox, called *FTA* (*Fun, Travel & Adventure* or *Fuck the Army*). The 1st issue stated: 'We're going to say what most of us say when talking to each other but we're going to put it into print. We want people to know they are not odd because they don't like what this man's army does to them. In fact we want to show just how many GIs feel this way ... ' There is also the much harassed *Fatigue Press*, from Fort Hood, Texas, *Shakedown*, Fort Dix and *Ally* from San Francisco, which has a GI membership of 30,000.

London there are several film and theatre propaganda groups, some co-ordinated under the title Agit-Prop, a revolutionary pamphleteering and street-theatre propaganda organisation. FM radio stations, and hip University stations in the US and what's left of the shipwrecked pirate radios in England all exchange material with the Underground press and derive mutual support from each other's existence.[25]

The next advance will be made in television. In New York there is an Underground Television workshop which experiments in political satire, obscenity and surrealistic fantasy, all interesting, but by comparison with the BBC of mid-60's, not particularly outrageous. In the UK the Arts Laboratories have discovered Sony portable video units and with them are revolutionising the possibilities of television, technically and aesthetically.

'I'm only in the underground press because I don't have enough money to get into television – underground television – that's where the underground will end up if we can ever get the bread together.'
> Jeff Shero of *Rat* speaking in *Rolling Stone*.
> October 4, 1969

Who reads the Underground Press? An *East Village Other* survey of 1,200 readers found that 71% had attended college, with 29% having graduated, and 13% having gone on to graduate school. It also showed that 98% had tried marijuana at least once and 77% had tried LSD. Among *EVO* subscribers are about 500 enlisted men in the armed forces, many of whom write to the paper.[26] Many assume

[25] The mid-July bulletin (1968) of Radio Love (the name chosen to emphasise the connection with the 'Underground Love Revolution'), London, announced: 'We hope to be able to help society to give its members more freedom without any need for revolution or chaos.' Society declined the offer. Radio Love was snuffed out pre-natally by a new Post Office Bill which contains such stringent conditions that it is now technically illegal to wear a hearing aid without a broadcasting licence.
[26] Quoted in *The Wall Street Journal*, March 4, 1968.

194

that the Underground press only preaches to the converted, although many of the 'converted' can't stand the Underground press: 'They're all the same', 'Sex obsessed', 'Too difficult to read'.

John Kois, editor: '*Kaleidoscope* has a circulation of eight thousand.'
Policeman: 'Eight thousand morons.'

Judging from the number of speaking invitations which flow into Underground editors from Young Liberal and Conservative organisations, high school magazine profiles, and from the reports of street sellers, readership is broad and variegated. An opinion not shared by Don Demaio, editor of Philadelphia's *Distant Drummer*, who has written to me that: 'While the purpose of the underground press must be, as I see it, to provide alternatives, the real purpose it serves right now is placating the straights who wish they were freaks. Ninety percent of our circulation is made up of people between 24 and 45 whose primary function is just to read what the freaks are doing. Depressing.' It would be even more so if it was 90% of the *freaks* who were reading what the freaks are doing. Underground editors should exploit their voyeuristic readership by speaking to them directly, attempting to harness their confused anti-society feelings—or if this seems too ambitious—at least defuse their animosity. G. William Domhoff, talking about the 'millions of well-trained, experienced, frustrated Americans who see stupidity and greed all around them' greatly stresses their importance to radical students, reminding them that: 'When people talk about the small percentage of Bolsheviks who took over Russia, they often forget the overwhelming numbers who passively accepted them, in that case out of disgust with war, despair, and a lack of a plan of their own that they really believed in.'[27]

[27] 'How to Commit Revolution in Corporate America', G. William Domhoff, speech given to the Student Strike Rally at the University of California, Santa Cruz, April 26, 1968.

Some indication of the commercial potency of the Underground press can be gauged by the attempts made by established media to woo their markets. Some fail, like *Cheetah* ('A magazine that could have succeeded', says Jan Wenner, 'if they had just copied *Rolling Stone* exactly. There was room for two'), others nearly make it, like Hearst's *Eye*. English overground magazines carry Underground supplements and a German corporation is currently considering whether to launch a European Underground *Nova*.

The Underground press can only escape the sweating clutches of boardroom executives by running into the streets, like the *Rat*. (Jeff Shero, has remarked that his newspaper will probably be 'liquidated'.) Some papers would collapse without revenue from 'straight' advertising and anyway, the very desire to distribute through national wholesale chains, highlights the dilemma of the Underground, which sometimes seems like the victim of a vast visionary exercise in world merchandising. A semiconscious counteraction to the Establishment's seduction attempts was embodied in the first declaration of the meeting of the Underground Press Syndicate in San Francisco in March 1967. Here the objectives of the Underground press were outlined as:

1 To warn the 'civilised world' of its impending collapse.
   (a) To set up communications among aware communities outside the establishment.
   (b) To reinstate reality-responsibility to mass media.
2 To note and chronicle events leading to the collapse.
   (a) To observe facts which reflect and unveil in advance the undercurrents dangerous to freedom.
   (b) To provide an accurate history of the rapid changes coming about through technological acceleration.
3 To advise intelligently to prevent rapid collapse and make transition possible.
   (a) To offer as many alternatives to current problems as the mind can bear.

196

(b) To consciously lay the foundations for the 21st century.

4 To prepare American people for the wilderness.
  (a) To instruct in survival techniques.
  (b) To seek out others of like thoughts and to recognise each tribe.
  (c) To prepare ways of living should the machine stop.

5 To fight a holding action in the dying cities.
  (a) To advise how to reinstate balance to the ecology.
  (b) Publish programs for conservation and reclamation.

A factor common to societies on the brink of revolution is the 'transfer of the allegiance of the intellectuals', a phrase borrowed from another historian by Crane Brinton in his *The Anatomy of Revolution* and applied with varying degrees of emphasis to the English Revolution of the 1640's, the American Revolution, the French Revolution and the Russian Revolution. Brinton points out that in all these cases, prior to the actual political upheaval, the journalism and literature of the day was directed against an existing government — as distinct say, from the Victorian period where intellectuals who, if they were alienated at all, were not alienated against the government, but against their 'environment' or each other. There was the French Enlightenment School: 'rebels all, men levelling their wit against Church and State or seeking in Nature a perfection that ought to be in France', the profound political and social criticism of the Russian novelists, and the vicious pamphleteering in England under the first two Stuarts: ' ... quantitively enormous, even by modern standards ... almost wholly pre-occupied with religion or politics — better, religion *and* politics — and is about as good an example of the transfer of allegiance of the intellectuals as could be found.'[28] Another example, surely, is contemporary Western Society, with the place of the pamphlets

[28] Crane Brinton. *The Anatomy of Revolution*. Vintage Books, 1965.

being taken by the Underground press and allied media, and where the preoccupations of religion and politics still remain but in a modified form: politics, in the broadest sense, has *become* a religion.[29]

Without our stretching the analogy, it seems Professor Gooch's[30] description of the period of James I: 'proclamation followed proclamation against the sale of "Seditious and Puritan books" and there was "much talk of libels and dangerous writings"' is oddly appropriate today. Indeed it is echoed by a speech to students at Yale: ' ... [Underground papers] encourage depravity and irresponsibility and they nurture a breakdown in the continued capacity of the Government to conduct an orderly and constitutional society' (Joe Pool, late Acting Chairman of the House Un-American Activities Committee).[31] Now, in the face of what Pool calls 'today's Molotov cocktails thrown at respectability and decency in our nation' the forces of law and order are beginning to fight back. An organisation called Media Laboratories Inc., has announced the first right-wing Underground newspaper, *Max*, aimed,

[29] For those who draw inspiration from comparisons, Professor Brinton's further preliminary signs of revolution include: ' ... government deficits, more than usual complaints over taxation, conspicuous governmental favouring of one set of economic interests over another, administrative entanglements and confusions ... loss of self-confidence among many members of the ruling class, conversion of many members of that class to the belief that their privileges are unjust or harmful to society, the intensification of social antagonisms, the stoppage at certain points (usually in the professions, the arts, perhaps the white-collar jobs generally) of the career open talents, the separation of economic power from political power and social distinction ...' A familiar tune, but Brinton warns that, 'some if not most of these signs may be found in almost any modern society at any time.' Ibid., p. 65.

[30] G. P. Gooch. *English Democratic Ideas in the Seventeenth Century.* Cambridge, 1927.

[31] The *Dallas Morning News*, November 7, 1967. Pool is also quoted as saying: 'This character-assassination plot is the most dastardly fifth column attack ever inspired by those who would destroy us here in America. They know that the more obscene and dirty their newspapers are, the more they will attract the irresponsible readers whom they want to enlist in their crusade to destroy the country. Responsible publishers know that freedom of speech can be lost if the First Amendment is abused by the mudslingers who tell one lie after another to destroy those who oppose them.'

according to its editors, at 'the Great Washed ... you know, that group of kids that want to carry our flag not shred it.' If it ever appears, interested readers will no doubt be able to order it through their wholesome family merchandiser.

ON
THE
ROAD
TO
KATMANDU

'The hippies are now, of course, the major British contribution to the Afghan scene.'

Philip Goodhart, MP – May, 1968.

The
Pot
Trail

A spectre is haunting the world; the spectre of long hair. In April 1966, French immigration officials were instructed to refuse admission in future to persons whose 'unkempt clothes, shaggy hair and evident uncleanliness might be thought to offer an undesirable spectacle'. Since then, gendarmes have been regularly flushing foreigners from beneath the bridges of Paris in sorties known locally as 'operations anti-beatnik'. In May 1967, in a joint statement, the Greek Minister of the Interior and the Minister of Public Order proclaimed: 'Entry is prohibited of any foreigner who is unclean and not dressed properly.' In November 1967, the chairman of a committee of British MP's who visited Turkey, reported to Parliament about the nuisance caused by hundreds of 'British hippies' swarming through the Middle East. 'They use drugs, have no money, and are in a very sorry state,' he told the House of Commons. The Consulate-General in Istanbul added helpfully: 'It is not only young men. Young women are also involved.' He went on to explain that the consulate had to deal with '1,000 problem youngsters a year'.

By December 1967, the virus had struck central Asia. In London, *The Times* revealed that ' "flower people" arriving in Nepal will now receive visas valid for only one week and not renewable'. A hippie camp near Katmandu was disbanded and the leader deported. Where to now? Further east, young man, to the remote retreats of South-East Asia – but not for long. By May 1968, a group of twenty-two travellers (the 'first batch') were expelled by the

Laos authorities, who, according to *The Times*, 'were disturbed at the increasing numbers of hippies, and the reputation they were giving to the country'. (A harsh condemnation, considering Laos' existing reputation.) Before these luckless deportees were admitted to next-door Thailand, they were made to shave their beards and cut their hair.

Meanwhile, harassment continued everywhere. In April 1968, the Italian newspaper *Il Tempo* complained of the disfigurement of Roman monuments by the ragged and longhaired: '[They] delouse themselves in the streets, camp on the steps, brawl, beg tiresomely, take drugs, undress, and anything else permitted them in the name of a misconceived liberty, which first of all offends against the liberty of the citizens and the decorum of the capital of Italy.' So the police swept the 'beatniks' off the Spanish Steps. In July 1968, Yugoslavia officially 'declared war on hippies' and the Belgrade newspaper *Politika Ekspres* reported that groups of boys armed with scissors had been forcibly carrying out haircuts on long-haired visitors. The paper continued: 'Modern tourist nomads, boys and girls from all parts of the world, have become a menace to the town.' In Mexico border guards began turning longhairs back with the words: 'No hippies, no Jews; on Presidential orders.' As one Underground paper explained: 'Mexico is having a spring cleaning and it's the hippies who are getting the broom up their ass.'[1] By April 1968, Argentinian police had arrested 133 'hippies' and sheared their hair to crew-cut length. In September, the Turks officially banned 'louseniks' from the country, and *Hurriyet*, the largest selling newspaper, warned that Istanbul was being 'stained by beatniks and hippies who have attached themselves to the city like ticks'.

In October 1968, the *Times of India* reported that:

[1] One year later: Señor Israel Nogueda, Mayor of Acapulco, in Mexico, has said he will mobilise the entire police force, to prevent hippies from entering the resort during Easter. He described a hippie as dirty, non-conformist, without a permanent income, dressing extravagantly and personifying vice and degeneration (*Times*, March 29, 1969).

'Some New Delhi magistrates are wondering whether there is a sinister pattern behind the hippie invasion of the capital.' Eighteen months later, the Government of Singapore pushed the fashionable fascination with ecology to ironic conclusions. Hippies were banned for 'polluting the social environment with drugs and other degenerate habits.' In Spain 'the hairy ones' are regularly evicted from their rented houses. Those who complain to the judge in Ibiza are told that the houses have no sanitation, a condition which, if consistently applied, would result in the eviction of most of the native population.

This hirsute new breed of travellers packs a socially disruptive valence way beyond the significance of its numbers, which are, anyway, soaring at a phenomenal rate. What goes on behind the spying eyes of local fishermen as a tribe of naked Californians frolic on the barren beaches? Here are the products of a civilisation which is the envy of most Spaniards, begging, living in caves, and dressing like madmen. On Sundays, when travellers happen to congregate near a church, one senses the bewildered curiosity of the children, and the hatred in the eyes of the priest. In Marrakesh, the bizarrely beautiful, velvet and satined Western girls tell stories of angry, veiled Arab ladies rushing up, shaking them and asking, 'Who are you? Who are you?' In Katmandu, a meditating hippie gives all he has to a Nepalese, but police return it. It is unthinkable for a beggar to possess £60. In Bangkok, Western travellers are cleared from cafés by nervous Thais with sub-machine guns, and debating the hippie influence is a national pastime. This letter in the *Bangkok Post* was written by a Thai —they are a deferential self-effacing people who normally accept the corruption of their administrators as cheerfully as the English accept bad food:

'Sir,
Parliament have nothing to talk about except how to prevent

long hair on men and short skirts on women ... Anything
they are not used to they condemn and try to stamp out.
What exactly are our elders used to? They are used to vice,
they are used to crime, they are used to corruption, they
are used to bad roads, they are used to bad drainage
systems, they are used to low pay for lower officials, they
are used to red tape for simple requests, they are used to
bullying the people, they are used to numbered Swiss
bank accounts, they are used to minor wives for themselves,
they are used to big cars, they are used to coming to the
office at 11 o'clock, and they are used to leaving at 2 o'clock
... It seems more convenient to sweep such things under the
rug, but long hair must be stopped because it is a bad
influence on our youth, ha, ha.
Taem.'

Bangkok Post, September 26, 1969

No wonder pot-trail countries want to outlaw these doped-
up refugees from the richest lands in the world; these
speechless missionaries, these gadflies on a country's non-
conscience.

'Who is in charge of you? What are your plans? Where
are your headquarters?' asked the Greeks when they gaoled
Neal Phillips, an American traveller, for hash offences.[2]
A hippie ban in Argentina was backed by the local 'Federation of Anti-Communist Democratic Organisations' who
warned: 'Hippies will become communist guerrillas after
they learn to live outdoors without food.' It is not only
fascists who are unnerved by the politics of long hair,
pot and communal living. 'Last year a group of long-
haired "hippies" who used to meet outside the Hotel Capri

---

[2] He was later to answer them, ' ... nor do we have a telephone, nor a
secret organisational chart nor any formal connection at all with each other,
but there are millions of us, we are all around you, everywhere, even under
the very ground you tramp with hob-nailed boots .... We shall simply
ISOLATE YOUR MINDS. This is the movement you feel all around you and
which you cannot understand, the vibration in the air which disturbs you
so, the thing you slash at with your swords but cannot kill, and which is
growing until it will engulf everything.' *OZ* 17, All along the Watchtower.

were rounded up and sent to cut cane in Camaguey. They were alleged to have been involved in organising prostitution for foreign seamen, but I had the impression that their long hair was the real offence.' (Michael Frayn, writing on Cuba in the *Observer*, 12.11.68.)

What sort of people are these itinerants who panic Greek officials into nagging prisoners for telephone numbers, prompt cynical Laotian bureaucrats to worry about their reputations, and propel Delhi magistrates into fits of hyperbolic hatred? Young Americans, Australians, Britishers, Canadians, French, German, Dutch, Italians, Japanese, Scandinavians, and South Africans who dress, talk and travel the same language. New gypsies who flow across the world; congealing in communal crash pads, caves, camping grounds, Youth Hostels, YMCAs and hotels. Hundreds of them dream months and even years away in Moroccan and Spanish pot holes. Thousands more press eastwards from Istanbul through Ankara, Erzurum, Tabriz, Teheran, Mashed, Herat, Kandahar, Kabul, Peshawar, Lahore, Amritsar, Patna, Katmandu, Calcutta, Rangoon, Bangkok, Vientiane, Phnom Penh, then south through to Kuala Lumpur, Singapore, Indonesia and Australia, there to recuperate physically and financially, before travelling on through the Pacific Islands (New Caledonia, Fiji, Samoa, Hawaii) or north-east to Japan, and back to Europe via the trans-Siberian railway. Nowhere is inaccessible. They tramp through Africa and South America. In Bangkok, I met a couple who had *hitch-hiked* through China. In Singapore I met young Americans who had thumbed through South Vietnam, only to be attacked – not by VietCong – but by 'Vietnik'-hating, uniformed fellow countrymen.

It is impossible to give an accurate estimation of the number of young overlanders, because visa applications are not categorised in age groups or by appearance. It has been roughly calculated that over 2,000 British 'hippies' passed through Kabul, Afghanistan, in 1967. That figure has probably more than doubled by now, and if you consider the influx of hippies from other affluent western countries, one can anticipate a traffic jam in the Hindu Kush by the mid-seventies. Not all are beaded trippers, preaching Haight-Ashbury. Gallant Land-Rover brigades head out from Earls Court with khakied Australians and tweeded secretaries determined to experience every square inch of mosque and desert. As the vehicles fall to bits, so do the travellers. This on-the-road dichotomy provides an instructive analogue with home sociology. Alf sets out with school blazer and golfing shoes; flag sewn neatly to rucksack, with maps, a compass and paraffin stove. He loathes the natives, collects local bus timetables and ponders the wisdom of his *International Hostels Guide*. But these days, Alf rarely makes it home intact. Circumstances force him to share the same cheap facilities as his beat counterparts, who, in the past three years, have come to outnumber him massively. Alf's stiff upper lip quivers under the aroma of kif, and home he eventually comes, in a Moroccan djellaba and Indian sandals, a gold earring through his left ear and carrying a Turkish carpet bag. The *Tibetan Book of the Dead* has replaced his hostels' guide, the stove has been swapped for a bamboo flute, and the compass jettisoned long ago. Alf will never be the same again.[3]

Whatever the navy may tell you, travelling overland is the best and cheapest way to see the world. You might miss the Topkapi Museum and the Taj Whateveritis; instead you can paddle your own canoe down the Mekong River, nibble aphrodisiac chocolate in a South Thailand teenage

[3] A 24-year-old journalist from Edmonton, UK, set off last year on a race around the world for a pint of beer, with £10 in his pocket. 'His luggage at the start of the race was a suitcase containing toilet requisites, maps and writing material, a sleeping bag, a track suit for use as pyjamas, four club ties, four pairs of socks, six white shirts and a coat hanger. When the shirts became soiled, he would have them laundered. He was resolved to be the perfect English gentleman in every situation, always smartly dressed and reasonably polite,' said *The Times*. Where is he now? Quite possibly stoned out of his mind in a Calcutta hippie commune, naked and unashamed.

brothel, be massaged in a steaming Moroccan bathing-dungeon by a fastidious Arab. Drift with the current and end up in places you never knew existed. On the way from Singapore to Dover, I rested awhile with a Malay in his local fishing village and saw coconuts harvested by trained monkeys, who, if they're underfed, organise strikes. A sick companion was cured by a licensed medicine man, trained cocks fought each other on our porch and I saw the son of the house married to a total stranger in a slapstick wedding ceremony.

In Phnom Penh an old woman loaded the pipes as I tried to smoke opium, and I sat in the temples of Angkor Vat watching the jungle make love to stone ruins of a medieval civilisation. On a Formentera beach I met a pop-art mermaid who lived on brown rice and talked like the *San Francisco Oracle*. In Rangoon my passport was confiscated and I sat in its only hotel, a lavish mausoleum to the British raj, watching a palm court orchestra play George Gershwin to an empty ballroom—as it had been doing every night since Burma closed itself off from the world. Outside, children slept on the roads and rats frolicked in the moonlight.

Fifteen thousand feet up the Himalayas I lost my Sherpa guide, cried a little, and was found by shepherds who took me to their camp fire, where we talked a special universal language. I slept among mountain villagers who wall-papered their mud huts with pages from my discarded *Newsweek*; at dawn I was aroused by cows who pissed on my sleeping bag. In the precious city of Katmandu—now already leaping headlong into the 15th century—I saw a beautiful 13-year-old official Goddess (who one day was to be pensioned off because no one would marry her); I met a yogi man who told me tomorrow; I watched a Tibetan girl weave rugs as she studied her paperback edition of *Playboy*'s Party Jokes...

You will see the most cosmopolitan examples of graffiti in the world (while discovering that fingers and water are better than toilet paper), learn to say 'I have no money' in seven languages and to communicate with anyone, anywhere, without any words at all. When you are lonely and broke in Amritsar, speeding towards the bus terminal at four in the morning in a bicycle rickshaw, you will crash into another rickshaw bound recklessly for the same terminal, with a similarly indisposed occupant, whom you once met three years before at a party in Maroubra, Australia, and who now as a gesture of companionship extends his second last morphine capsule. There is the 'hitch' you will never forget. Mine happened at the wrong end of New Caledonia, after jumping a Noumea-bound bus. It was a heatwave, the ex-army truck had no springs, one Melanesian too many had used my lap as the luggage compartment, and the capital was twelve hours away. Although I would lose my fare and there hadn't been another car for hours, I got out. A decision immediately regretted as I sat by the empty roadside watching the bus disappear into the horizon. The first car that came by was someone on his way to a private plane. 'I need a co-pilot,' he laughed, and two hours later, I was back in Noumea, swimming. On communal floors all across the world, you will participate in a turned-on league of nations; around a chillum with a Thai girl on her way to a finishing school (she will never make it of course), a middle-aged Danish beatnik with his wide-eyed Prince Valiant son, an American Vietnam deserter heading for Switzerland, an Israeli poet whom you last saw swimming down the main street of Bangkok in a flood with an umbrella, gentle Jeffrey from Wiltshire, who sings English madrigals, unaccompanied, the failed immigrant Dutchman returning home from a hated New Zealand, French hippies, Canadian poets and Australian surfies on their way to Cape St Francis in South Africa to ride forever the perfect platonic wave.

Some are folk heroes, whose names echo across the globe; like 'eight fingers Eddie', an involuntary father figure to what he calls 'the white tribe' and who, judging from the prolific gossip, possesses an enviable capacity to materialise in several world capitals simultaneously; the Customs officer at the Afghanistan border who smokes hash with the travellers, and offers a bed in return for more tangible demonstrations of companionship; Fritz, pink-shirted, intellectual extrovert painter who roams the world with a baby gibbon on his shoulder and who has been everywhere and knows everything; 'Most snake bites are a good trip, man'; the aptly named Fuzz, a hefty British Columbian, who's famous for greeting every new environment with 'Let's haul ass outa here', and single-handedly tearing apart inhospitable hotels; Pancake, a travelling Dutch chef who knows 101 ways of boiling water and has kept alive hordes of hungry hippies with his ingenious batter mixes. In Tangier, there is Achmed (along with Brion Gysin and the unclad mid-day meal of William Burroughs) whose superpotent repertoire of narcotics is legendary and who is credited with having first blasted the Rolling Stones into that other dimension. In Ibiza, there's a man, from Lancashire, who made his fortune drug-running, and now hosts real life, *Time* magazine, hippie spectaculars on Formentera, with champagne, pot and venison for all, and at last report is in a gaol in India. Hopefully, you won't have to deal with the British Consulate in Kabul, which vents such spleen on the dishevelled refugees, that even under such emergency circumstances as losing a passport, it is still considered safer to smuggle yourself to the less intolerant bureaucrats in Delhi.

Notes
on
Survival

The going is tough. I've met many a despondent traveller, languishing in unsympathetic surroundings, awaiting, at the Post Restante, an air ticket home from his father.

Despite copious supplies of pharmaceutical wonder drugs, you are sure to suffer the oozing results of eating unfamiliar foods. Hepatitis is common-place.[4] Everyone has their pet theory as to what causes it (excreta in the drinking water, foul vegetables, shared syringes) and you can find yourself wasting away in an unspeakably depressing ethnic hospital for months. An all-purpose prophylactic gamma-globulin injection will temporarily immunise you.

As you read this, hundreds of world travellers are huddled together in crash pads, town squares, or on the backs of buses, gnawed at by an identical craving: hunger. Although in most countries, even with a few pennies, it is difficult to get a worse meal than you do at a typical London café, people get embroiled in mystic drug rituals and forget to eat. Often, some time passes before it is realised that one is on the brink of starvation.

Like a young Englishman who arrived at the Benazir Hotel in Kabul, after days on the road without food and immediately devoured one entire, giant-sized melon. He was very soon carried off to an Arab doctor, shrieking from stomach cramps. Local foods are generally safest to eat, especially when they are cooked in front of you. Bed bugs, you will just have to sleep with, but keep them out of your hair, with the help of dog insecticide shampoo unless you fancy a bald spell. The safest way to receive money is through banks, but allow three weeks for express cable transactions. It is less wearisome, restricting and costly, to carry it with you – in US dollars, if possible. You will not receive cash sent through the post, whether it is hidden in carbon paper, or sent registered.[5]

Use aerograms for your own letters in poorer countries,

[4] Laughingly dubbed 'hippytitis' by Consular officials.
[5] Oriental thieves are cunning: All mail to Nepal must pass through India. Every Christmas the Pakistani Consulate in Katmandu is sent a crate of whisky from its Foreign Office. Every year the crate arrives, seals and bottles unbroken, but with the precious liquid drained away.

or, if you use stamps, insist on having them franked in your presence, otherwise the postal clerks will detach them to sell again. When you're sending hash, compress it between two sellotaped post cards in an envelope and omit name.

Embassies are an extension of Governments, so remember the anti-hippie mania when applying for any visa. French diplomats have instructed consular officials in Nepal to refuse visas to their hairy countrymen. This innovation may be imitated. A sign outside the Afghan Embassy in Iran reads: 'Visas will not be given to people with long beards or hair like that of beetle.' Berets are ideal for secreting long hair in, borrow a grey flannel suit, or wear a short-back-n-sides wig. Carry a biro. A favourite Embassy ruse is not to lend you one—i.e. if you are kept waiting long enough, you might go away. Pool money to cover any 'minimum currency requirements'.

You can buy forged student cards almost anywhere (three dollars in Istanbul, two dollars in Kabul, one dollar in Katmandu) which save money on trains and some airways. For a little more, you can buy *genuine* student cards at the Turkish Students Union. Fifty forged student cards printed in India cost one dollar, and you can sell them to fellow travellers for a dollar apiece.

Begging works in the outer city areas and especially in countries where Europeans are considered a novelty. You can assuage your guilt by dashing off a few pavement drawings, earning up to fifteen shillings a day. In emergencies girls can fuck repressed Moslems for a fortune. Couples can make money by letting them 'just lookee'. Throughout the Arab world the youthful male is regarded as having charms quite equal to those of your overworked girl friend.

Your blood value varies from £3/10/- a pint (Turkey) to £28 (Kuwait). Most world markets are flooded with folksingers, but you're rich if your guitar is electric. You can offer English tuition privately or in schools; price

213

depending on appearance. Useful if in town for a while. Make scarves, sandals, belts.

Small-time smuggling is rewarding and risky. Pick up the hints on the road. When buying lapis lazuli in Kabul, choose stones with fat gold seams for India and ones of rich, broad blue for Europe. Take free-port electronics to the east and return with turquoise, rubies and assorted antiques. (One man became rich by buying batches of sitars at 25 dollars each.) You can carry pot back and forwards from a Pakistan canning company, which tins it with a delicious apple jelly. A factory in Lahore makes firearms to any specification for the price of toy ones, and many a flower child has kept alive by gun-running. (Don't ever fire them, they're made of cast iron). Men in tight, checked suits and horn-rimmed glasses will offer you small black cases to deliver to Copenhagen in return for a free air ticket to anywhere in the world, but don't.

Sell your western-styled jeans in Nepal, and your long leather boots in Morocco. Once you could make 500% profit bringing back sheepskin jackets from Kabul, and you can still triple your money with antique robes. Your passport can fetch up to £200 in Istanbul or Tangier. In Calcutta you will be pestered with dealers wanting to buy your *unsigned* traveller's cheques at half the nominal value. Write lengthy articles for local newspapers on how much you like the country and its government. Film extras are in constant demand in Algiers, Colombo and Tokyo, and are said to be well paid. In Bangkok, many travellers keep alive by selling little white pills (probably aspirins) in a routine as bizarre as it is cynical: Thai employer introduces traveller to an unsuspecting, trusting village audience, as, say, Dr Schweitzer from Harley Street. Traveller recites Shakespeare or dirty limericks to the crowd, while enthusiastically waving a little bottle of white tablets. Thai accomplice 'translates' this into an exciting sales blurb. The tablets sell swiftly, and traveller reaps a fat commission. Variations on this theme can be played to native communities throughout India and the Far East. When it comes to exploiting innocent primitives, hippie nomads can be as ruthless as governments.

Thailand seems a long way to go to sell pills. Some travellers set out with the intention of merely navigating from A to B and end up meandering through the entire geographical alphabet. Others because it is a fun way to fill in the months between university and the executive desk. For the more introspective, the drift east conforms with an involvement in Oriental mysticism and philosophy. (' ... if religion is the opium of the people, the Hindus have the inside dope' Alan Watts.) Some took Kerouac's *On the Road* too literally, others are belatedly following the trail of the Maharishi's famous summer school. Some are petty criminals, seeking a slow buck, others are escaping from themselves, their families or Interpol.

My impression is that there are more young overlanders than ever before, that they are staying for longer periods, and that they believe the drastic reduction of physical amenities is matched by a concomitant increase in spiritual well-being. Jacques Ellul in *The Technological Society* has demonstrated man's inability to elude omnipresent 'technique'; sport, media, amusement, medicine and so on have been centralised and technologicalised. Even escape, recognised as necessary, is organised. Holidays involve complicated transport arrangements, compulsory camp sites, licences and regulations ... 'The erstwhile act of free individual decision becomes a purely a technical matter.' The plight of Britain's 25,000 gypsies, bullied and harassed from their traditional sites and roadside verges, in some cases by 'licensed thugs', and granted registered plots by the more progressive councils, reflects the final assault of bureaucracy upon a race of people who for so long have managed to resist it. Ellul observes that 'Modern men, however, are beginning to be aware of their need at all costs not to challenge the technical situation, and to

recognise that technical means exist to meet this very need.'
He then goes on to cite the fantastic success of Butlin's
holiday camps:[6] 'The whole thing represents an elaborate
and rigorous enterprise for becoming unconscious ... [a
vacation] which gives the impression of freedom, but never
allows the individual to come face to face with himself,
even materially.'

However, on a lonely trek from Marrakesh to Agadir, in
the Atlas Mountains, or 17,000 feet up the Himalayas,
there is no one *but* yourself to come face to face with. In a
Greek or Spanish cave—not for three packaged weeks—
but for months, even years, the lost experience of solitude
can be revived.

Any self-enlightenment is often ushered-in by drugs
—for the road to Katmandu is paved with cannabis.
It is still possible, even in these days, to live in hip
urban communities and maintain your pharmacological
innocence. But how can you refuse a joint extended
by a dazzling blonde tramp at a charcoal fire-side in
Kabul, having just survived a two-hundred-mile desert
journey? Apart from any spiritual bounty, intoxicants
ease physical hardships along the route. They possess a
secret mileage ingredient. Daylong trips across corrugated
deserts in converted army trucks can seem like minutes.
Hunger and sex pangs are soothed. A friend once wrote to
me: 'The months I spent as a depraved pot-head in
Tangier were the healthiest in my life. I put on a stone in
weight, slept like the heroine of an Ovaltine ad and ate
like a farm hand. My consumption of normal cigarettes
dropped ... my cough (notorious on three continents),
shakes, frustrations and general neuroses quietened down;
I was contented for the first time in years. Most of the

[6] Even Professor Ellul may be surprised to learn that each year, Butlin's
immunise *one million* people against themselves and each other. These
family vacation camps were launched in 1936 by (now Sir) Billy Butlin:
'The important thing is that no one is ever left to himself even for a moment.'
Fred Pontin's more recently established organisation operates on a similar,
perhaps a little more relaxed, basis.

216

other foreigners felt the same way.' For those who return, affection for the weed will be a lasting souvenir of the journey – based not so much on psychological dependence but on realisation of the absurdity of the drug laws.

There are other, broadly political connotations to this manifestation of world-wide drop-outism. Not merely in the shallow, and often temporary rejection of their mother's cooking, but in the accomplishment of the creation of an international community. Asked about any philosophical changes of mind after his trip around the moon, astronaut Frank Borman replied that he now realised that the peoples of the world would soon have to think of themselves as Earthmen, rather than as members of any particular race. Already the hairy tribe have spiritually abolished their nationality, and see themselves as a vast, unconscious international conspiracy. Marx's famous rallying cry, 'workers of the world unite, you have nothing to lose but your chains,' captured the imagination of the international proletariat, but little else. Workers did not unite; instead they went to war against each other. But this present generation are uniting instinctively, erasing national barriers, and losing nothing but their passports.

For some, the pot trail represents a wholesale rejection of the political arena. As Richard Horn put it in 'Letter from Katmandu' in the *East Village Other*:

'There is a kind of emergent feeling that the road is its own cure for what ails you (spiritual – political – total) and so, if I may be granted a word of advice, leave it behind. If the summer's action – up-tight scenes in Chicago and Czechoslovakia and wherever else, have not convinced you that politics always shits on freedom and the arts, then I can never. But maybe somewhere on the road between Kabul and Delhi ...'

So while their brothers in the West build barricades, the flower children, officially pronounced dead on October 6,

1967, are ghosts along the pot trail, haunting happy hippie love-ins and tribal weddings.

> *How*
> *ya*
> *gonna*
> *keep*
> *'em*
> *down*
> *in*
> *the*
> *factory*
> *after*
> *they've*
> *seen*
> *Katmandu?*

That peripatetic child of the marriage between Baden-Powell and John F. Kennedy, the US Peace Corps, is entrenched throughout the Third World in conditions that vary from the spartan to the luxurious. The Peace Corps recruits are jealous of their personal involvement with the local communities. They resent the intrusion of 'hairy parasites', and sometimes, as we have seen by their pill-selling antics, this attitude is jsutified. There are notorious instances of travellers sabotaging the goodwill painstakingly established by squarer Peace Corps workers; the Germans who hire bicycles for sixpence then ride them to the border and sell them; the French who ostentatiously eat during the Muslim fast month of Ramadan; even the occasional violent hippie drug rampages. In the past few years, however, there has been a definite thaw in this expatriate cold war. Inspired by mass media and the State Department, youth has come to see itself as a class, no matter how offensive that may sound to the doctrinaire. LBJ once said that his one ambition while President, was to have united the country. In this he partly succeeded.

He united the youth of his country (and the world) against him. A favourite game of travellers is to 'turn on a Peace Corps man' and some of the post-Hashbury Corps workers, who have slipped through the CIA net, are infusing a more radical attitude among the veterans.

The sociologically irritant effect of the new gypsies upon recipient communities has already been noted, but of course, the influence is mutual. It is generally believed that the flow of US civil rights workers from the North to the economically backward, agrarian Southern states in the early sixties, was associated with a desire to escape the anonymity of plastic city environments. One volunteer, who had been living in primitive conditions among Mississippi negroes, wrote:

'There is some strong ambivalence which goes with this work. I sometimes fear that I am only helping to integrate some beautiful people into modern white society with all its depersonalisation (I suppose that has something to do with its industrial nature). It isn't 19th century pastoral romanticism which I feel but a genuine respect and admiration for a culture which, for all the trouble, still isn't as commercialised and depersonalised as our Northern culture.'[7]

to which Jack Newfield has added:

'What I am trying to suggest is the ultimate irony of the New Left's assault on the Closed Society. It is that the liberators have so far benefited more from the struggle than those in bondage ... and it may be an enduring paradox that all through Mississippi the lives of the white volunteers have been more enriched, more fundamentally changed, than the lives of the maids and tenant farmers whom they came to help.'

How much more acute is the influence of primitive foreign

[7] From *Letters from Mississippi*, quoted by Jack Newfield in *A Prophetic Minority*. New American Library, 1966.

cultures on today's thousands of urban refugees? These travellers are considerably further afield, spiritually and geographically, than their civil rights prototypes, linked to their homelands only by a precarious mail service and the odd glimpse of *Newsweek*. Their sexual and dietary habits are disrupted. They discover that squat lavatories are more natural. They are confronted with a different theology, a mysterious concept of 'time', a pre-linear style of communication.[8]

Many Peace Corps workers and travellers are particularly impressed (at times, overawed) by the 'quality of life' in these countries and become more native than the natives. Some Peace Corps workers I spoke to were distressed by their roles as harbingers of masscult and Rank Xerox. Fortunately the consciences of some of them were relieved by bureaucracies which had assigned them useless (and thus harmless) tasks—like the two Britishers sent to teach hardy mountain villagers Physical Education (villagers who can lug 70lbs of baggage up perpendicular heights with a forehead strap).[9] Other missions are more destructive: like those sent into remote tribal areas to teach English, with disastrous results. Young children, once they believed that the language was mastered, would migrate to the nearest city under the impression that there would be a market for their new-found talent. At home, the centuries old harmony and filial routine was upset. In the city there was no work and the children became beggars—albeit English-speaking ones.

The task of these zealous volunteers is generally to pre-

[8] e.g. Some Asians believe it is offensive to say 'no'. 'Can I have a pound of butter?' is likely to be greeted by a shopkeeper out of stock with: 'The lemonade is good this year.'

[9] Some Peace Corp workers do question the apoliticality of such seemingly innocuous assignments: 'I taught physical education at a University in Colombia. The plan was simple: give the discontented students tennis balls and teach them how to bounce them well, and their excess energy, which had previously been used in political agitation, would be used up, safely, within tennis courts. Can you think of a better way to alleviate the problems of a poor country?' (Don Torrence, *News from Nowhere*).

pare the community for vast injections of US Aid. Peace Corps workers survey roads, prepare farmers for mechanisation, train factory workers. Their invasion is justified by demonstrating the consequent increase in the standard of living and amelioration of poverty—measured in financial terms. One cannot measure the happiness of individuals by the outward appearance of the public, but a walk through, say, the dour streets of Carlisle and the cheerful markets of Katmandu leaves little doubt as to who, as the admen say, is getting the most out of life.

This is not to under-estimate the barbarities, injustices and unpleasant superstitions which abound in primitive communities, and which are sometimes overlooked by myopic itinerants, but it is to suggest, at the risk of being sentimental, that the new refugees from the West are profoundly and permanently affected by the fresh simplicity and sylvan logic of such a lifestyle.

The desire of young expatriates to savour the 'backwardness' of these communities, like anthropological gourmets, is equalled only by the determination of the natives to catch up. Because of its inaccessibility, Nepal is one of the few remaining countries which has so far not been penetrated by the exporters of Coca Cola. However, so anxious are the villagers to enjoy the liquid fruits of a civilisation that they admire from afar, that empty Coke bottles are salvaged from across the border, and filled with a hideous home-brewed imitation.

One day the Tibetan girl I saw reading 'Playboy Party Jokes', will be a night-club bunny.

Perhaps young Westerners realise that now is the last chance to see the world before it finally dwindles into comprehensibility, when it will offer all the excitements and horizons of a baby's play-pen, unless—like babies—we re-learn how to play. Overlanders are anti-lemmings, scurrying across previously unexplored terrain as it slowly subsides into a deathly sea of uniformity. A final inspection of the bits between encroaching petrol stations, Wimpy

221

bars and Hiltons; a last look at tribal and kinship communities before they are uprooted from cheerful complacency, and their members re-planted beside the conveyor belt. OUT go fuddy-duddy emotional ties between men and their inherited crafts; IN come brisk 'human efficiency units', job detachment, boredom.[10] The Western equation will soon be universal: success/happiness=material consumption. The gospel spread by 2,000 Soviet experts resident in Afghanistan, the swelling GI forces in North Thailand, and Columbo Plan Asian graduates from Australian universities.

As we are plugged-in to the same sensory stimulators, everyone is converted to McLuhan's global villagers. Interestingly, the famous television programme, 'Our World',[11] seen by 400 million people in 23 countries, was obsessed with babies. They sprouted from wombs of all nationalities, various colours and physiologies. Confronted by identical environments and experiences (media), these children of tomorrow could all grow up to be the same person. That is why the hippies are hurrying to the last frontiers.

[10] 'In most of the poor countries an emotional loyalty to a way of life continues. Unless we realise the difference between the present loyalty patterns of the rich and poor countries, intervention to cause more 'efficient' production can lead to widespread misery and hardship. The people in the poor countries of the world are still generally attached to their trades and professions; their satisfaction is greatly decreased if they are forced to change from one type of employment to another.' Robert Theobald. *The Challenge of Abundance.* C. N. Potter, 1961.

[11] Broadcast, June 25, 1967.

Popeye
in
Panama

Record
of
a
conversation
with
a
'head'
seaman

Tiger: 'Panama Red is strong stuff—I'd put it through a potato masher to get all the seeds out, and put two pinches in a pipe, and couldn't smoke it, it was so strong. It's very violent, like the people in Panama. I have an idea that the kind of marijuana varies according to the native people who smoke it. In South Africa they call it dagga and it is laughing grass. It is very green and the best stuff comes from Durban. The Bantus smoke, and so do some of the whites. A guy in Durban has an overcoat with lots of pockets and he walks into the docks, and sells to the dockers and Cape Coloureds. They had a chilum which they had made out of a Coke bottle, knocking the end off and breathing in at the drinking end. He went to all the ships, the police would be watching him. They knew who he was and he never got busted, because if he got busted there would never be any work done. The dockers work, then stop for a cup of tea and a smoke. I got busted and the judge said that as I was a European it was a very serious offence, and I was treated as severely as the law would allow, which, because of the quantity I had on me, was a £2 fine. If you have under twenty sixpenny deals, then you are a smoker, but if you have more, you are a seller, and can be put into prison for up to five years.

There is a lot of grass in South Africa and there are small quantities of hash. The best quality stuff is grown by the Indians. They take the seeds off and manicure it finely, but the Cape coloureds just ram it into the end of a broken Coke bottle.

I went to central America in November. I spent three years around that area — Trinidad, Barbados, Jamaica, Venezuela, Colombia, Panama, Costa Rica, Honduras, Guatemala, Nicaragua, San Salvador, Haiti and Dominican Republic. The scene is pretty much the same from country to country. Most people smoke even though it's illegal. But five minutes after being inside the solitary confinement cell in Panama, I scored. I scored from a guy who was also in 'solitary confinement' and was doing a year for selling marijuana. He bought his shit from the guards. It's completely corrupt. It's done on the rota system. The pushers take it in turns to get busted. When it's his turn to get busted, the police give him a yell, he gets a lot of stuff together, and he gets busted. They take his shit as well, and he is installed in jail with his supply of shit, which he sells to the guards, and the guards sell to the prisoners. When he's done six months or so, or his supply of shit has run out, that means his sentence is over. The letter of the law is still observed and they can say they busted a pusher last week. It keeps the jails happy too, because there are people there doing twenty years, and the only thing which keeps them together is playing their guitar and smoking.

The last five years I've been picking ships which have been going to countries with good shit. I've always been in a different position from other seamen because I am a smoker and have gone ashore looking to score, and have been treated in a completely different way from the other seamen who are drinking. Even with people who didn't speak English I was able to talk the same language if they were a smoker. It's a kind of telepathy. I've been in a strange place with money in my pocket wanting to score, and I always can if it's possible. But it's no use looking for shit in Libya for example, because it's rich and people drink.

Once I was on a ship, with 43 crew, none of whom smoked, and we were away from England for 7 or 8 months and by the time we came back, over half the crew were turned on and I had the captain's permission to smoke. I used to freak out in my cabin or sit on the poop and watch the sunset and play my flute, and one by one they would come up and ask for a try. We used to keep the different kinds in little bottles. Marijuana from different countries. The quality varies according to the time of the year. The Panama Red comes onto the market about the second week of April. This lasts for three months and then you get russet marijuana and after that red marijuana which is better than the russet but not as good as the spring. The Panama stuff is really strong but in Somalia, for instance, you had to smoke a small plant before you felt anything. Lots of moisture and violent heat makes strong grass. Hash comes from places of high altitude such as the Himalayas. If the plant is grown at a high altitude it produces a lot of resin. In Panama they cure hash with very hot sun, brown sugar, and water. They turn the leaves, like making hay. It's illegal, but it's hard to stop people growing it. In Jamaica, they fly over the island in a helicopter with binoculars, looking for marijuana fields. The last time I was in Jamaica, some guys asked me for a gun which they wanted to use to shoot the helicopter.

The hitch-hikers in Central America rarely get off the highway. A few go and live with the Indian tribes, like a French boy I know, who was taking peyote in Mexico, but the Central American countries know about violence. Costa Rica is the most peaceful country as they haven't had a war or revolution for 180 years. I'm going back to live in Costa Rica, even though it's corrupt, the people are kind.'

Many travellers share his opinion of Costa Rica. On

December 15, 1968, the local newspaper, *La Hora*, reported that 'over 1,000 hippies from several countries have set up a "Hippie Republic".' The move was said to have been started by some 70 hippies from abroad, who recruited Costa Rican boys and girls, saying they wished to live in a world without frontiers and without laws.

Pot
Trail
Casualties

'I've seen people who've got beaten half to death, some who got beaten even to death. I've seen people dying because there was no doctor ... 450 people, 150 beds, the rest sleeping on the floor, 4 toilets ... I've been here 5 months ... Getting slightly crazy ...'

Hans Van Der Aar, 22-year-old inmate of a Turkish gaol. Sentence: *30 years.*

'It is true that conditions in Turkish prisons are not up to British standards and this is something, of course, which those who choose to commit offences of this nature in Turkey must recognise.'

Foreign and Commonwealth Office, London

At least forty-six young Europeans are, at the time of writing, in Turkish gaols for possessing, smuggling or selling cannabis. Six Americans are in Spanish gaols, and four more are awaiting trial. In 1968, twenty-one other Americans were held there for varying lengths of time, and then released owing to lack of sufficient evidence against them. There are five Britishers in Spanish gaols, and two in Moroccan gaols. Six Americans were arrested in New Delhi in 1968, and received sentences ranging from fines to gaol sentences. This is only a partial summary of the number of young people either arrested or gaoled along the pot trail, as authorities are not over-anxious to release statistics. The figure in Turkey has been established from information passed on by prisoners. With the exception of America, the legations of Western countries in pot trail lands are not particularly candid. The German Consul in Istanbul refused to disclose any information whatsoever, whereas there are, in fact, at least eight Germans in Turkish gaols. In an edition of the *Times of India*, which reported the two months' 'rigorous imprisonment' of two French students for possession of hash, and a six-week 'rigorous imprisonment' for an unemployed Japanese youth, appeared this item: 'An increasing number of hippies are being found in possession of "charas". The nuisance has grown so much that *some foreign missions have told police that they need not comply with the formality of informing them whenever a hippie is arrested.*'

In Turkey, the methodical harassment of stoned Europeans is a phenomenon which is being carried out with ostentatious ferocity, and I suspect that this game may catch on in other countries where the weed is a Way of Life. The rumblings in Turkey began in 1966 when extravagant publicity was given to what were then called beatniks. A typical feature from the *Sunday Telegraph*'s man in Istanbul ended with the sentence: 'The British consular authorities are embarrassed by their being here. But they can do nothing until the Turks find some legal way of kicking the Beats out,' which they did — within two years. Their expulsion policies were coupled with macabre gaol sentences for young foreign offenders — full use is being made of the new legislation which, in some cases, provides for the death penalty. The clampdown on longhairs coincides with a fanatical boosting of the tourist industry. The tourist and the road fraternity eye each other with mutual contempt and embarrassment, rejecting each other like molecules, but it is an uneven contest. The tourists have the money so the hippies have to go. As the package deal penetrates more remote areas, further persecution is sure to follow.

The correspondence of the unfortunate convicts delineates

227

a harrowing picture of degradation, corruption and futility. Some of the arrests involve *agent-provocateurs*, who are allegedly recruited in collusion with American narcotics agents. Others are trapped by police informers. Under Turkish law, an informer is not only exonerated, but rewarded with money and the return of his contraband. Police agents now sleep at the famous Gulhane Hotel, and some travellers are coerced into netting their companions. The prosecution often seeks the death penalty, and although murderers enjoy regular amnesties, 'hash fiends' do not.

In 1965, 27-year-old Robert Pontin was returning from Pakistan by train through Turkey. Having disembarked at one point for refreshments, Robert returned to find both his train and his rucksack had moved on. He cabled the police at the next stop to rescue his belongings. Meanwhile, another passenger delved into the rucksack, stole some hash, and reported the existence of the rest to the police. When Pontin arrived to collect his belongings, he confidently admitted to owning the hash and complained that some was gone. He is now serving an eight years and four months' sentence, plus an extra year slapped on for an obscure offence against the Turkish flag.

Another Britisher, Raymond Ansboro (26 years old), is serving a similar sentence. He was once stabbed in gaol, 'but this was a period when there was no hashish to turn on with, and everybody was hung up. But that isn't often.' One inmate had to wait two months for an operation after swallowing a fish hook, and when he went to hospital, he was chained to the bed.

Perhaps one of the most outrageous cases is that of Hans Van Der Aar, a 22-year-old German, who has lived in Holland all his life, thus providing both the German and Dutch consuls with the excuse to nominate each other as the more responsible. He was arrested at the border with two kilos of grass, and convicted of smuggling (15 years), and selling (15 years), although there were no witnesses in court to verify that he intended to sell. Turkish officials have gloated that he had been selected as an example, to deter other young people from abusing the drug laws. Here is an extract from a letter Hans Van Der Aar sent to a friend in London in November 1968:

'My parents, family and consulate doesn't help,[12] so I'm doing my best. But I've need of everything: extra food (weight 50 kg. lost 15), winter clothes, winter is coming etc. etc. Here in Turkey you're not alone in a cell, they have rooms for 10, 20, 30 and more people. So as you see, no comforts, nothing at all. If I have to live on what the Turkish Govt gives us I'll be dead in a few years. With money you can cook your own food, buy yourself a bed etc. A Turkish prison doesn't know what privacy is. Every minute of the day you've Turks around you. No jobs, no work. Some people work but for a foreigner, no chance. I get up about 8 o'clock, go to sleep again about 10. I'm trying to fill my time with writing, reading, but it is impossible to do something all day. Nobody to talk to, nothing else to do but write or read, the time doesn't go at all.

I speak Turkish pretty well, but between only Turks, I'm never at ease. I've been here 5 months now, all alone, no foreigners. Getting slightly crazy because I don't know what will happen in the future. Now winter is coming, it is getting cold, no heating, no clothes to wear. If you got sick, you can go to the doctor once a week. He'll write you a prescription for some pills or so. Before they take you to a hospital you've to be nearly dead. I've been in a mental hospital for about 15 days. For what I don't know. They were supposed to make some blood tests. Instead they put me into the insanity ward. I've travelled much, seen many things, but never a hospital so dirty without sanitation like this. Try to imagine 450 people, 150 beds, the rest sleeping

[12] cf. 'The American Embassy of Athens has done absolutely nothing to help me. I must put the thumb on those people, they are offering zero and I am in terrible trouble without even a tiny bit of aid from them, like acknowledgeing my existence as a human being or something.'
Neal Phillips in *The Book of Grass*. Grove Press, 1967.

on the floor, 4 toilets. No warm water. Food we wouldn't give to a dog. People without clothes. After 6 in the morning, everybody gets kicked out of the building, old and sick, without any clothes. If you've not seen it, you won't believe it. There are so many other things I could tell but maybe you wouldn't believe it. You've to see it with your own eyes. Life and treatment in a Turkish prison is like in the Middle Ages, not always, but 75% of the time, if you've not got the money.

I've seen people who've got beaten half dead, some who got beaten even to death. I've seen people dying because there was no doctor. A few things more I've got to say. I think that if the European governments want and would do something altogether it would be possible to get the sentence of the foreign prisoners reduced or maybe even to get them out. It is for example, very strange that 95% of all Americans who get busted get out. Most of them on bail. Several of them, good friends of mine, got out, with another nationality they sure would have got sentenced. I told you already that I was German, I feel more Dutch though. One day if I get out I'll be going east again ...

love and peace
Hans Van Der Aar

P.S. Tomorrow morning I'm going to Edirne in solitary confinement.'

Hans recently received a note informing him of his time of release: *6 a.m. March 10, 1998.*

The British appear somewhat more sympathetic than the Germans. They gave Raymond Ansboro 'two old curtains' for him to sleep in. It is customary in Turkey for prisoners to be kept alive by their families, who provide food, clothing and companionship. Foreigners must rely on the man in the bowler hat.

Fortunately the plight of some of the Turkish prisoners has received international publicity through the perseverance of the Underground Press. Little is known of conditions in other countries. Spanish law provides punishment of *prison menor* with a minimum sentence of six years and one day, and a maximum of twelve years for persons who are convicted of a crime against the public health of Spain. The Spanish Supreme Court has ordered all lower courts to be most rigorous in their prosecution of narcotics cases and to apply the strict letter of the law.

The American Vice-Consul in Madrid wrote me that: 'Large amounts of low grade narcotics are smuggled into or through Spain each year, mostly from North Africa. Since some 16 to 17 million tourists visit Spain each year, it is impossible for the Customs to stop more than a small percentage of the total amount of drugs which enter the country. One well-known ruse is played by Moroccan dealers, who sell dope to the unwary tourists and then tip off the Spanish customs agents, who apprehend the amateur smuggler and deliver a reward to the dealer. Sometimes narcotics are planted in the luggage or car of an innocent tourist, and later picked up in Spain by a member of a ring without the knowledge of the carrier.'

Early in 1969, Morocco's historically laissez-faire attitude towards Western drug-takers was savagely swept aside. Sandy, a Scotsman I met in Marrakesh, was arrested last year in Casablanca for possessing 350 grams of hash, and gaoled for four weeks. To make him admit to pushing it, Sandy was tied to an iron pole like a butcher's carcass and left to hang. Police flayed the soles of his feet with a cowhide whip, wrapped his head and face in a wet towel and forced water into his nose and mouth. 'I am 26 years old', wrote Sandy, 'and it's the first time I've cried since I was ten.' The British Vice-Consul in Rabat later asked Sandy to warn hippie travellers that Moroccan pipe dream days were over. The country is being cleaned up for tourists. At Easter 1969, an organisation called KK was formed in London to collect information on overseas imprisonments and to provide comfort, where possible, for the victims.

Report
from
Marrakesh

' ... the great central square, Djmaa el Fna, is the centre of
all the action, packed with drummers, story tellers, snake
charmers and rather unpopular English hippies looking for
hash.'
Brenda Jones, the *Sunday Times*. January 1969

Brenda, they're neither necessarily English, hippies, unpopular, nor looking for hash. (It looks for them.) The
travellers, of many nationalities, are of varying social
persuasions: beats, bums, Boy Scouts, Maoists, mystics and
rather unpopular English journalists looking for some human
interest. Berber vaudeville teams love overlanders grooving
on their antics—it lures the moneyed tourists. Charmed
cobras must make fascinating slides, but they are toothless
and harmless. The Medina could have been the set for
Tod Browning's once banned movie, *Freaks*: truncated half-
men jut from wheel chairs, pin-heads are on public display
and occasionally, a neighing, hoof-footed gentleman
gallops by, wearing a saddle.

Typically, I arrived a day late for Otis Cook's Christmas
Eve love-in, where hundreds of itinerant heads had freaked
out on acid punch and a potent range of improvised narcotics, including marjoon (literally jam, but universally
understood to be jam containing cannabis)—which is a
fudge made from many mysterious ingredients including
walnuts, figs, dates, raisins, honey, ground ginger and
cinnamon. Otis showed me the special passport stamp he
had created specially to commemorate the event—
'BROTHERS OF ETERNAL LOVE—FIRST ANNUAL LOVE-IN
—24-12-68—Marrakesh/Maroc—LOVE'—The 'eternity' of
the brotherly love had been temporarily theatened when
several of the more voracious trippers developed dehydra-
tion symptoms, landing in hospital, where the un-

Florence Nightingale nurses proved an effective ant-acid.

Otis took me to his international crash pad in the Mellah, the Jewish section of town, which is renowned for its cleanliness, unlike, as it turned out, Otis himself. An Indian chilum was instantly produced, whereupon some of the inert cadavers who littered the floor came to, well, not *life*, exactly, but to a ghostly caricature thereof, a state of befuddled vegetable-like expectancy, as the water pipe was passed from communal hand to mouth. Cream's *Wheels of Fire* was on the cassette, but rotating wearily, as the batteries in Marrakesh are from Shanghai, called White Elephant, and they're not joking. A friendly neighbourhood policeman called by to share the pipe and improve his English. Ingrid, a bald-headed Swedish girl sat becalmed in the corner, mumbling and scratching. ('Shaving's the only way to get rid of head lice, man,' said Otis, who had wielded the razor.) Three weeks later, Ingrid had still not recovered from the love-in. She could still mouth only one sentence: 'I don't know,' and the last time I saw her, she was being helped aboard a Casablanca-bound bus by friends who were shipping her home to hospital. A local boy, Mohammed ('He's OK. He takes acid') passed around fried fish and bread. A Danish couple projected a light-show on the ceiling — the usual confused homage to abstract expressionism — and a silent Australian wrote poetry in a ledger book.

And so a pot cloud descended within minutes of my arrival. All attempts to retrieve a few unstoned moments for the next weeks proved fruitless. Which is as it should be. Staying cool in Marrakesh would be like Alice not falling down the well. Mohammed found for me a suspiciously cheap four-room Moroccan house built around a tiled courtyard, with orange and lemon trees and sparrows. A friend warned us that the house had a madman attached — my landlord apparently, at present in hospital, but if ever he escaped my life would be in danger. It was thus

233

unnerving when the Arab lady upstairs began affixing great iron bars to our shared doorway.

It is said that 57% of Moroccans smoke kif; none of the remaining 43% ever seemed to show up in Marrakesh. Travellers stay stoned there, without buying an ounce, as the Arabs are aggressively anxious to share their pipes. The ancient pop-eyed merlin who sells candy to the kids on the way to school, distributes delicious hash cookies at twilight.

Otis kept calling round to make sure I stayed high. The January days were warm and wandering through the markets could unearth rich velvet caftans, antique Berber satchels, embroidered sandals and the sort of jewellery which became the rage in Paris for a while. At night I bathed like I never had before, in a dim steamy dungeon under wooden buckets of hot and cold water, among writhing, silent dark bodies.

Apart from the hard core, communal beat crowd, mystical and moneyless, the Marrakesh scene was split into (i) Paris, Chelsea, East Village, San Francisco drop-outs, stray Living Theatre members, and pretty blacks living in the Hôtel de France, huddled around Beatleful cassettes. (ii) *Vogue* and whisky upper class freak-outs who orbited around Paul Getty's holiday house and sipped coolness in the twilight shade of outdoor cafés.

'I can ignore the published figures, and forget about dollar values, and say truthfully that the standard of living is higher in Morocco than the standard of living in the United States.'

Tuck Milton, a traveller

He's right in a way, although few Moroccans are in a position to evaluate his claim, as most of them are denied equivalent freedom to travel. Certainly the beggars, the editors of censored newspapers and (untried) political prisoners may opt for the standard of Mr Milton's own country. And yet, Marrakesh did throb with a magic and fraternity that soothed my Anglo-Saxon pores. All men are brothers, even beggars, so wasteful welfare agencies are not necessary because traditionally, every Moroccan passes change to his less fortunate brother.

Everyone seemed to be speculating on the home market by exporting kif-stuffed camel saddles, but cheques are difficult to clear in Marrakesh even if they survive the postal gauntlet. Letters were either opened or lost and the girl at the Post Restante provided the ultimate hazard— she had an eccentric command of the alphabet.

Like a dream, Marrakesh evades objective description.

In the drugged haze of my last few days there, countless clowns began popping out of mirages. The blonde Texan lady whom I had last seen naked inside the Albert Hall in London floated into the courtyard one afternoon and giggled tumultuously. A soft, gentle trio of Americans who slept in a walnut factory wove spells of magic and mystery. Breathless friends brought urgent and nonsensical gossip from London. A long time resident came with tales of local fuzz busts and warnings of mass deportations. Finally, inevitably, on the last night, the madman slid silently into my courtyard while I was engrossed in shadow patterns projected on the ceiling by a paraffin heater. There was a brief struggle, which I lost, and he towed inside a whale-like Moroccan prostitute wearing a white bridal dress and flamenco lipstick, whom he proceeded to cunnilinger under a lemon tree, much to the dreamy fascination of my stoned companions. I danced about like an epileptic faggot, ordering someone to go find the cavalry. Why was I so afraid? The madman was harmlessly exploring the bowels of his beauty, and offering now, extra portions of the house rent free if only I would 'turn up zee moozic'. His grinning maiden lumbered towards me, intent upon my genitalia, and a drawling neighbour from the Mid-west corn belt who arrived to rescue the situation, took one look

235

at the chaos, goggled incredulously and fled. The madman had spotted some pale Western flesh and was anxious to barter.

Perhaps we could have reached a deal, but marjoon has a habit of making even the mundane sensational, so that this particular evening's not uneventful circumstances were rendered, to say the least, farcically incomprehensible. And this was just the prologue to a night rampant with insanity. I know that the madman kicked in the door of a nearby travellers' commune and that the police were foiled in an attempt to raid my house by the fact that no one opened the door; Otis Cook strayed into the dream, somehow frightening a pregnant Moroccan, getting locked in a room, and beaten by half a dozen of her outraged relatives. At dawn friends bundled me onto the Casablanca bus. The tambourine man pressed a hash cookie into my hand. The watch said four hours, but I knew the journey took two minutes. Next I sat in a Paris transit lounge, being laughed at by jet set stockbrokers, and woke up in London, in bed with Marrakesh flu. Something Alice never caught.

Otis Cook— A Hippie Odyssey

'I had been in Korea with the US army. I didn't know anything about dope or things like that. When those hippies started I hated them. I didn't get what they were doing. One day down at Laguna Beach I picked up a hitch-hiker, a long-haired guy about 19 or 20 and he rolled a few joints. I had my first experience with dope. It was beyond words.

I went to a love-in in Los Angeles. I was walking around

236

on two capsules of acid, when someone handed me a joint. I walked over to a bunch of drummers. I passed the joint around. Next thing I knew, some of the cats sitting there weren't flower children; they had flowers in their ears and beatnik clothes but they were cops, and they hauled me away.

I was going to play the game and go to jail, but I was friends with a lot of people down in the canyon. They had a thing going up in mountains where you could take acid with no one bothering you. Well, I went with them, took some mescalin, and walked round getting stoned on the birds and the bees, picking up pretty things. Then we all lay down on a rock and they started reading from Timothy Leary's *Psychedelic Prayer Book*. He has published two and I want to put in a plug for both of them. I didn't understand at first, but he says if you do anything in the wrong way, everything you do would be a conspiracy against yourself, and I believe with that book and the right mescalin or acid, you can experience beyond your five senses. I went through lots of different changes. It's fantastic when you get exclusive with nature. You really get close to something. You never stop enjoying your movie as long as there's breath in your body. My lawyer told me he couldn't get me off. I was on a few charges of various kinds. I didn't want to play games with them in their cubby holes. It was more important to find myself. So I told Kathy I had decided to split. She said 'That's cool.' I got a visa for India, because my Brothers of Eternal Love in Laguna told me I would find my guru there.

In Hong Kong I bought some ginseng root, the purest thing in the world. It glows in the night. Eaten over a period of 21 days it is like taking acid, only a body purifier as well. It is very rare. The guy in the shop didn't think I had the money for it. I went next door, which looked like it hadn't had no customers for 20 years. They had it for 250

237

dollars. I went to the bank, and when I got back to the store, the whole family was waiting to see me buy the stuff. It was in a tin box. Inside the tin box was another old and wooden box and inside that was about thirty pieces of long sticks.

When I opened the box in Calcutta everyone in the hotel wanted some. You know; "I got a sick mother" and all that. Next thing I knew I was down to one piece. When I got to Katmandu I had to camp outside of town. There was a Danish camera man taking pictures. So I went to my suitcase and showed him the ginseng root and an Indian statue I had. I went to show him the tent and when I came back, the kids had broken the root up into little pieces and passed it around. I blew my mind. All gone.

I put my machine and all the records I had got in India, in the Blue Tibetan restaurant. Everyone played it while smoking their chilums. After about 2 weeks of this, the restaurant owner and neighbours got uptight. The restaurant opens at 10 a.m. and could seat 30, but the ones who got there first would just sit there all day stoned and he wasn't making any money. He would throw them all out at 10 p.m. and I would end up paying their bills, if they had no bread. Well, it was a good trip. A friend said he would take me out of town to see the countryside. I thought it was meant to be a private bus but it turned out to be a regular city bus. There were about 30 of us so I said why don't we just rent it. We did, and drove out to this place called Dhulikhel with tents and blankets. It was like a commune. One night we tripped on the idea of building a temple. In Katmandu there are 2,500 different temples and different religions, so every day is a holiday. We figured if we called our commune a temple, they might let us stay there. We had visas for 15 days. After that, they start looking for you. Katmandu is full of spies. They all knew where I was because an Indian newspaper had done a story on us about building a temple. So they grabbed us and threw us out. They accused us of thievery. Someone had picked up some souvenirs from one of the temples and put them on one of the tents. That was just an excuse. I don't know what their real reasons were, whether about drugs or what, I didn't think about it.

All these officials came out to the camp, wanting to talk about me building a temple. So I turned to Paolo, this Italian cat, an artist, on acid every other day and said: "Hey, come and explain your temple bit." He said: "Sure, I'll come," and we had a final blast on the chilum and walked up the hill to their little office, full of little men with glasses, shirts and suits. One said in English: "You have 12 hours to leave this country." I said: "You motherfuckers, you can't see beyond your eyes. You don't give us a chance to get accustomed to your country, just your selfish money." They said they were just following orders, but they'd take us to Katmandu to see about it, so I said all right, and we went—Paolo and me and this guru, a beautiful Nepalese — in a jeep with two policemen, and suddenly I had a feeling I'd never see the camp again. This was it. I knew they were heading for the Indian border so I jumped off. Paolo put up a fuss too. They turned the jeep round and started into Katmandu, but I wouldn't go with them. I walked. Got rides. Ran into several roadblocks. At one they chased me, but I got through. I walked into the Blue Tibetan for my passport. I was really mad, cussing those Nepalese who were my friends but were actually spies, all the time, and doing their thing with the Government and getting paid for it. I was blowing my mind, not knowing which ones were cops. Eventually they came and got me. Three of them. I chucked them off and threw one sideways. That was it. I had taken action so they weren't going to let me get off. They started kicking and stomping. It wasn't a good trip. Tied up in chains and dragged through the streets. They were so frightened and paranoid. I put up a hell of a fight. I was in jail for ten days. Pretty good. They kept me loaded with hash. All the brass generals came and shook my hand, played their little game.

The Times 12 December 1967
Katmandu—A hippie camp at Dhulikhel, a mountain village 19 miles from here on the Katmandu–Tibet Highway, has been disbanded by the Nepal police. They are said to have deported the camp leader and warned others to leave the country soon.

The camp was to have become an international temple for the hippie cult. It had been decorated with photographs of King Mahendra and Queen Sita, but these proved of no avail against police action.

Paolo and his wife had gone while I was in jail. I told him to take a room in a hotel in New Delhi and wait for me there … he's not a hippie and took advantage of the situation because he stayed in the richest hotel with room service and I had to pay for it. He sold his camera to pay for souvenirs to take back to Italy while he dined at my expense. He was in the hotel for 10 days before I arrived. I paid the bill. It was in the past. I had told him I would.

We went from there to Kabul. Paolo had an idea about going to see the Pope in Rome. It was just one of his trips. We wanted to give the Pope everything that our camp represented—all the art work, the pictures, the souvenirs, Buddha statues, scrolls, the tonka. We wanted to do this because the Pope had just gone on TV in America asking for peace. We were going to give peace to the Pope. It was Paolo's bag, though. For me it was just a trip. I thought, OK, it's as good as anything else.

While we were in Kabul I got a package in the post from my friends in Los Angeles, the Brothers of Eternal Love, and it was just outasight. In the package, 250 caps of Blue Cheer, so I thought I would give a party. It was Christmas Eve. We had it in a hotel and it was the most beautiful party you ever have seen. Everyone took the capsules. 150 hippies freaking on acid at Christmas. Wow! In Afghanistan.

Well, we took off again on our way to Rome, but the money ran out in Iran. I had this Nepalese bank draft for 2,000 dollars, but no bank in Iran would touch it. Now I had no money, Paolo and his wife left me. I dumped all their stuff they had left with me at the American Embassy, in hopes they would send it on to the Pope. That was end of that trip. All I had was a passport and no money.

When I finally cashed that cheque the first thing I did was buy a cassette, and 12 tapes. It was great to have money again. I had a pad in Copenhagen for the winter, with the Danish photographer from Katmandu. So I bought an air ticket. I knew I could get dope there. On the plane I had my cassette playing some music. A Swiss guy asked me politely to turn it off. Then the steward asked me. I said I didn't see why I should. They got uptight about it. I turned it off. Then later I put on the tape and began talking into it. "I'm on an airplane above the clouds, soon we will hear the wheels touching down." As we landed, I said into it. "I'm going to leave this on and tape me going through customs." It was just a trip. When I got off the plane I had it under my sleeve. I went towards the waiting lounge, not customs. There were two airline officials there, one a very nice guy.

I says "Which way do I go?"

He says "Well, where do you want to go?"

"I want to go home to God."

He says "Well, this is Copenhagen, Denmark, and this is God to us, you go through there."

I says "Well, thank you very much."

I went through this door and up to a little window, but before I got there a door went sliding shut and I says "Oh, you're locking me in, huh?" They say "This is passport control, your passport please?" I says "Outasight, outasight, outasight," handed my passport over. They say "Where are you coming from?" I says "I just been round the world, I'm coming from San Francisco." He says "I can see that by your hair ... you do not have a return ticket?" So I says "Well, I don't need one when I'm coming home." He says "This is your home?" "Yes, the whole world is my home." Well, they objected to that. "Do you have any money?" I says "Money, do you want to see money?" By this time I was getting mad and I pulled out this 2,000 dollars which I had in traveller's cheques, and said "Is this 2,000 dollars enough, or do you want 10,000 more?" They kept throwing this "Oh, so you're rich man" stuff at me and I really flipped out. I tore all the traveller's cheques up.

They were needling me. At one point they were going to let me in, and in fact even started to open the door, but when they seen the microphone he said "What is that there?" I said "It's a microphone." He says "You're recording this conversation? Turn that thing off." I said "Why?" He said "You're in a democratic country here, we don't record your voice, so don't record ours." I said "If this is a democracy I don't want any more of it." They said "Sit over there and we will see if you can be let in." After I tore up the money they locked me up. I recorded the whole thing. "There's 4 policemen taking me up the stairs, they're putting me in an elevator." One was the big chief, who had denied me entry. In the elevator, I says "First floor." He says "Second floor." I says "Third floor." We go into a room. I says into the tape: "Three customs, four cops and one big cheese." He says "Take everything out of your pockets." I do and he says "Give me that machine." I said "Oh, no, you don't get this away from me." He started wrestling for it so I shout "I'll give it to you, just let me turn it off." So that was the end of the tape. When the American consul man came down I played it to him and said "It's because he didn't like me and I didn't like him they refused me entry." He said "Tonight they're going to put you on a plane and they are to fly you back to Zurich."

They radioed ahead to Zurich that I was a dangerous

man. Two cops came on the plane with me and delivered me to two other cops. I just changed hands. They denied me entry. I spent the night in gaol. Next day they took me into an office and say "What are you doing in Zurich?" I say "I've been forced here against my will." They said "You can't stay here, where would you like to go?" I say "Paris, France." After signing some papers, off I went. They put me in this little cage on a train. And this is a bum trip, this little train. I was thirsty and they just put me in there, no matches, I was a prisoner. I banged on the bars but there was no one to do anything for you. The 2 police just left me and said someone would take me off at the other end. Half-way through I had made so much noise that someone complained. At the next station 2 policemen got on. I asked for some water. They quickly shut the door and radioed ahead that I was a very dangerous man.

At the border, there were about 4 or 5 cops standing there with guns ready to do me in. One had heard about me and the tape recorder. He was outasight, he couldn't believe this had happened to me. He showed me the order they had been sent down from Zurich. He said, "You sound like a real dangerous man," and laughed. He was really nice, I recorded his voice. They let me go eat until train time, they didn't bother me. Then when we were talking this enormous thing came in the door, I never saw such a big huge enormous policeman, he was fantastic. I talked about this into my tape, low, as the other policeman was on the phone. I said, "Oh my God, the jolly green giant just walked into the room." I said to him, "What is your *nom*?" I held the microphone up to him and he says, "Mr Green." It blew my mind.

On the train to Paris, someone had the idea I looked like Rasputin, so I asked how to spell that. He wrote it on a card for me and I was going to use it as my name. I went into a hotel and tried to get a room, but I couldn't get one there or anywhere in Paris. Finally I got one for 25 dollars a night and I telephoned home. Next day I went to see a kid I had known in Katmandu. He said, "Oh, you can't stay here, it's my dad and mother, I will try and find you a place somewhere," so I quickly got out of the house. You know, I'd like to help you so long as you stay on the opposite side of the street. Back at my hotel, I started smoking and painting my room psychedelically, but a big fat woman threw me out, she blew her mind when she seen that room and I was out on the street again. I went to a town in the country. I had some good hash from Paris. I bought a car there, painted it psychedelically so the cops grabbed me and I had no licence or insurance. They let me sell the car back but I only got half price.

I went down to Marseilles, lived in an old abandoned beatnik house. Someone told me about Tangier, so after about a week I caught a plane but the plane went to Casablanca. I met some kids there and went down to Marrakesh with them. You know, when you try to describe a movie, you have a picture in your mind but you can't get it out into words. That's how I am about Marrakesh. I don't really know, I was stoned out of my mind the whole time. After I was there for a while someone ran off with my passport and I was the happiest man in the world without that thing. The Post Office gave me my mail and the bank cashed my cheques.

Then it all happened so quickly it was like a nightmare. One minute I'm in my house with all my cats and a bunch of friends, sleeping up on the roof because it's getting hot, a little music now and then, people dropping by. There was a knock on my door bright and early and when I answered it, there was the whole street watching the performance. There is no privacy in Morocco and they were leaning out the windows, over the roofs, 30 or 40 people waiting to see what the cops would do. So they asked me for my passport and I didn't have one. They took me to the guard room at the palace. I wasn't the only one being pulled in. About 6 of us were held in the main square for three days. Then Wednesday they said we could go, but to come back on Friday because they were going to deport us.

Meanwhile my house had been there for one and all to come and take things and a lot of my memorable and religious things had gone. The house was a mess and the rent was due so I grabbed all my cats and gave them to a very dear friend of mine, Sidney Bigman who is a blind writer living there. Not wanting to be deported, I hitch-hiked to the same village near Essouira where I had given all those penicillin shots to the kids another time and they gave me permission to live without a passport in Peace. Wow, it was outasight to live there without identification and no rubber stamps. Everything was sweet and dandy. Everyone in the village was happy and we had a celebration in my room. It was one beautiful party.

I decided to return to Marrakesh to pick up my mail. First thing, I went to Paul's to see if my cats were all right and then I discovered that a lot of things had happened. Paul was dead, Gary was in a mental hospital and an American girl named Dorothy was walking round in a state of shock. They were trying to ship her home. I couldn't work out what had happened. I went to the square to get some coffee and a policeman recognised me. I was arrested and turned over to three — I don't know what you call them — they were brutal sadists, you can't call them police-men. When I tried to get out of their car at the Post Office to get my mail they put handcuffs on me. I spent the next two hours in the back of the car being tortured with cigarettes. They beat me with fists, pulled out bits of my beard and kept giving me chops to the ribs. It was a bum trip all the way to the central police station in Casablanca.

They put me in gaol. Everything was a downer. One night

245

I had three or four babies in my bed and one 15-year-old girl sleeping on my blanket. One afternoon I watched about 30 Moroccan prisoners getting their hands beaten with a rubber hose. About 10 hits on each hand. I just sat there smoking kif and I says: "Isn't this a groovy movie, man, real groovy. Man, it's just too much." What can you do? You're a prisoner yourself, you can't say anything or do anything, it's a real downer.

The consul representative came round, a big fat American, and he said: "Mr Cook, we're going to fly you home to Ohio." Like I was a destitute criminal or something. "What for?" "You've been ordered out of this country, and we're going to give you a passport and fly you back to where you were born." "I'm wanted on several charges back home and I'm not going to accept a passport. I don't want that fucking piece of paper. I got rid of the last one and I just want to live here in peace." He said if I didn't take the passport I would be kept in prison. I said "Whatever they want to do is all right with me."

Well I was 4 days on bread and water which is all you get if you don't have any money, which I then didn't. When the consul guy showed up again I told him to jam his passport up his arse. Two days later he showed up with two kids from the Living Theatre, who had heard about me being there. "They are going to buy you a passport," he said, "I don't want no passport. I want you to cut off my money and letters. I ain't signing nothing." The kids left me fifty dirhams which was real groovy. After listening to police gossip I could see I would be a long time in jail. Next time they brought over a different guy from the Embassy, a guy with horn rims, really hung up with knowledge. One of those high class pinball machines. He says: "We're not fooling around with you any more. Either you take this passport or you can sit here and rot for all we care, American citizen or not. You've got to have a passport to move in this world." I said, "OK, if you're going to put one of those things on me, I'll accept it."

246

They put me on a bus to Ceuta. The policeman hadn't tied me up, but when I left the bus of my own accord to take a leak, he handcuffed me to the seat, but they were simple to get out of. When he saw this, he vented his rage, kicking and beating me. I was released into no man's land. I walked to the border, and I told the Spanish about the torture and all, but when they saw the stamp the Moroccans had put on my passport, they refused me entry into Spain. So for several days, I was in a piece of no man's land, shaped like a crucifixion. The hills came down to where there was a bridge over a river bed, with a little wooden shelter for a Spanish soldier. There were boys who smuggled goods into Morocco, and women who put on all these clothes and carried large bundles over the mountains to a Moroccan village. In the day there was a teahouse and a place to buy food, beneath the bridge. During the night, I would go down there and I became friendly with some of the boys. We would go into Ceuta and rob the apple and pear trees.

One day the Spanish guards beat me up, and I returned to the village between the borders where they make fishing boats. I had been crying and one of the men made motions as if to say "What's wrong?" I pointed to the Spanish guards and unbuttoned my pants to show them my thigh which was red. Later it turned black and blue. I made a motion for food by putting my hand up to my mouth and speaking a few words of Arabic. These Spanish guys got uptight about it and made a protest to the guards about beating me up. That afternoon a waiter from the teahouse showed up and said "Where's the American?" They had this four-course dinner for me on a big tray, all kinds of food. Later that night I sneaked into Morocco to a little village and had supper and some kif. When I got back I found another dinner waiting for me that the Spanish guards had brought me. They had been looking all over for me. That day I really had food.

I was on the border for 20 days. Then I was escorted to the police station in Tangier and a representative of the

247

American consul walked in and said: "Are you Otis Cook? How would you like to go to Paris?" I says, "Wow, outa-sight!" He said: "Sign here," and I did. Kathy had sent money for the ticket and 200 dollars as well. In an hour I was in the sky, flying high.

I got out of Paris just as quick as I could make it. Nothing but no room, no room. Fermé, fermé. I showed them my money but they take one look at my hair and they don't want to know me. I got a room the first night with a friend by wrapping my hair in a towel but in the morning when the landlady found out why I had the towel on she threw me out. At night I took the train into the suburbs and slept in churchyards. I decided to split to Pakistan and I bought a player and a whole bunch of records; but I met two Danish boys going to London so I said why not and here I am.

I got a lift with a friend down to the Isle of Wight Dylan concert and it was fantastic. There's no way I can express my feeling for what I seen out there. It really is a message, a spiritual message. The night I arrived, I met a couple of guys with electric light yo yos. Red and green ones that would light up. They would go round twirling these things and they were the ones you could buy any amount of shit from. Later there was a big show going on, a light show with music until four in the morning in this enormous tent, which was nothing but row after row of bodies. Next day, near the food stalls, we had a small crowd of 15 or 20 kids sitting around and smoking a chilum, right there in the open.

I don't know what to say. There was hash coming from every direction. I was turned on by everybody that knew me. And I was stoned on acid the whole time I was there. Early in the morning on the last day there was one thing that really blew my mind. I was walking through the crowd in the sunshine, tripping on acid and I came upon a couple of guys who had a big box of incense in front of them. I said, "Oh, could I have one of your incense, please?" and they said, "No, we've only got enough for ourselves." That really blew my mind, and I said, "Well, I wouldn't want to take anything from any selfish motherfuckers like you," and walked off. It took me quite a few minutes to get over the shock of that. Anyone who's taken acid knows what the smell of incense does to you, and how bad you would like to have one at the time ... At the moment Dylan left the stage I was very quiet, but at that exact time when they announced "He is not here," I jumped up on a little car in front of me, on the hood, and started shouting, "Bring him back, bring him back. You can't do this to us, we gotta have him back." And the guy says, "He isn't coming back. He did his thing and he's gone." I says, "Wow, maybe he didn't want to overdo it." I think that was the reason. I don't know what to think. I better stop thinking. But the whole week end was fantastic. The vibrations were just outasight.

Last night I went to the Wimpy bar and had a meal. Some skinheads come in and sit in a corner booth, and they were yelling and cussing. I jumped up, and, I don't know, started to put my two cents in, and they started to call me all kinds of names. I was so stoned I really don't know what happened, except I came to blows with one of the guys. I invited him outside to finish it but he refused to come out of the door. I went on down the street, looked back and saw a whole bunch of them, 7 or 8, gathering outside the restaurant. They all began following me. Some kid I knew had a tyre pump on his bicycle, so I asked him if I could use it for a minute. Had a hell of a time getting it away from him without explaining what I wanted to use it for— as protection. That got me half way down the street, with them keeping their distance, not knowing whether to attack or not. Just then, a brick went flying by and hit the side-walk, so I set my radio down and went off chasing them. That got them far enough away so I could make it across the highway. When I was out of sight, I split to a friend's house. I had a girl take a look out the window once, and she said the whole bunch of them was standing on the corner. After about ten minutes a police car started pulling up and they went scattering in all directions. So I went on home in peace.

I don't know. Why? Why? A guy just wants to practise his religion, just wants to do his thing, man. All I want to do is smoke, stay stoned and just groove. Why is it so hard for a man to breathe—this damp air in England?'

THE
POLITICS
OF
PLAY

'Same thing Day after day—Tube-Work-Dinner-Work-Tube-Armchair-TV-Sleep-Work. How Much More Can You Take. One in Five Go Mad, One in Ten Cracks Up.'
                                    Wall Graffiti, Notting Hill, 1968

A COUPLE'S MIDSUMMER MADNESS

Gwyn and Mary Thomas were pillars of their local community. For years he served as a member of the council where his wife worked as a clerk.

Then their cosy little world collapsed round them. Both became ill and had to give up their jobs. They struggled along on a £15 a week pension and National Assistance ...

Then this quiet, middle-aged couple decided to go on a spree. They booked in at London's Hilton Hotel (cheapest double room, 15gns, without breakfast). They ran up a bill of £130 before moving on to the Cumberland and Savoy hotels.

Their bills for hire cars alone amounted to £90. Mrs. Thomas opened an account at Harrods, the big store.

In five weeks they lived like lords and ran up bills of more than £700.

Their behaviour was so inexplicable that Lord Justice Phillimore, in the Appeal Court, said it must have been the result of 'some kind of midsummer madness.' ...

Each was sentenced to nine months.
                                    News of the World. Oct 12, 1969.

'Sha da da da

Sha da da da da,

Sha da da da

Sha da da da da,

Sha da da da

Sha da da da da,

Sha da da da

Sha da da da da,

Yip yip yip yip

Yip yip yip yip

Mum mum mum mum

Mum mum

Get a job.'

The Silhouettes–1957. Kae
Williams. Inc. & Wildcat Music. Inc.

'I think the whole concept of the Underground is ridiculous. What it is I don't know. What does it mean?'

Richard Ingrams, Editor, *Private Eye*

'WORK = CASTRATION
   Join the gentle strike.'

Graffiti, Eros, Piccadilly, 1969

Question:

Dutch crazies, *Dallas Notes* street sellers, Munich hippie hustlers, Notting Hill astrologers, stateless occultists, angry teenage witches, Eton 'heads', Easy Riders, Situationist-Provocateurs, UFO spotting mystics, titled flower gypsies, breathless Women's Liberators, full-time surfie nomads, peripatetic prankster editors, rock stars kicking out the jams ... The yippies before the House Un-American Activities Committee, dressed as Viet Cong, or throwing away free money in the Stock Exchange, or posting 30,000 joints to 30,000 weary housewives. Otis Cook's pot-trail acid parties, his outlawed shrines to Hippiedom and Brothers of Eternal Love. Hitch-hiking Honeybunch Kaminskis ('aged 13—what a little yummy') bound for greased Cornwall pill boxes. Provo poets, white chickens, happenings and smoke. The Living Theatre. Danny Cohn-Bendit making mockery of national borders, singing the Internationale in every courtroom out of tune. British radicals who flush plain-clothes detectives from their ranks with harmless ridicule, disrupt parliamentary investigations with sulphurous stink bombs and go naked to the David Frost TV show. The wonderful wizard of Aussie, Ian Channell, inaugurator of ALF—Australian Liberation Front for Action, Love and Freedom, and official resident merlin of the University of New South Wales. The Crazy World of Arthur Brown, Louis Abolafia and his tribe of pubic presidential candidates, the screams of yesterday's Lord Sutch, the group-groping clowning decibelic anarchy of the Fugs, the Jimi Hendrix Experienced Autonomes of Zurich, Doggs Troupe Moonmen bleep bleeping into Adventure Playgrounds with guerrilla theatre, the laughter-plating Plaster Casters, Tiny Tim, Mad Mel, the Exploding Galaxy, Grateful Dead and Kommune K's courtroom theatre of the absurd. A buzzard in Macy's, Santa Claus in Selfridges, fire-bugs in Brussells. THE DROP-OUTS OF THE WORLD—high on dope, hope, each other or the Himalayas —WHAT UNITES THEM ALL?

Answer:

Their attitude to work. They don't.

' ... purposeful work is a necessary part of all human fulfilment ...'
> Dave Dellinger, Editor, *Liberation—A magazine of The Left*, March–April, 1969

The Underground does not agree. Nor do its members accept the other axiom of the old New Left that repressive institutions can only be exterminated by 'immense sacrifice, dedication and responsibility'. It is this opposing instinct within the Movement which causes so much conflict. The sober, violent, puritan, Left extremists, versus the laughing, loving, lazy, fun-powder plotters. It split the annual SDS conference in Chicago in June 1969. In the same month, when Frank Zappa came to London, he told an earnest audience at the London School of Economics that student revolution was 'this year's flower power'. You couldn't have heard a bomb drop. 'But you said once before', shouted a student above the commotion, 'someone has to do something before America shits on the whole world.' Replied Zappa: 'What do you expect me to do? Sit here with my finger up its arsehole?' The Prankster versus the Politicos.

The Movement's essential anti-work, pro-play ethic explains why—for all the New Left's braying flirtation with the working class — the affair rarely blossoms into marriage. It is a phony courtship. Sometimes it is the young members of the Left who realise this themselves and change their style, like those who dropped out of Civil Rights when they became aware that the 'equal work opportunities for blacks' that they were championing, meant only jobs they would *never* ever do themselves.

What about the workers? They're not fooled by the rantings of obsequious students. They know the revolution's done for fun — not them. And anyway, they hate the dirt and hair and polysyllables. This exchange between students and workers at Essex University during a Revolutionary Festival is exceptional only in its amiability:

Militant Students to construction workers on campus site: We are struggling so that you too get higher wages.
Workers: Thanks mate, but I've got my union to take care of my wages. And anyway, you're living on a grant paid from my taxes.[1]

Even in France, where there had allegedly been a blood-brother relationship between the two groups, Jean-Jacques Lebel can say, nine months after the revolution: 'If twenty students were killed during a demonstration tomorrow, I guess there would be something like rejoicing in the working class districts of town.'[2]

---

[1] Adapted from *Solidarity*, Vol. 5, No. 8. Rockers who wandered the campus were apparently not thought deserving of approach. Cf. an exchange between Senator Abe Ribicoff of Connecticut talking to union militants after he had returned from a TV confrontation with Chicago's Mayor Daley:
Union man: We saw you on television, Senator, and it seemed like you were for those hippies. You're not getting our vote this time.
Ribicoff: Look, suppose your kid was beaten up by the cops, how would you feel?
Union man: Those hippies the cops beat up were wearing beards and anybody who wears a beard, he deserves to get beat up.
Ribicoff: Christ wore a beard. Abraham Lincoln wore a beard.
Union man: Obscenity.
Newsweek, January 27, 1969

[2] *Village Voice*, February 27, 1969.

The Underground's dialogues with many of the working class are usually confined to interrogations at immigration barriers ('Bend over, boy. Shine the torch, Harry. Can you see any pot up there?'), scuffles outside National Assistance offices and flights from tough, crew-cut skinheads ('Weirdos is no fun to jump though, because they don't fight back, they just curl up while you kick them.')[3]

How can hippies be attracted to the idea of 'radicalising the trade unions' when the implicit goal — higher wages — seems obsolete to them? Although, ironically, it is with the most oppressed section of the working class that the Underground has spiritually, and in some cases, politically, aligned itself: the blacks.

Michael X once told me that hippies were the only whites his people could talk to. When Eldridge Cleaver was the Peace and Freedom Party's candidate for President of the United States, he chose a yippie, Jerry Rubin, as his running mate.

They jointly published the YIPANTHER PACT:

'Disenchanted, alienated white youths, the hippies, the yippies and all the unnamed drop-outs from the whiteman's burden are allies in this human cause.' — Cleaver

'Release a Black Panther in the Justice Department ... don't vote in a jackass elephant cracker circus' — Jerry Rubin

Later, Eldridge Cleaver withdrew from the elections in favour of the yippie candidate, Pigasus, conceding: 'The pig is mightier than the Cleaver.'

The prank is mightier than the politician. LSD in the drinking water.

Grubby Marxist leaflets and hand-me-down rhetoric won't put an end to toil. It will be an irresistible, fun-possessed, play-powered counter-culture.

[3] A skinhead talking to UK *Rolling Stone*, July 26 1969.

'You know the *young* workers are with us', says Jean-Jacques Lebel, 'they suffer from a sort of racism of age, They are impatient with the system and the old order. And, you know, they have a lot in common with the students. We listen to the same kind of music, wear long hair, like to fuck ... '[4] Presley, pot and pornography may mobilise them faster than Union resolutions, apprentice picnics and promises of collective farms. Listen to this May Day appeal to British workers (Socialist Worker 1969):

'This year we hope for an even bigger turnout, but it will be a demonstration with a difference. We are not marching through London to shout at the so-called citadels of power. Unfortunately there are no Joshuas in the working class movement and the walls of the stock exchange will not fall down as we shout slogans.

HAVE FUN.

We are marching from Tower Hill through the East End to Victoria Park where we will enjoy ourselves. There will be jazz bands, pop groups and dancing.

As one building worker said at the first meeting, "My governor is going to be choked when I take the day off. He's going to be double choked if I enjoy myself".'

Flower Power in Victoria Park, 1969. Maybe in the 70's it will be Mick Jagger, marijuana and multiple sex—then the governor will be treble choked.

> *But,*
> *What*
> *About*
> *My*
> *Right*
> *To*
> *Work?*

'My husband is a good man, a good father. His whole life is spent providing for his family. At 47 years old he is a

[4] *Village Voice, op. cit.*

second grade signalman and has now been made redundant. How dare anyone rob him of the right to work! No man forced into idleness at 47 is a happy man, nor for that matter, a good citizen.'

Letter to the Daily Mirror, August 1967

'Pavoir, Mr Leonard Wesson reached the end of the road today ...

For after 50 years, Mr Wesson, 64, is retiring. In his time as a pavoir, Mr Wesson reckons he has laid over 100 miles of roads and pavements in Middlesbrough.

"It's been a good life and I made a lot of friends," said Mr Wesson. "But now I will have more time to look after my wife".

On behalf of his colleagues, the Borough Engineer presented him with a chair.'

A North Country Newspaper, Oct. 7, 1968

Man has been taught to cherish his right to toil. His reward is subsistence income, a joyless task and working conditions which are often unsafe, usually unhealthy. Man's right to work is the right to be bored for most of his natural life. In *Work*, a Pelican collection of Twenty Personal Accounts,[5] which could have been sub-titled An Anatomy of Melancholy, there is one factor common to each occupation; the unbearable, day-to-day monotony endured by man in the course of earning his 'living' [*sic*].

Factory Worker: Work to me is a void, and I begrudge every precious minute of my time that it takes ...

Journalist: To myself I was nothing much more than a machine.

Warehouseman: Now there is little interest in the job other than getting money on Friday ... There is a general feeling of frustration, a feeling that life has such little purpose ...

Nightwatchman: It was boring on the second night, and turned into a slow torture that lasted all the time I was

---

[5] Edited by Ronald Frazer. Pelican Original 1968. (The essays were first published in *New Left Review*).

awake, until I could have gone mad – or worse – got used to the job's madness.

Civil Service Clerk: At first I liked it, till the novelty wore off and the chronic, stagnant boredom began to take over ... it's how prison must be.

House surgeon: It became routine ... I realised that I actually hated my work ... Done properly the work is the nearest thing to voluntary slavery I can think of.

And so it goes on: for the term of most men's unnatural lives.

For some, the degree of monotony entailed in the work situation varies in inverse proportion to the attached amount of power, prestige and wealth and other carrots.

Apart from the very rich, who 'transform work' into a luxurious sinecure, other groups of non-workers include artists, craftsmen and media men. Media men? Compare the atmosphere of a bank to a newspaper office; of a factory to an advertising agency ... media people enjoy their work. Today, media is substitute play. The play element fizzled out of established culture in the 19th century, when work was sanctified. In the last hundred years, media has kept play alive, if not kicking. That is why the Underground is obsessed with media in all its forms; why most of its enterprises are media enterprises and why the Underground's most brilliant media manipulators are those with the greatest flair for fun. Media is armchair play.[6]

We are born into a world where work is considered ennobling, unlike the lucky ancient Greeks, for whom a life of leisure was essential for a man of wisdom. It was during his full-time leisure that man could cultivate his mind and seek the truth.[7] Work was considered degrading.

[6] See *The Play Theory of Mass Communications*. William Stephenson, University of Chicago Press, 1967.

[7] See *Of Time, Work and Leisure* by Sebastian de Grazia, published by Twentieth Century Fund, New York, 1962. Lengthy extracts of this and

261

It was something done by slaves. As the centuries rolled by, we *all* became slaves, and it was the unemployed who became 'degraded'. Not that 'work' always had its contemporary unpleasant connotation: 'Formerly, when a New England family convoked a 'bee' (that is, a meeting for working in common), it was for all concerned one of the most memorable times of the year. The work was scarcely more than a pretext for coming together.'[8]

Then came the Industrial Revolution. The working conditions publicised by Dickens may since have gone, but the melody lingers on in the Backing Britain jingoism of today's headlines. Everyone is asked to get out of bed half an hour earlier, mothers are invited to take part-time jobs and the elderly and infirm urged to do their bit by collecting old newspapers and milk bottle tops.[9]

'What has replaced Christianity is not hedonism, but its opposite; the gospel of work, accompanied by its theological abstractions, such as the Balance of Payments, its totems in the shape of parities and the monthly trade returns, its deadly sins like 'higher productivity', and its exhortatory slogans bidding 'earn our way in the world'. Not far from the pop festival, at the Trades Union Congress in Portsmouth, Mr Wilson was preaching the new gospel. And Mr Wilson, we suspect, reflects the prevailing orthodoxy far more accurately than Mr Bob Dylan.'

New Statesman, 5th September, 1969

The Underground has abolished work. There are no

---

other important contributions are reprinted in 'Play Orbit', a beautiful catalogue prepared for an exhibition of the same name at the ICA gallery in London. Edited by Jasia Reichardt. Published by Studio International. London, 1969.

[8] Quoted by Jacques Ellul. *The Technological Society*. Knopf, 1964.

[9] These suggestions, and many more, were part of the I'm backing Britain Campaign, conducted, among others, by Robert Maxwell, Arnold Weinstock, Lord Thomson, Marks & Spencer Ltd., David Frost and Bernard Delfont.

Positions Vacant columns in the Underground press. Hippie hands do not say housework. No one takes vacations — do children holiday from play? Instead, Underground people:

    (i) Transform Work (i.e. Work=Play).
    (ii) Sow their own wild oats.
    (iii) Fuck the System.

' ... where men and women do not determine how they do their work ... where they have become merely components in the production system ... they have during their working lives, lost their identity as individuals.'
    TUC President, John Newton, speaking at the Trades Union Congress, Portsmouth. September 1969

Work
Transformed

— Work is done only for fun; as a pastime, obsession, hobby or art-form and thus is not work in the accepted sense. Underground people launch poster, printing, publishing, record and distribution companies; bookshops, newspapers, information bureaux, video and film groups, restaurants ... anything that they enjoy doing. First advantage: Every Monday morning is a Saturday night.
— Most Underground ventures are under-capitalised; their precariousness means it is often necessary for those involved to work hard at not working.
— But because the motive is fun and freedom, not profit or power, the laxity of (non) working conditions is beyond a shop-steward's dream (or nightmare?). Gone are contracts, time checks, fixed holidays, strikes, division of labour and doing things in triplicate.
— Ever tried to contact an Underground organisation before 11 a.m.? On a sparkling spring day? When there's a free rock concert nearby?
— Head-shop motto: The customer is always wrong — unless he's stoned.

—We humans are such an unpleasant species, that there is still bickering, backstabbing and sporadic dishonesty; but then few people get fired, you can non-work alongside your girlfriend, and no one minds if you freak-off to Katmandu for a few days, or years.

—When Underground organisations can afford to pay wages, everyone usually gets the same, which isn't much, but without property or status fixations, who needs money?

—It is true that some ventures do make an unhealthy profit. Accidents can happen, but most windfalls are then wasted on some idiosyncratic community-enriching private circus.

—A qualification: Money-making ventures may be launched as a side-line to prop up an ailing propaganda organ—yet the fun-element is preserved, as in the case of the Underground porn industry.

—The do-it-for-fun, do-it-for-free spirit entices an amazing selection of individuals who contribute generously and tirelessly to whatever the project in hand happens to be.

—Underground organisations are inherently political—even the restaurants. You are what you eat. When you change people's diet, it is argued, you change their heads. Those who start macrobiotic restaurants believe it is just as important for their food to *do* good, as taste good. That's why there's free brown rice and vegetables every day.

Sowing
Wild
Oats
(and
other
goodies)

The generation which one day awoke to protest, not only altered the course of politics, but altered their relationship to one another. On those long marches from Aldermaston to London, Selma to Montgomery, people came to know

264

each other again. Of a 1964 Free Speech Movement sit-in, Gerald Rosenfield once wrote: 'We spent that night together, some in gaol, most of us sleeping-in in the hotel lobby, a small army camped in the fortress of the enemy. Instead of returning to our private lives we stayed and lived together that night and through the next day, and when it was over we were no longer strangers to one another. For twenty-four hours we were a community.'[10]

It is not surprising that over the next few years, many hundreds of young people should want to nourish this novel cameraderie, extending it in time, consolidating it in space, so creating the commune movement which has spread across the world, most spectacularly in south-west America: the photogenic Drop City, near Trinidad, Colorado, where inhabitants make films, paint, create free form music, meditate, eat macrobiotic food and generally slave over growing-their-own-thing, amongst a bright cluster of Buckminster Fuller inspired geodosic domes.

Libre, New Buffalo, Drop City South, Arroyo Hondo and scores of others are all developing with astonishing speed in the mountains and plains. Within teepees and domes, white tribes are learning to eat weeds, heal themselves with herbs, build solar water-stills, and re-discover secrets of the gypsies and Indians. The outmoded family structure is being extended. Children of the communes are ultimately accountable to their mother, but in most respects children belong to all, each realising parental intimacy with every member of the commune. 'These people *know* each other, in a true sense. They live together, work together, share an idea, a feeling; they watch each other under stress and above all, they share adversity and deprivation. These are the binding factors in a life. These are the things that lead to a true sense of family.'[11]

[10] Quoted by Paul Jacobs and Saul Landau in *The New Radicals*. Random House, 1966. A lesson relearnt in Paris, where 'Almost overnight, atomised individuals turned into vital groups, into genuine communities'—The Cohn–Bendits (*op. cit.*).

[11] Vivian Gornick, 'Mecca on the Mesa.' *Village Voice*, May 29, 1969.

No commune is an island; and inhabitants are often invaded by vigilantes searching for drugs, criminals and runaways. At Dixon, New Mexico, a commune had to be abandoned after its members were arrested for growing marijuana amid the roots and vegetables; at Meadville, Pa., after complaints from local residents, a commune was closed by State Police—the charges against it were maintaining a disorderly house and corrupting the morals of a 16-year-old girl. Not the real objection of course.

Drearier communes are dotted throughout the UK and Europe. The Selene Community in Wales is the fastest growing of these rural ventures and their invitation is addressed to people who are 'Introverted, roughly in the upper 10% intelligence bracket, progressive in social views' but still interested in that old-time pantheism. *Communes*, their monthly magazine, is a chronicle of day-by-day activities which provides sobering insight into the troubles of the modern utopian. Of an unwelcome visitor they record:

'When we left him alone in the room, we heard drawers opening, and when he left (we gave him a lift to the village) we discovered that he had found the biscuit tin and helped himself to about half a pound (selectively taking all the chocolate ones) and had taken the only piece of fruit in the house, without asking, or even informing us. And he left the ladder where he placed it by the bedroom window, upside down and back-to-front, its top buried in the flower bed and its retainers scraping against the wall. An altogether unthinking, unfeeling and boring person with little idea of socialisation.'[12]

The agrarian commune movement can be seen as a retreat to an era when work was directly related to basic human needs. Growing your own cabbages may not exactly be a laugh every sunrise, but for many it offers more reward than selling shoes—even if their satisfaction is merely a

[12] *Communes*, June 27, 1969.

variation on that sentimental respect all city dwellers have
for those who till God's soil. The new communalism reacts
against Western style family 'units' and their seedy inventions of old peoples' homes, mother-in-law hatred, baby
sitters and baby bashers. The bank manager's ideal family
isolates one from another, ill-preparing its offspring for
relating to the outside world. Love thy neighbour—so long
as he is safely ensconced within his capsule. The primary
importance of the commune movement lies in these efforts
to reinterpret the family role as well as in the determination to minimise the significance of money, if not of
chocolate biscuits.

Fucking
the
System

The crucial battles for a new lifestyle are in the cities. The
skirmishes have begun already. In every major Western
capital there are communal centres which operate to ease
the discomforts of dropping-out in an unfriendly environment.[13] Haight-Ashbury 1967 was the scene of the most
famous attempt to cope with urban drop-outs on a grand
scale. Emmett Grogan, now embittered by the glamorisation of the Underground, was once a key member of the

[13] Even if this means dropping into an unfriendly commune. Here's a
farewell letter from an ex-Hyde Park Digger communalist: 'People thrown
together by necessity (usually financial) although sharing in the true community spirit, food (usually stolen), experiences (usually hallucinatory),
and pot (usually not enough) still tend to split into little camps: i.e. Joe
hangs up Bill and Bill hangs up Fred which upsets Jim because Jim likes
everyone. Which is a big hang up for him, for if he refuses to bend in one
direction or another, he's on his own, man! Most conversations in turned-on
scenes are mainly turned-on to "my best trip" or various "freak you out
cocktail recipes" and little else is discussed ... the people wanting to be in on
the love commune thing seem to be sitting around on their arses drawing
NAB and waiting. Waiting for what? For things to be arranged for them by
the Diggers? (That mythical race of people) Dharma, Kharma, Smarma!
Each of us should be a digger, for fuck's sake, otherwise there's not going to
be any communes, because we'll all die of old age, waiting." *OZ* 13.

San Francisco diggers, and has said that they simply made available to the public what was already happening in private. The local free-orientated community pooled all resources so that the 'transient hordes who came to town without knowing that the average temperature is 49 and that everyone has cold fog with their supper ... could eat every day and be warm every night.'[14] Food was hustled from wholesalers and rural communes cooked in vats and ladled out free to the hungry. There were free clothes (from free stores which were open 24 hours a day) free accomodation, free dope, free love and free money.

Over the next two years, while the eyes and ears of the world focused on campus rebellion, informed social observers issued their confident predictions that the hippies would soon drop out of dropping out. Major Fred Brown and friends wrote to *The Times*: 'the True Flower Child is a responsible member of society, holding down a steady nine to five job', and the nation's boardrooms heaved a sigh of relief. In fact, true flower children were surreptitiously digging in at home or roaming the international pot trail, one stoned step ahead of the highway architects. Suddenly last summer, they reappeared in cities all over the world. Some had come back from Katmandu, others had finished school. Those who could not find 'transformed work' situations within the Underground network lay around national monuments, their presence a picturesque repudiation of the ideals symbolised therein.

Everything was done to make the hippies disappear. Munich police confiscated sleeping bags, Amsterdam council workmen hosed benches around the Dam. The Eros fountain at Piccadilly was discreetly turned up to splash the surrounding steps — symbolising society's wishful reaction to their alienated children. Wash them away. To prevent youngsters congregating beneath the statue of King George III, Dorset council used the ultimate deterrent:

[14] *IT* 54. April 1969.

'The dried blood which smells like rotten meat, was sprayed twice and the hippies did not come back.

Daily Telegraph

Just as those who believe class barriers no longer exist should ride the breakfast Pullman from London to Manchester any morning of the week, so too, those who doubt the flowering of an anti-work ethic among the young, should spend a few hours 'desecrating' their local monument. While there you may be sold a booklet—your first mistake. It's free. Called 'Project London', it is a survival manual for full-time drop-outs. (See Appendix IV). Like its New York counterpart, 'Fuck the System' (reprinted in Abbie Hoffman's *Revolution for the Hell of It*), 'Project London' is published on the principle that the best things in life are free, if only you have the necessary information to obtain them. The morality of the booklet is the morality of the Underworld—minus the profit motive. The Deviants, a London rock group, sing 'Let's Loot the Supermarket' and many fans ask 'why stop there?' The world is overproducing already ... and everyone, except the Underground, seems embarrassed by it. Silos of surplus wheat rot in Canada. The Common Market considers feeding its excess butter back to the cows. Thousands of tons of coffee are dumped off the Ivory Coast, not far from Biafra.[14a] None of this can make meals for Starving Millions (except in tax-deductable Oxfam containers) because rival exporters would suffer, economies tremble and the whole house of cards collapse. So while there is money, there is scarcity. A truism, of course, but it is curious that it is the drop-outs, not the New Left pamphleteers, who, without tortured intellectualisation, are training themselves for a moneyless society.

Again, while Marx's reminder that All Property is Theft is re-etched every year on the walls of scores of student pubs, it is Piccadilly's 'Commune of the Streets' who, prepared for the creeping chill of an English winter by

[14a] See *The Food Explosion*. David Ramsay-Steele *OZ* 19.

occupying a deserted eighteenth-century mansion near, appropriately, the Hilton Hotel. Thundered *The Times* and Left Militants in rare unison—'This action is totally irresponsible ... not one homeless family has been installed.'

That's because several hundred homeless hippies were housed instead, and anyone was welcome to join them. For a time, the squatters *were* a family, a communal one. Everyone talked to anyone, free food was served, animated and intelligent young children played among the debris. (In terms of morale and survival capabilities, the occupation began deteriorating when people split-off into small family-type units, erecting barriers between each other instead of between them and the police.)

'We are the secret agents of a future society free from the routine degradation of work.'

'Dr John', Leader of the London Street Commune

Guaranteed Leisure

Tomorrow you may be paid NOT to work—can you take it? The drop-outs are anticipating future economic policy. People will be paid to stay away from factories, just as some farmers are paid *not* to harvest crops. At existing levels of consumer demand, automation and cybernation are rapidly replacing workers. In his study 'Automation and the Work Force',[15] Ben B. Seligman disposes of two myths: (i) that automation produces as many or more jobs than it eliminates, (ii) that it upgrades employees.

In 1962, the US steel industry employed 28% fewer

[15] From *The Guaranteed Income. Next Step in Socio-economic Evolution?* edited by Robert Theobald. As well as setting out the details of the Guaranteed Income proposal, this book contains ten important essays, including a discussion of the Psychological Aspects of Guaranteed Income by Erich Fromm, and Marshall McLuhan's Guaranteed Income in the Electric Age. Anchor Books, 1967.

workers than in 1951. The decline of man-hours was 34%. 'As a direct result of automation', writes Seligman, 'over 80,000 fewer production workers could produce as much steel at the end of the eleven-year period as at the start.' An analysis of the rest of manufacturing produces the same conclusion. The computer eliminates jobs in government occuaptions as well. And Seligman estimates that the number of white collar workers displaced by computers 'has grown from virtually zero a decade ago to as much as 100,000 persons a year ...'

Robert H. Davies[16] records that the first computer was delivered to the US Bureau of Census in 1950. At the beginning of 1965, approximately 25,000 computers had been installed by American-based companies. In 1970, it is estimated that there will be 52,000 computers installed in the US.

By the end of 1962, 434 computers had been installed in the UK. At the end of 1969 this number had risen to 43,000. The automated Victoria line on London's other Underground requires a work force of 719, instead of the 1,025 necessary if it had been a regular line.[17] When I telephoned to obtain these figures, the London Transport Board were very apologetic about this reduction and wanted me to point out that as it was a new—not converted—line, no one had actually lost their jobs. The National Giro Centre said that 2,500 staff can handle one million trans-actions a day with the National Giro System, which, if it was not computerised, would require an 'astronomical' task force. In Europe, research into the overall effect of computerisation on employment is surprisingly sparse. In *Computers, Managers and Society* (Penguin, 1969), Michael Rose cautiously concludes, after surveying available (and contradictory) evidence, that 'a contraction in general clerical opportunities may begin to occur within the short rather than the long period.'

[16] Advance of Cybernation.
[17] *160* train operators instead of *292* guards/drivers if the line was not automated. *8* traffic regulators instead of *22* signalmen. *551* technicians instead of *711* ticket collectors, booking clerks, etc.

271

This worker-displacement tendency is unwittingly aggravated by Government fiscal policy; which, after Keynes, aims for full employment by stimulating consumer demand. But this artificially created demand, argues Robert Theobald, 'will lead to purchases of highly efficient and productive machine systems that need few men to control them; i.e. to the installation of cybernation. Thus, in the relatively near future, a policy of forcing rapid growth in demand in order to increase employment opportunities will actually lead to the opposite result: it will raise unemployment rather than lower it.' Theobald believes that the aim to provide everyone with a job is no longer valid; instead everyone should have an absolute right to a guaranteed income. In the future there will be more unemployment. We shall come to regard this unemployment as desirable.

Obviously Theobald's analysis is controversial. J. K. Galbraith[18] for instance, who regards projections of increased leisure time as a 'conventional conversation piece', believes the opposite. He argues that as incomes rise, 'men will work longer hours and seek less leisure.' Among his reasons for this belief, Galbraith states that (with exceptions) within the present industrial system, 'work is unlikely to be painful and may be pleasant', an assessment of such sweeping optimism that perhaps his vision is not entirely to be trusted.

As the saying goes, if every economist in the world was laid end to end, they would never reach a conclusion. If Theobald is correct, and Galbraith wrong, then we had better learn how to use the leisure bonus. Look what happened to Sparta. 'The Spartans remained secure as long as they were at war; they collapsed as soon as they acquired an empire. They did not know how to use the leisure that peace brought.'[19]

[18] John Kenneth Galbraith. *The New Industrial State*. Houghton–Mifflin, 1967.

[19] Sebastian de Grazia, *op. cit.* (*Of Time, Work and Leisure*).

Incidentally, in our cosy projection of a cybernated age, there will still be room for anyone who wants to launch 'custom built' industries, orientated towards a specialised market. Technology will provide basic needs. And individuals can produce for other individuals. But, unless you *want* to build a better mousetrap, it will be your duty to live off National Assistance.

When I once asked Tuli Kupferberg—the author of *1001 Ways to Live Without Working*—what the West Coast drop-outs did with their time, he said they spent all day playing Frisbee. Frisbee? A Frisbee is a saucer-shaped plastic dish which glides gracefully through the air and is easy to catch. Person A throws it to B, who throws it back (or to C, D, or E, etc.). That is all. It is a game played for fun—not profits, not points.

It is somehow divinely appropriate that this game is favoured by drop-outs. Frisbee is non-competitive. It has no rules. No one could sell tickets to it.

Like a child taking its first steps, members of the Underground are learning how to live in that future where work is rendered obsolete.

They are re-learning how to play.

**Play
is
Fun.
Play
is
Freedom**

Play is a voluntary activity. If it is compulsory, then it is not play. J. Huizinga in his famous study of the play element in culture,[20] defined freedom as its major characteristic.

The *essential* characteristic of play is fun. Play 'adorns

[20] J. Huizinga. *Homo Ludens, a study of the Play Element in Culture.* Beacon Press, 1955.

273

life, amplifies it and is to that extent a necessity both for the individual—as a life function—and for society by reason of the meaning it contains, its significance, its expressive value, its spiritual and social associations, in short, as a culture function. The expression of it satisfies all kinds of communal ideas.'

When did *you* last play? Was it fun? Play has been abolished in contemporary society—except in children, until we knock it out of them—and in its place there is recreation—human maintenance. Recreation repairs man from toil, 're-creating' him to live to die another day. Organised sport isn't play either; it's a ritualised, legitimised aggression narcotic; hard work, competitive, corrupt. Ever seen an Olympic contestant smile?

Those most caught up in the syndrome of work/family/ machine/sport/success/failure/guilt ... are those most outraged by the evolving Underground alternative. At student sit-ins, it is the 'jocks' who try to toss the anarchists out. The hippie-haters with shaved heads, uniform clothes and boots-made-for-kicking, seek out the most menial of manual jobs. Football every Saturday. Train wrecking on the way home. Always aggressively upon the scene of a hippie happening. At 144 Piccadilly, occupants fought them off (and police) with brightly coloured beach bowls discovered in the building—i.e. their weapons were toys.

Sex
is
Pure
When
it's
Playful

Infants get the most out of their sex life. They play with themselves unashamedly, anarchistically, freely, and solely for the purpose of gratification. As they grow up, their sexuality becomes repressed, neurotic, perverted. In his *Life Against Death* Norman O. Brown stresses that 'Freud's definition of sexuality entails the proposition that infants have a richer sexual life than adults ... Children explore in indiscriminate and anarchistic fashion all the erotic potentialities of the human body.' Sounds like the sex habits of the Underground, which is still, like children, narcissistic and guiltless. Remember the last time you saw a love scene with Robert Mitchum? Heavy. Tense. Serious. Adult. Like most cinematic sex scenes. Like most marital sex scenes. What is it? It's work. The Underground is turning sex back into play.[21] Underground culture revels in the easy sexuality found in pop, the Underground Press, language and lifestyle (drugs help promote it). An important event at Bob Dylan's famous Isle of Wight concert was an unplanned side-show — a group of children playing/fucking in some foam in front of thousands of people. Out goes Reich's fuddy duddy orgone box ... in comes happy, hippie playful sex. When did you last play with your lover? Not the ancient 'romantic' ritualistic ego games (=toil), but free, uninhibited, fun-oriented sexual anarchy. Pure play has no rules. On your mark; get set ...

[21] Read *Life Against Death* (especially Chapter 3) where childhood is seen to be man's indestructible goal. Freud's 'pessimism is in his inability to see this goal reconcilable with man's equally deep commitment to culture and cultural progress.' One solution, of course, is to imbue *culture* with the freedom and playfulness of children so the twin goals are no longer contradictory. However, Brown goes on later to discuss the one 'fatal flaw' in the return to the pleasure principle — it cannot come to terms with the reality principle. Finally, two quotes used by Brown:
(i) From Schiller's *Letters on the Aesthetic Education of Man*. 'Man only plays when in the full meaning of the word, he is a man, and he is only completely a man when he plays.'
(ii) Sartre *Being and Nothingness*. 'As soon as man apprehends himself as free and wishes to use his freedom ... then his activity is play.'

Play
Culture
is
Coming
Back

Once upon a time, culture was fun and games. Then it became earnest, drab, puritan and anti-play. Now it is being 'played' again, its quotient of fun, freedom and games proportional to its depth Underground—rock, fashions (dressing up), happenings, movies, street theatre and living. Purposeless play is creative. The most inventive scientists and researchers play.[22] Many new inventions started out as toys. Artists play. Why? Because as John Cage has written, purposeless play is 'affirmation of life—not an attempt to bring order out of chaos, nor to suggest improvements in creation, but simply a way of waking up to the very life we're living, which is so excellent once one gets one's mind and one's desires out of the way and lets it act of its own accord.'

The Underground's devotion to mystologics is chance/ play oriented (tossing coins for the I-Ching, spotting UFO's ...). Drugs, especially psychedelics, put the play back into culture. The best Arts Laboratories are play pens. When did you last play in an art gallery?

The play element, as we have already seen, flourishes in the Underground culture and work (non-toil) situations, and is beginning to flow into its political non-organisations. Affinity Groups (New York) and Action Committees (Paris, May) try to head in this direction (loosely structured, anti-organisational, flexible, potent), as do London's street guerrilla theatre troupes. The Chicago Festival of Life was its ideal, but here fun, freedom and play clashed bloodily with work, enslavement and brutality.

[22] See Nigel Calder, *Technopolis: Social Control of the Uses of Science*, Chapter 4—In the Automation. Also, Edward de Bono, *New Think: The Use of Lateral Thinking in the Generation of New Ideas*, which was cited in Chapter I when I was discussing chance. ('Vertical thinkers are ashamed to play, but the only shameful thing is the inability to play.')

The best outline of how Underground politics should work is Chester Anderson's afterword to Domhoff's *How to Commit Revolution in Corporate America*. (Entwhistle/West, Goleta California 1968.)

Here is part of it:

'It would appear that in the new society organisation increases at function's expense, and that organisation *per se* tends to perpetuate itself and increase in size like a galloping cancer until the original purpose of the organisation withers away to a scrap of sentiment and a rag of tradition wholly without meaning or importance—stealing the other school's mascot (a stuffed & mounted long-haired goat) and dyeing it green.

Traditional organisation theory, as practised by even the most radical organisations, is built upon a framework of power & control that's totally irrelevant to half the revolutionaries & the whole revolution. Organisation in terms of linear sequence is more than obsolete in the present technological environment—a thing of synchronicity & circuits—it's virulent, a social pathology, neither fun nor useful. Who needs it? ...

Instead of the American Revolutionary Party, I propose a casual association of revolutionary gangs, not bothering to co-ordinate or otherwise inhibit them, caring more to maintain good communications among them. A national urban-guerrilla club, fun-orientated & irresistible.

Fuck leaders & uniforms & holy causes more important than people. A gang that playfully corrupts the mayor's teenage son produces more important & enduring changes than does the strictly disciplined, grim & earnest assassination squad that gets his father.

We can't begin to match the Establishment's present firepower & other resources, but there's been no Mace deployed yet to the future, and the kids give us unrestricted access to next week. The future is ours now to make what we will of, and to turn on, ball or otherwise recruit & indoctrinate any kid at all is an act more politically significant even than Oswald's one-shot demonstration. And more fun, too.

Point is, we can't conduct the present, any part of it,

with the techniques of the 19th century. The Industrial Revolution is over & we lost ...

Instead of an American Revolutionary Party, or an armed band of Black Guerrillas, or any other such Establishment stereotype, something altogether different is necessary, and if the opposition fails at first to recognise the revolutionary nature of our invention, that's the opposition's problem.

Innovate now.'

The politics of play. The strategy which converts the Underground to a brotherhood of clowns; the lifestyle which unites a generation in love and laughter. In Chicago, it's Pigasus the pig for President. In Nanterre, it's a horse nominated by students for local councillor. 250 acid trips in Afghanistan. 500 *Other Scenes* in John Wilcock's travel bag. Abbie Hoffman throwing a kiss to the Chicago jury. The politics of play.

One weekend a lonely sailor strolls through Hyde Park and hears King Crimson shout: 'What's it All About?' and he spends the weekend with new-found hippie friends. On Sunday night, they take him to Waterloo station for the ship-bound train and he's haunted by his own face in the sunken, drunken eyes of every other kit-bagged man, so he deserts the navy there and then. 'I'm outside trying to lose myself in the Underground while they're still inside roasting.' The politics of play. The new sex helps break-up unhappy families, deconditions us from toil and introduces more of us to one another. The new beautiful freaks will teach us all how to play again (and they'll suffer society's penalty). In the land where the court jester is King, there is only one political question—is he funny enough?

Careerists read *Playboy*, insurance men get rich on fear, the politicos wage their deadly peace, the machine grinds on until the Underground puts enough acid in the petrol tank. The politics of play: the international, equi-sexual, inter-racial survival strategy for the future, the laughing gas to counteract tomorrow's Mace. Onward to the eighties, Motherfuckers.

278

APPENDIX ONE

DOING IT IN THE ROAD

'Ach, how mein arm does ache'—German policeman.

Germany

Berlin, June 2 1967[1] Several thousand demonstrators and observers witness arrival of Shah of Iran at opera. Crowd begins to disperse when police attack, without warning, swinging clubs. More than twenty students are hospitalised, and one, Benno Ohnesborg, is fatally shot from behind. A nurse comes to his aid and is clubbed by police. At least fifteen witnesses have given testimony confirming this story. Other independent eye-witnesses report that police 'began ganging up on single demonstrators and youthful-looking bystanders, in some cases dragging them, and then beating them, kicking them as they lay upon the ground'. The Mayor of Berlin who was saddened by such behaviour:

'The patience of the city is at an end. A few dozen demonstrators, among them students, have earned the sad credit to have offended and insulted a guest of the Federal Government of Germany in the German capital; they are also to blame for injured demonstrators and policemen and one dead student.'
Quoted by Hermann Kai in *Die Revolte der Studenten*, Christian Weger Verlag, Hamburg, 1967.

Berlin, Easter, 1968 Students conduct peaceful demonstration. Leaders continually call for non-violence. Police attack, one roughly arresting a non-demonstrating elderly lady. 'When I asked for an identity number', reports an observer, a professor of city planning, 'four policemen attacked me, tore the buttons off my coat and arrested me.' On Easter Sunday, demonstrators drive to three police stations to await the release of previously arrested students. The police attack the cars as soon as they arrive, smashing headlights and windows and beating up the occupants.
Hamburg One young student is savagely beaten about the head. It is reported that his face is 'totally deformed'.
Munich The majority of West Germany's politicians blamed students for the violence of the Easter weekend. A comprehensive survey of the population of West Berlin revealed that: 80% of the West Berlin population had less sympathy for the students after the violence than before it.

---

[1] The German Union of Students has published a well documented report of the demonstration and subsequent developments—Knut Nevermann, *Der 2 Juni* 1967, Pahl Rugenstein Verlag, Cologne 1967.
Much of the information in this section has been obtained from a document *Student Revolts—The New Left in West Germany*, by F. C. Hunnius who prepared it originally for a Canadian journal, *Our Generation*. Mr Hunnius derives most of his examples from objective non-student sources. A similar policy has been adopted for this appendix.

France

Paris, May 1968[2] A demonstrator, apparently unconscious, was lying on the barricade. A CRS man was hitting him repeatedly with a baton while the barricade was beginning to burn. A Red Cross man, wearing signs on his cap, his chest and his back so that he was easily identifiable even from a distance, approached to try to remove the wounded man. The CRS man hit him straight in the face and knocked him down, then went back to work on the still motionless demonstrator.

A boy who was beaten up while being taken to the police station, reports that on arrival:

'To get to the cells you still had to pass between the station desk and a row of CRS and *gardes mobiles* who struck very methodically and with special brutality. I was hit on the head, the stomach and the legs. But I stayed upright, because a young man ahead of me fell under the blows and was absolutely smashed with kicks. Then I was pushed into a cell about two and a half metres by four with about 60 to 80 people in it ... A girl asked to go out because she felt ill; the CRS let her out, then we saw them hitting her with batons. After that we didn't even dare to ask for help when someone fainted!'

A woman tells how she took refuge in an empty flat with some others, including a young couple:

'The wife was three months' pregnant. They hid in the bathroom, and almost at once the CRS smashed the door and rushed at them, shouting furiously. I was hiding in the next room, where by some miracle they never came in. I could hear the young woman shouting "I'm pregnant!" and being beaten up to the accompaniment of cries of "You'll soon see if you're pregnant, you tart!" I skip the details, I could go on for ten pages. They beat her husband almost unconscious, beat up another boy and took them both off, leaving the pregnant girl nearly passing out in the doorway, with her head covered in bruises and in a shocking state. As I picked her up she cried: "My husband, my husband, they're going to kill him, he's got a fractured skull already." We went out on the landing and a door on the second floor opened. A gentleman told us to come in quick .. We stayed there in the dark till five in the morning, the building was surrounded. All that time we could see them beating up the wounded, arresting people walking home alone, baiting them, and finally throwing grenades at the flats. We couldn't get help until five o'clock. The pregnant girl started to have contractions and the nurse who examined her said she was in danger of losing her baby. She was taken to hospital at once and I've heard no news of her since.'

A nurse was arrested and taken to the detention centre at Beaujon:

'We got out of the bus and were beaten up; then, going between the two ranks of CRS, I reached a stadium surrounded by barbed wire. I waited, standing

[2] Information in this section is taken from an article by Mervyn Jones in *The New Statesman*, 5 July 1968. The article itself is compiled from *Le Livre Noir des Journées de Mai* (Editions du Seuil), and from a collection of testimonies available to him in mimeographed form.

in the rain. From time to time, CRS buses delivered men and women, hit or gassed, with very bad head wounds, broken arms, etc. Chinese or Vietnamese and blacks specially were treated with great violence. Then we were taken indoors one by one. A CRS man said to me: "Come along and I'll shave you, curly locks." He hit me. An officer intervened but the girl ahead of me had all her hair cut off. I was taken to a cell, three metres by six. After five hours, it contained 80 of us. We had to stand up. I could see the courtyard; a young man went by half naked, legs lacerated with baton blows, bleeding, holding his stomach, urinating everywhere. A young woman who'd been with him told me the CRS beat him till he fainted, then undressed him and hit his sexual organs till the flesh was in ribbons.

Some girls arrived, among them a schoolgirl of 16 who told us she had been arrested by CRS at St Michel. They took her into their bus and four of them raped her. She told me she let them do it, otherwise they'd have beaten her up and shaved her head. Her clothes were torn and she was bruised. Another girl was crying, she had a broken finger. She had to wait 18 hours in that cell before she got medical attention at a hospital—then she was brought back to the cell.'

United States

Chicago, August 1968 Chicago's Mayor Daley, the Cecil B. de Mille of violence, gave an unforgettable welcome to the youth of America at the Democratic Convention in August 1968. This occasion was graced by an unusually luxuriant attendance of journalists, many of whom got in the way of police truncheons. Their tears flowed on to front pages all around the world.

Max Hastings of the London *Evening Standard* made front page headlines with this eye-witness account:

' ... the police smashed their clubs into the human mass, aiming between their legs, at their heads, shoulders—anything. They used chemical spray to disable them and were still hitting them as they lay on the floor ... after the events of the last twelve hours in Chicago it will never again be possible to think of either the city or Mayor Daley without feeling slightly sick.[3]

In the same issue, James Cameron wrote: ' ... in Paris, in Berlin, in Hong Kong, even in London, there is now a recognised reflex action against beads and beards and the contemporary juvenile thing. I would say I have never seen it so coldly and cruelly systematised as here in Chicago.'

Here are some brief, almost random extracts from the massive Walker Report to the National Commission on the Causes and Prevention of Violence.[4]

'A priest who was in the crowd says he saw a "boy", about fourteen or fifteen, white, standing on top of an automobile yelling something which was unidentifiable. Suddenly a policeman pulled him down from the car and

[3] *Evening Standard*, Thursday, August 29, 1968.
[4] *Rights in Conflict*, The Walker Report to the National Commission on the Causes and Prevention of Violence. Signet Books, 1969.

beat him to the ground by striking him three or four times with a nightstick. Other police joined in … and they eventually shoved him to a police van.

A well-dressed woman saw this incident and spoke angrily to a nearby police captain. As she spoke, another policeman came up from behind her and sprayed something in her face with an aerosol can. He then clubbed her to the ground. He and two other policemen then dragged her along the ground to the same paddy wagon and threw her in.'[5]

The tape of the Police Department radio log discloses the following conversation at 1.29 a.m. on Tuesday morning:

POLICE OPERATOR: '1814, get a wagon over here at 1436. We've got an injured hippie.'
VOICE: '1436 North Wells?'
OPERATOR: 'North Wells.'

In quick sequence, there are the following remarks from five other police cars:

'That's no emergency.'
'Let him take a bus.'
'Kick the fucker.'
'Knock his teeth out.'
'Throw him in a wastepaper basket.'[6]

Winston S. Churchill II, reporting for the London *Evening News*, and James Auchincloss of NBC were standing together in front of the Hilton Hotel, apparently after the first police sweep, when, they report, they saw a plain-clothes man catch a girl demonstrator and beat her with a blackjack. Both of them went to help the girl and asked the man to identify himself. They say that Auchincloss was hit twice by the plain-clothes man as a result, and Churchill was knocked to the ground. As Churchill rose, a policeman on a three-wheel motorcycle charged them, pinning both of them against the hotel wall for a moment.[7]

The Walker Report estimated that the 'weight of violence was overwhelmingly on the side of the police'; just as Professor Skolnik's more thorough study, 'The Politics of Protest'[8] concluded that in America: 'Nearly all violence that has occurred in mass demonstrations has resulted not from the demonstrators' conscious choice of tactics, but from the measures chosen by public authorities to disperse and punish them.'

Berkeley, May 1969 'With 51 arrests yesterday, total arrests now number 272. Horror stories of police brutality continue to gain credence. Twenty-five-year-old James Rector is dead, Alan Blanchard has lost his sight and

[5] ibid. p. 10.
[6] ibid. p. 183.
[7] ibid. p. 323.
[8] The Politics of Protest, 1969, prepared by Professor Jerome Skolnik, head of a task force on Violent Aspects of Protest and Confrontation.

scores of other people have been seriously injured in the disturbances ...
Alameda County Sheriff Chief Frank Madigan, who is in charge of all police
activity, has defended his department's use of shotguns with the words,
"that's the way the ball game has to go".'

Evening Standard

APPENDIX TWO

DIRECTORY TO THE WORLD'S UNDERGROUND PRESS

UNDERGROUND PRESS SYNDICATE—AMERICA/CANADA: Box 26, Greenwich Village Post Office, New York, 10014. Box 1832, Phoenix, Arizona, 85001.

ANN ARBOR ARGUS: 725 North University, No. 7, Ann Arbor, Michigan.
BALTIMORE FREE PRESS: 2601 Madison Ave. Apt: 1205 Baltimore.
BAULS (Of the Brickyard): P.O. Box 2340 West Lafayette, Ind. 47906.
BERKELEY BARB: Box 5017, Berkeley, California 94715.
BERKELEY TRIBE: 1708 Grove St, Berkeley, Cal. 94703.
BUFFALO CHIP: Box 1122, Omaha, Nebraska 68101.
CANADA GOOSE: 10133 99th St., Edmonton, Alberta, Canada.
THE CARILLON: University of Saskatchewan, Regina, Canada.
COMMUNICATION COMPANY: 26 Bond St, New York, NY 10012.
CONNECTIONS: 217 S. Hamilton St, Madison, Wisconsin 53703.
DALLAS NOTES: Box 7140, Dallas, Texas 75209.
DISTANT DRUMMER: 1736 Pine St, Philadelphia, Pa. 19103.
DWARFFE: Box 1832, Phoenix, Arizona 851001.
EAST VILLAGE OTHER: 105 Second Avenue, New York, NY 10003.
ECO CONTEMPORANEO: Correo Central 1933, Buenos Aires, Argentina.
EXTRA: Box 2426, Providence, Rhode Island 02906.
FIFTH ESTATE: 1107 W. Warren, Detroit, Michigan 48201.
FLORIDA FREE PRESS: 602 1/2 N. Adams, Tallahassee, Florida 32301.
FREE KAZOO: 604 University Ave, Apt. 5, Syracuse, NY 13210.
GEORGIA STRAIGHT: 217 Carrall St, Vancouver 4, BC, Canada.
GOOD TIMES: 1550 Howard St, San Francisco, California.
GREAT SPECKLED BIRD: 187, 14 St, NE, Atlanta, Georgia.
HAIGHT-ASHBURY TRIBUNE: 1778 Haight St, San Francisco, Cal.
HARBINGER: Box 751, Station F, Toronto, Canada.
HELIX: 3128 Harvard St East, Seattle, Washington 98102.
HETERODOXICAL VOICE: Box 24, Newark, Delaware 19711.
KALEIDOSCOPE (Milwaukee) P.O. Box 5457, Milwaukee, Wisconsin, 53211.
THE KUDSU: Box 22502, Jackson, Mississippi 39205.
LAIR: 360 71st Ave, St Petersburg Beach, Florida.
LIBERATION: 5 Beekman St, New York, NY 70116.
LIBERATION NEWS SERVICE: 160 Claremount Ave, New York 10027.
LOGOS: Box 782, Montreal 101, Quebec, Canada.
LOS ANGELES FREE PRESS: 7813 Beverley Boul, Los Angeles, Cal. 90036.
LOVE: 656 Eureka St, Reno, Nevada 89502.
MIAMI FREE PRESS: 3305 Grand Avenue, Coconut Grove, Fla.
MIDDLE EARTH: No 1, Iowa City, Iowa 52240.
MINNEAPOLIS FREE PRESS: 908 13th Ave, Minneapolis, Minn. 55404.
MODERN UTOPIAN: Starr King Centre, 2441 Le Conte Ave, Berkeley, California 94709.
NEW HARD TIMES: Box 3272, Clayton, Mo. 63105.

NEW LEFT NOTES: 1608 W. Madison St, Chicago, Ill. 60612.
NEW YORK ROACH: 14 North Gate Rd, Great Neck, NY 11023.
NORTH CAROLINA ANVIL: Box 1148, Durham, NC 27702.
OCTOPUS: Box 1259, Station B, Ottawa, Canada.
OLVIDATE: Apartado Nacional No 8873, Bogotá, Colombia.
OMPHALOS: 971 Sherbrooke St, Winnipeg, Canada.
OTHER SCENES: Box 8, Village Post Office, New York 10014.
PEACE AND FREEDOM NEWS: c/o Peace Action Centre, 2525 Maryland Ave, Baltimore, Maryland 21218.
PENINSULAR OBSERVER: 180 University Ave, Palo Alto, Cal. 94301.
PROBE: Box 12629 UCSB, Santa Barbara, California 93107.
RAG: 609 W. 23rd Ave, Austin, Texas 78705.
RAT: 341 East 14 St, New York, 10009.
REBIRTH: P.O. Box 2628, Phoenix, Arizona.
RESISTANCE PRESS: Box 892, Chicago, Illinois.
SAN DIEGO DOOR: 6389 Imperial Avenue, San Diego, Calif. 92114.
SAN DIEGO FREE PRESS: 751 Turquoise, San Diego, Calif. 92109.
SAN FRANCISCO ORACLE: 460 Magnolia Avenue, Larkspur, California.
SEED: 837 N. La Salle, Chicago, Illinois 60610.
SEVENTY-NINE CENT SPREAD: Box 5134, Carmel, California, 93921.
SMALL CHANGE: 124 North Syndicate, P.O. Box 833, Port William, Ontario, Canada.
SPECTATOR: 423 S. Fess St, Bloomington, Indiana 47401.
SPOKANE NATURAL: Box 1276, Spokane, Washington 99210.
STRAWBERRY FIELDS: 8/63 NE 2nd Avenue, Miami, Florida.
SUN: 1510 Hill, Ann Arbor, Michigan 48104.
TRIBAL VILLAGE: 17 Paton Rd, Toronto 4, Ontario, Canada.
VANGUARD: 203 Clayton St, San Francisco, California 94117.
VIEW FROM THE BOTTOM: 532 State Street, New Haven, Connecticut.
VORTEX: P.O. Box 16016, Kansas City, Missouri 64112
LE VOYAGE: 3577 de Bullion, Montreal 18, Quebec, Canada.
WASHINGTON FREE PRESS: 3 Thomas Circle, NW, Washington DC 20005.
WATER TUNNEL: Box 136, State College, Pennsylvania 16801.
WESTERN ACTIVIST: Western Michigan University, Box 147, Stu Ctr, Kalamazoo, Michigan 490001.
WILLIAMETTE BRIDGE: 522 W. Burnside, Portland, Oregon 97204.
WIN: 5 Beekman St, New York, NY 10038.
WORD: 411 Frenchman St, New Orleans, Louisiana 70116.

ALBION: 12A Camelford Street, London W11.
AMBIT: 17 Priory Gardens, London SW10.
BLACK DWARF: 7 Carlisle Street, London W1.
FIRE: 20 Fitzroy Square, London W1.
FRIENDS: T. F. Much Publishing Co., 305 Portobello Road, London W10
GANDALF'S GARDEN: 1 Dartrey Terrace, London SW10.
HOTCHA: Postfach 304, CH 8025, Zurich, Switzerland.
ICA NEWS: Nash House, The Mall, London SW1.
IETS: Box 876, The Hague, Holland.
IT: 27 Endell Street, London WC2.
KARUNA: Opnaesgard 23, Horsholm, Denmark.
LINKECK: Rollbergstrasse 67, 1 Berlin 44, BRD, Germany.
OM: Kaizerstraat 2A, 11 et, Amsterdam, Holland.
OZ: 52 Princedale Road, London W11.
PEACE NEWS: 5 Caledonia Road, London N1.
PENG: Altemayer, Postfach 2815, 56 Wuppertal 1, BRD, Germany.
PIANETA FRESCO: 14 Via Manzoni, Milano, 20121, Italy.
PUSS: Hillersberg, Fleming 42, Stockholm, Sweden.
REAL FREE PRESS: Wolstraat 41, Antwerp, Belgium.
REVO: Box 252, Brussels, Belgium.
SIGNAL INTERNATIONAL: Box 8150, Lahti, Finland.
TLALCO: BCM/Cavas, London WC1.
ZIG ZAG: 7 Fiveoaks, Caddington, Luton, Bedfordshire, England.

OTHER PUBLICATIONS OF INTEREST—AMERICA AND CANADA

ABAS: 420 Summer Avenue, Newark, NJ 07104, US.
ALBANY LIBERATOR: 172 N. Pearl St, Albany, NY 12207, US.
ALICE: Box 459, Blackbury, Virginia 24060, US.
ALTERNATIVE PRESS INDEX: c/o Radical Research Centre, Carleton College,
    Northfield, Minnesota 55057, US.
ALTERNATIVES: Nudist-Sex Directory. Box 1264, Berkeley, California 94701,
    US.
ALTUS: c/o James Skilman, 1130 Piedmont Avenue, NE, No. 32, Atlanta,
    Georgia 30309, US.
AMERICAN AVATAR: 27 Fort Avenue, Roxbury, Mass. US.
AMERICAN DREAM: Box 820, Tempe, Canada.
THE AMERICAN EXILE IN CANADA: Box 759, Station F, Toronto 5.
ANARCHOS: Box 466, Peter Styvesant Station, New York 10009, US.
ANVIL: Box 1148, Durham, NC 27702, US.
ASPECTS: Box 3125, Eugeno, Oregon 97403, US.

ASTERISK: Old Market News, 1112 Howard Street, Omaha, Nebraska 68102, US.

ASTRAL PROJECTION: P.O. Box 4383, Albuquerque, New Mexico 87106

AUM: Alliance of Underground Media, 528 Lambert Road, Orange, Connecticut 06477, US.

THE BLACK OBSERVER: 757 Kaighns Avenue, Camden, NY 10010, US.

THE BLACK PANTHER: & A BLACK COMMUNITY NEWS SERVICE: Black Panther Party, Ministry of Information, Box 2967, Custom House, San Francisco, Calif. 94126, US.

THE BOND: Rm 633, 156 Fifth Avenue, New York, NY 10010, US.

BROADSIDE: P.O. Box 4219, San Rafael, Calif. 94903, US.

CAMPUS UNDERGROUND: Campus Publications, 401 1/2 Main Street, Cedar Falls, Iowa 50613, US.

CANADIAN DIMENSIONS: Box 1413, Winnipeg 1, Manitoba, Canada.

CAPITAL EAST GAZETTE: 109 S. Street, NE, Washington DC 20002, US.

CAW: Box 333, Cooper Station, New York, NY 10003, US.

CHANGES: 5419 Foothill Boul., Oakland, Calif. 94601, US.

CHANGES: 80 Fifth Avenue, New York, NY 10011, US.

CHEVRON: University of Waterloo, Waterloo, Ontario, Canada.

CIRCUS: 201 E. 42nd St., New York, NY 10017.

COBWEBS AND STRANGE: Box 84, Sidney, British Columbia, Canada.

COMMON SENSE: First Unitarian Universalist Church, 245 Porter Lake Drive, Springfield, Mass. 01106, US.

CORPUS: Sons of Light, 14 Cooper Square, New York, NY 10003, US

COUNTERPOINT: 1201 Illinois Avenue, Stevens Pt, Wisconsin 54481, US.

COUNTRY SCENES: Box 465, Woodbury, Connecticut 06798, US.

CREEM MAGAZINE: 3729 Cass Avenue, Detroit, Michigan 48201, US.

THE DAILY MEADOW MUFFIN: 41 Park Row, New York, NY 10038, US.

DAILY PLANET: Apt. 4, 58 East 55 Street, New York, NY 10022, US.

DAILY WORLD: 205 W. 19 St, New York, NY 10011, US.

DAMASCUS FREE PRESS: 24524 Fossen Street, Damascus, Maryland, US.

DIRECTORY OF LITTLE MAGAZINES & SMALL PRESSES: Box 123, El, Verrito, California 94530, US.

DOUGLASTON FREE PRESS: 40-24 Main Street, Douglaston, NY 11363, US.

DRUID PRESS: 2345 E. Speedway, Tucson, Arizona 85719, US.

DRUM: c/o Gilbert Moses, Ft Green Community, 649 Fulton Street, Brooklyn, New York 11217, US.

EARTH PEOPLES PARK NEWSLETTER: Box 313, 1230 Grant Street, San Francisco, California 94133, US.

EARTH TIMES: 746 Brannon Street, San Francisco, California 94103, US.

EGG: 11 ½ Spadina Rd., Toronto 4, Canada.

ELECTRIC NEWSPAPER: 875 E. 9 St, Salt Lake City, Utah 84105, US.

EL GALLO: 1265 Cherokee St, Denver, Colorado, 80204, US.

EL GRITO DEL NORTE: Box 466, Fairview Stn, Española, New Mexico.

ENTMOOT: 64 Taylor Drive, Fairfax, Cal. 94930, US.
FATIGUE PRESS: c/o Oleo Strut, 101 Ave. D, Killeen, Texas 76541, US.
FEATHERSWORD: P.O. Box 1648, Gulfport, Mississippi 39501, US.
FERAFERIA: 3737 Canyon Crest Road, Altadena, Calif. 91001, US.
FILM CULTURE: Box 1499, New York, NY 10001, US.
FIRING LINE: c/o Join Community Union, 4401 N Broadway, Chicago, Illinois 60640, US.
THE FIRST ISSUE: 308 Stewart Ave, Ithaca, NY 14859, US.
FOCUS MIDWEST: Box 3086, St Louis, Missouri, 63130, US.
FORT LAUDERDALE FREE PRESS: P.O. Box 23584, Ft. Lauderdale, Fla. 33165.
FOUNTAIN OF LIGHT: P.O. Box 69, El Prado, New Mexico, US.
FREEDOM: 427 Las Vegas Blvd. South, Las Vegas, Nevada 89101, US.
FREEDOM INFORMATION CENTRE: c/o Jan Hillegas, Tougaloo, Miss. 39174, US.
FREE PAGAN TORCH: Box 3932, Rosedale Stn, Kansas City, Kansas 66103, US.
THE FREE YOU: Midpeninsular Free University, 1061 El Camino Real, Menlo Park, Calif. 94021, US.
FTE: Nowhat Co, 5228 Hollywood Blvd, Los Angeles, Calif. 90027.
FUN: Fuzzy Wuzzy Productions Inc., 207 East 14 Street, New York, NY 10011, US.
FUSION: 0899 Boyleston St, Boston, Mass. 02115, US.
GAY: P.O. Box 431, Old Chelsea Station, New York, NY 10011, US.
GAY POWER: 105 Second Ave, New York, NY 10003.
GLEBE: Box 1056, Greenfield, Calif. 93927, US.
GOTHIC: BLIMP WORKS: 116 St Marks Place, New York, NY 10009, US.
GRASS ROOTS FORUM: Box 472, San Gabriel, Calif. 91778, US.
GUARDIAN: 197 East 4 Street, New York, NY 10009, US.
GUERILLA: c/o Allan Van Newkirk, 1107 W. Warren, Detroit, Michigan, 48201, US.
THE HARD CORE: Columbia SDS Newspaper, c/o Morris Grossner, 780 West End Avenue, New York, NY 10025, US.
HARD TIMES: P.O. Box 3573, Washington DC, 20007, US.
HAWAII FREE PRESS: Box 352, Haleiwa, Hawaii 96712.
HORSESHIT: Scum Publishing Co., Box 361-E Hermosa Beach, Calif. US.
I.F. STONE'S WEEKLY: 5618 Nebraska Ave, NW, Washington DC 20015, US.
THE IMAGE: 4514 Fountain, Hollywood, Calif. 90029, US.
INDEPENDENT EYE: c/o Alex Varonne, Antioch Union, Yellow Springs, Ohio 45387, US.
INDIANAPOLIS FREE PRESS: P.O. Box 88253, Indianapolis, Ind., US.
INNISFREE: Rm. W20/485, 84 Massachusetts Ave, Cambridge, Mass. 02139, US.
INQUISITION: 716 Bertonly Avenue, Charlotte, N. Carolina, 28211, US.

INSTITUTIONAL GREEN: 865 West End Avenue, New York, NY 10025, US.

JAZZ & POP: 1841 Broadway, New York, NY 10023, US.

JEWISH CURRENTS: Suite 601, 22 E. 17 Street, Apt. 3, New York, NY 10003, US.

THE JONES FAMILY GRANDCHILDREN: Box 2626, Norman, Okla. 73069, US.

JOURNAL OF THE RESISTANCE: c/o New England Resistance, 27 Stanhope Street, Boston, Mass. 02116, US.

KARMA: 4373 Wayside Drive, So., Saginaw, Michigan 48603, US.

KISS: 105 Second Avenue, New York, NY 10003, US.

LANCASTER FREE PRESS: Box 592, Lancaster, Pa. 17604, US.

LA RAZA: 2445 Gates Street, Los Angeles, Calif. 90031, US.

THE LAST HARASS: Box 2994, Hill Sta., Augusta, Ga. 30904, US.

LE CHRONIC: 158 Highland, Roxbury, Mass. 02119, US.

LEVIATHAN: 250 Mullen Avenue, San Francisco, Calif. 94110, US.

LONG BEACH FREE PRESS: 326 Locust, Long Beach, Calif. 90812, US.

LUV: Luv Productions Inc., 509 5th Ave., New York, NY 10036, US.

EL MALCRIADO: Box 130, Delano, Calif. 93215, US.

MARIJUANA REVIEW: LeMar International, Box 71, Norton Hall, Sumy, Buffalo, New York 14204, US.

MARK TWAIN COLUMN: c/o Prisoners Information and Support Service (PISS), P.O. Box 387, Boston University Station, Boston, Mass. 02215, US.

THE MILITANT: 873 Broadway, New York, NY 10003, US.

MILWAUKEE COURIER: c/o David Novick, 2118 W. Fond du Lac Ave, Milwaukee, Wisc. 53206, US.

MINORITY OF ONE: Box 544, Passaic, NJ 07055, US.

MINORITY REPORT: P.O. Box 252, Dayton, Ohio 45401, US.

MONTHLY REVIEW: 116 W. 14 St, New York, NY 10011. US.

MOUNTAIN FREE PRESS: Box 304, Denver, Colo. 80201, US.

THE MOVEMENT: 55 Colton Street, San Francisco, Calif. 94103, US.

MOVEMENT FOR A DEMOCRATIC SOCIETY: (MDS) NEWSLETTER: Box 57, Cathedral Sta., New York, NY 10025, US.

NEGED HAZEREM: c/o Hashomer Hatzair, 150 Fifth Ave, New York, NY 10011, US.

NEWS FROM NOWHERE: P.O. Box 501, Dekalb, Illinois 60115, US.

NEW BABYLON TIMES: Box 160 RFD No. 3, Brattleborough, Vermont 05301.

THE NEW HARD TIMES: Box 3272, 6515 Wydown Blvd, Clayton, Mo. 63105, US.

NEW LEFT NOTES: 1608 W. Madison St, Chicago, Ill. 60612, US.

NEW PATRIOT: 308 Stewart Ave, Ithaca, NY 14850, US.

NEW PENELOPE: Box 8473, Phoenix, Arizona 85001, US.

NEW SCHOOLS EXCHANGE NEWSLETTER: 2840 Hidden Valley Lane, Santa Barbara, California 93103, US.

THE NEW SOUTH STUDENT: Box 6403, Nashville, Tenn. 37212, US.

NEW TIMES: 377 Park Avenue South, New York, NY 10016, US.

NEW YORK FREE PRESS: 200 W. 72 St, New York, NY 10023, US.

NEW YORK HIGH SCHOOL FREE PRESS: 208 W. 85 St., Apt. 2E, New York, NY 10023, US.

NEW YORK HERALD TRIBUNE: 110 Riverside Drive, New York, NY 10024, US.

THE NEW YORK REVIEW OF SEX: Suite 23, 200 W. 72 St, New York, NY 10023, US.

NEW YORK SCENES: 377 Park Avenue S, New York, NY 10011, US.

NOLA EXPRESS: Box 2342, New Orleans, La. 70116, US.

NORTH AMERICAN CONGRESS ON LATIN AMERICA (NACLA) NEWSLETTER: Box 57, Cathedral Sta., New York, NY 10025, US.

NORTH WEST PASSAGE: 2616 Maplewood Ave., Bellingham, Washington 98225.

OBERLIN OTHER: 285 E. College St, Oberlin, Ohio 44074, US.

OLD MARKET PLACE: 208 Kentucky Ave, Paducah, Ky., US.

OLD MOLE: 2 Brookline, Cambridge, Mass. 02140, US.

OM: c/o Roger Priest, US Navy, P.O. Box 1033, Washington DC, 20013, US.

OMEN: P.O. Box 12457, Tucson, Arizona 85711, US.

THE OPEN DOOR: 1021 E. Wright, Milwaukee, Wisc. 53212, US.

ORPHEUS: Bin 1832, Phoenix, Ariz. 85001, US.

OUR GENERATION: 3837 Boul. St Laurent, Montreal 18, Quebec.

OUTCRY: Radical Student Union, Eshleman Hall, UC, Berkeley, Calif., US.

OVERLOAD: New People Media Project, P.O. Box 4356, Salter Gate Station, Berkeley, California 94704, US.

THE PAPER: Box 4576, Toledo, Ohio 43620, US.

PAPER HIGHWAY: c/o Rich Balagur, 169 Nott Terrace, Schenectady, NY 12308, US.

PEACE BRAIN: 3430 N. Elaine Pl, No 2, Chicago, Ill. 60657, US.

PEACEMAKER: 10208 Sylvan Ave, Cincinnati, Ohio 45241, US.

THE FREE MAGAZINE OF THE PEACE AND FREEDOM PARTY: 619 South Bonnie Brae, Los Angeles, Calif. 90057, US.

THE PEOPLE YES: 154 E. 11 Ave, Columbus, Ohio 43201, US.

PHILADELPHIA FREE PRESS: 1237 Vine Street, Philadelphia, Penn., US.

PITTSBURGH POINT: Box 7345, Pittsburgh, Pa. 15213, US.

PLAIN TRUTH: Box 2148, Sta. A, Champaign, Ill. 61920, US.

PLANET: Media Research Institute, 746 Brannan St, San Francisco 94103, US.

PLEASURE: 200 W. 20 St, New York, NY 10011, US.

POPPIN: 1249 Howe Street, Vancouver 1, British Columbia, Canada.

PRISM: 311 Green Annex, Princeton, NY 08540, US.

PROBE: 701 Bolton Walk 101, Goleta, Calif. 93107, US.

PTERODACTYL: Grinnel College, Grinnel, Iowa 50112, US.

PUNCH: c/o Paper Book Center, 569 Main St, Worcester, Mass. 01608, US.

PUSSY CAT: Ansonia Station P.O. Box 1165, New York, NY 10023, US.

QUICKSILVER TIMES: 1932 17 St, NW, Washington DC, 20009, US.

RADICAL AMERICA: 1237 Spaight St, Madison, Wisc. 53703, US.

RADICALS IN THE PROFESSIONS NEWSLETTER: c/o REP, Box 625, Ann Arbor, Mich. 48108, US.

RAGS: Rosy Cheeks Publications Inc., 30 East 20 Street, New York, NY 10003, US.

RAMPARTS: 495 Beach, San Francisco, Calif. 94133, US.

THE REALIST: 595 Broadway, New York, NY 10012, US.

THE REBEL: An Exile Publication, Box 611, Station H, Montreal, Quebec.

A REBIRTH OF WONDER: 41 W. 72 St, New York, NY 10023, US.

RESISTANCE PRESS: Box 592, Chicago, Illinois, 60690, US.

THE ROACH: Box 352, Haliewa, Honolulu, Hawaii, 96809.

THE ROAD: Box 352, Haliewa, Honolulu, Hawaii, 98762.

ROLLING STONE: 746 Brannan St, San Francisco, Calif. 94103, US.

SAGE: P.O. Box 1741, Sante Fe, New Mexico, US.

SCANLANS: 143 West 44th St, New York, NY 10036, US.

SCIMITAR: 308 Stewart Avenue, Ithaca, NY 14850, US.

SCREW: P.O. Box 432, Old Chelsea Sta., New York City, NY 10011, US.

THE SEARCHER: c/o Dave Perry, 115 Suffolk Road, Wellesley, Mass. 02181, US.

SECOND LOOK: c/o University Christian Movement, 475 Riverside Drive, New York, NY 10027, US.

SHAKEDOWN: Fort Dix, New Jersey, US.

SHORT TIMES: Fort Jackson, S. Carolina, US.

SNATCH: P.O. Box 31075 Diamond Heights, San Francisco, Calif. 94131, US.

SOMETHING: c/o John Sara, 1002 Broadview Ave, Toronto 6, Ontario.

SOUTHERN PATRIOT: 3210 W, Broadway, Louisville, Ky. 40211, US.

SPACE CITY NEWS: 1217 Wichita, Houston, Texas 77004, US.

SPECTRUM: 1047 31 St, NW, Washington DC 20007, US.

ST LOUIS FREE PRESS: 4487 McPherson Ave, St Louis, Mo., US.

STREET NEWS: Box 4576, Toledo, Ohio, US.

STUDENT TIMES INC: 719 Boyleston St, Boston, Mass. 02116, US.

STUDENT VOICE: Apt. 4, 501 W. 121 St, New York, NY 10027, US.

TAKE ONE: P.O. Box 1778, Station B, Montreal 110, Canada.

THE UNGARBLED WORD: 918 Kerlerec St, New Orleans, La. 70116, US.

THE WALRUS: 1312 W. Main St, Urbana, Ill. 61801, US.

THIS MAGAZINE IS ABOUT SCHOOLS: c/o S. Spinks, 84 Aua Rd, Toronto 10, Ontario.

TRANS-LOVE ENERGIES: 1510 Hill St, Ann Arbor, Mich. 48104, US.

TRAVELLERS DIRECTORY: 5104 39 Ave, Flushing, New York, NY 11377, US.

TRICONTINENTAL: OSPAAAL POB 4224, Havana, Cuba.

THE TRUMPET: P.O. Box 232, Goleta, California 93017, US.

VERITAS: Box 381, Boonton, NY 07005, US.

WORCESTER PUNCH: Box 352, Worcester, Mass. 01601, US.

VETS STARS AND STRIPES FOR PEACE: 1608 W. Madison St, Chicago, Ill. 60612, US.

VIETNAM GI: Box 9273, Chicago, Ill. 60690, US.

VILLAGE VOICE: Sheridan Sq, New York, NY 10014, US.

VISION: 2441 Le Conte Avenue, Berkeley, California 94709, US.

VOCATIONS FOR SOCIAL CHANGE NEWSLETTER: 2010 B. St, Hayward, Calif. 04541, US.

WHOLE EARTH CATALOGUE: Portola Institute, 558 Santa Cruz, Menlo Park, Calif. 94025, US.

WORLD COUNTDOWN: 1209 N. Western Ave, Hollywood, Calif. 90029, US.

WYSO NEWS: c/o Jo Anne Wallace, Antioch Union, Yellow Springs, Ohio, 45387, US.

XANADU: c/o P. Rothschild, 204 N. Rockhill Road, Webster Groves, Mo. 63119, US.

ZAP COMIX: Print Mint, 830 Folger Ave, Berkeley, Calif. 94710, US.

PUBLICATIONS OF INTEREST—EUROPE AND ELSEWHERE

ABENG: Kingston, Jamaica.

ALOHA (formerly Hitweek): Alexander Boerstraat 30, Amsterdam 7, Holland.

ANNA LOUISE STRONG'S NEWSLETTER: I Tai Chi Chang, Peking, China.

ANTI/PRO: Sreenath, Prabhat Colony, Santa Cruz, Bombay 55, India.

ARROWS: Union of Students, Sheffield University, Western Bank, Sheffield, England.

ARTS LAB NEWSLETTER: 141, Westbourne Park Road, London W11, England.

BLACK DIMENSIONS: Ladbroke Grove, London W11, England.

BLACK DWARF: 79 Cromwell Rd., London SW7, England.

CAMBRIDGE VOICE: 147 Chesterton Road, Cambridge, England.

CATONSVILLE ROAD RUNNER: 132 Muswell Hill Broadway, London N10, England.

CIRCUIT: 1 Robert Street, London NW1.

COCK: Cockerel Print, P.O. Box 2538, Wellington, New Zealand.

COMMUNES: Selene Community, Can-y-Lloer, Ffarmers, Llanwrda, Sir Gaerfyrddin, Cymru, Wales, UK.

THE CONTINENTAL NEWS: 1, Britto Road, Karachi 5, W. Pakistan.

DADD: 103a, Brankston Gardens, London SW5, England.

DE ANDERE KRANT: de Klerklaan 58, Eindhoven, Holland.

DREAMER: c/o Brian Mills, Derby College of Art, Kedleston Road, Derby, England.

EL CORNO EMPLUMADO: c/o Meg Randall, Apartado Postal 13–546, Mexico 13 DF.

EMBRYO: c/o Ysteffan Cooke, 73, Kensington Road, Reading, Berks, England.

ESPERIENZA: G. Rossi Buno, Via Lunari 5, Lucca, Florence, Italy.

EUROPEAN UNDERGROUND PRESS SYNDICATE: c/o Mazin Zeki, 4 St George Terrace, London NW1, England.

FREEDOM: 17A Maxwell Road, London SW6, England.

FRIENDS: The T. F. Much Publishing Co. Ltd., 305, Portobello Road, London W10, England.

FRIENDS (of Rolling Stone): no fixed abode at time of writing.

FRONT: 44, rue Vieille-du-Temple, Paris 4, France.

FRONT UNI: 17, rue du Sentier, Paris 2, France.

GRANMA: Apartado 6260, Havana, Cuba.

GOD NEDERLAND & ORANJE: Postbus 3612, Amsterdam, Holland.

GRASS EYE: 52 Corporation Street, Manchester 4, England.

GROWTH: 56, Crow Hill North, Middleton, Manchester, England.

L'HEBDO DARA KIRI: 35, rue Montholon, Paris 9, France.

HOD: 440 Selby Road, Leeds, LS15 9AN, Yorks, England.

HOTCHA: Postfach 304, CH 8025, Zurich, Switzerland.

THE HUSTLER: 70 Ledbury Road, London W11, England.

IDIOT INTERNATIONAL: 32, Paul Street, London, EC2, England.

IL CANGURO: Via G. Bellini 10, Milan 20146, Italy.

INTERLUTTES: BULLETIN D'INFORMATIONS MILITANTES: 13 Rue Pascal, Paris 5. (B.P.65–05 Paris).

INTERNATIONAL FREE PRESS: no fixed abode at time of writing.

KING MOB ECHO: BCM/King Mob, London WC1, England.

KREA TIDINGS: 18, rue des Eperonniers, Brussels 1, Belgium.

LAMBI: Haiti.

L'ACTION CULTURELLE DU SUD-EST: 27 Rue du 11 Novembre, 13 Aix-en-Provence, France.

LEMURIA: 142 Prins Hendrikkade, Amsterdam, Holland.

LEVELLER: quarterly of Synic, Room 209, Abbey House, Victoria St, London SW1, England.

LIBERATION NEWS SERVICE EUROPE: 30 Holland Park Gardens, London W14, England.

LIGHT: 200d, Railton Road, Herne Hill, London SE24, England.

LE LIBERTAIRE: 220 rue Vivegnies, Lieges, France.

LINKECK: Roll Bergstr. 67, 1 Berlin 44, BRD, Germany.

LOVE: Kompagnietreade 20, Copenhagen, Denmark.

LUNG: c/o Durning Hall, Earlham Grove, Forest Gate, London E7, England.

MARE BOX: 58 Dordrecht, Holland.

MOLE: The Students Union, Hull University, England.

THE MOLE: 83 St Ambyne, Hove, BN3 2TL, Sussex, England.

NEW LEFT REVIEW: 7 Carlisle St, Soho, London W1, England.
OEUF 16: Communes-reunies, 1212 G. Lancy, Geneva, Switzerland.
ONTBIJD: Op bed Hermeleinstraat 15, Breda, Holland.
OPEN SECRET: 20, Greek Street, London W1, England.
OPS VEDA: 16 Woodholm Road, Sheffield 11, England.
OUTSIDE REVIEW: 17 Cocksmead Croft, Kings Heath, Birmingham 14, England.
PARADOKS: Zagreb, Nikole Tesle 1/1, Yugoslavia.
PENG: Altemayer Postfach 2815, 56 Wuppertal 1, BRD, Germany.
PEOPLES' NEWS: 60, St. Ervans Road, London W10, England.
POP EXPRESS: Izdaje Centar, za Kulturnu djelatnost omladine, Zagreb, Yugoslavia.
PO PO PO: 5 Köln 10, Postach 178, Germany.
PSY: in Westerstraat 235, Amsterdam, Holland.
RED MOLE: 182, Pentonville Road, London N1, England.
RED NOTES: 160 North Gower Street, London NW1, England.
REVO: P. O. Box 252, Brussels 1, Belgium.
ROLLING STONE: 19 Hanover Square, London W1, England.
ROTTEN: Gernersgade 7A, 1319 Copenhagen K, Denmark.
ROUNDABOUT: 40 Abbey House, Victoria Street, London SW1.
SEED: replacing Interzone A. 50a, Princedale Road, London W11, England.
SETTANTATRE: V. Calzolari 11, 50061 Compiobbi, Firenze, Italy.
SHILLING PAPER: Queen's College, Cambridge, England.
SOLSTICE: 21A Silverstreet, Cambridge, England.
SOLIDARITY: c/o H. Russell, 53A Westmoreland Road, Bromley, Kent, England.
SPEAK OUT: National Council for Civil Liberties, 152, Camden High Street, London NW1, England.
SUCK: c/o Alexander Boersstraat, 30 Amsterdam, Holland.
SUPERLOVE: Larsbjornstraede 13, 1454 Copenhagen, Denmark.
SYNIC: Room 209, Abbey House, Victoria Street, London SW1.
SYNTHESIS: 11 Florence Street, London N1.
TIME OUT: 70 Princedale Road, London W11, England.
UBU NEWS: 54 George Street, Redfern 2016, NSW, Australia.
UNDERGROUND: 6 Frankfurt Am Main 1, Hebelstrasse 11, W. Germany.
VITO: Box 2025, Curaçao.
WORM: The Students Union, Hull University, England.
WYVERN: University of Essex, Colchester, Essex, England.

APPENDIX
THREE

TRAVELLING—
TRANSPORT
GRASS
CRASH-
PADS

λ

Transport

Istanbul, as they say in the geography books, is the gateway to the East, and by judicious use of local buses and trains you can make it all the way from there to Katmandu for £12. Intrepid beats and 'The Marco Polo Hitch' journalists still prefer to hitch-hike, although it is exhausting, dangerous and boring. Travel with a girl or fair-haired companion. A long blonde wig is useful. One Australian boy hiked from Bondi to London with a portable prop from a novelty shop—a shapely pair of inflatable rubber legs. There are plenty of petrol trucks, although the drivers expect payment. Most comfortable are the express Mercedes lorries which speed non-stop from Munich to Teheran. You can also pick up £50 pocket money in Teheran if you 'import' a car from Germany for a local dealer. Make sure you are not landed with the duty for it yourself.

From this point, hitching becomes even more arduous and again, most drivers will want you to pay. If you are dropped between Mashed, Kandahar and Kabul, you will find yourself in the middle of the desert. The road through the north of Afghanistan is the most fascinating (via Mazar-i-Sharif), although sometimes impassable. The buses for Kabul take the other route, through Kandahar. From Kabul to Amritsar, take a bus or hitch, unless the Moslems and Hindus are warring again, in which case you will be turned back at the border. (Both sides claim it is the other side who won't let you pass.) Afghan Airways offers a cheap joyride over their heads. Once in India, use trains. Third-class compartments break the Geneva humanitarian codes, but then, most hitch-hikers escape payment, so you can't complain. Look the Indian railway guard in the eye and say: 'I am not going to pay.' He will go away. If he persists, ask: 'Didn't I meet you at Oxford?' For the less unscrupulous, your forged student card will cut the third-class fare to a pittance, but the bureaucratic formalities you have to endure to gain the concession make Kafka an understatement. At every station you are revived with cheap cups of tea in disposable earthenware cups, the liquid having a surprisingly amphetamine quality.

In Katmandu, you can choose between buses, bicycles and being piggy-backed by Sherpas.

From Calcutta to Bangkok, fly United Burmese Airways. Their fares are £10 cheaper than IATA fares, and you'll get another £10 cut with a student card. Thailand is a hitch-hiker's paradise. Cars will commit a U-turn for the privilege of your company; not, like the Arabs, because they want your money. When hitching to Vientiane in Laos, you will probably catch a large Shell petrol truck, on its way to stock up with opium, or a tedious timber lorry. Be careful in northern Thailand. Communist guerrillas sometimes attack the buses and rob the passengers. First, they shoot the driver, then board the bus like Hollywood Apaches. One traveller who refused to give up his watch was summarily shot. Several travellers have disappeared from this area. If you want to avoid paying bus fares, (1) pretend not to understand what the conductor requires, at the same time creating an embarrassing exhibition, with wild gesticulations and shouting, and he will soon leave you in peace, or (2) point to another European and say that he has paid. He can return the gesture. These two ploys are common throughout the East, although in Thailand you won't have to pay anyway. Not due to any discriminatory generosity on the part of the Transport Minister, but because the Thais are too polite to ask you.

In Laos, there's nothing much to hitch, except US aid planes dropping supplies to farmers. A hustle, but many have swung it.

Drug
Bulletin

'As long as it fucks you up, it's good for you.' *Anon.*

This survey is by necessity personal and sketchy. Prices vary with season, the nature of the market, and your own gullibility.

Morocco
Kif has been the staple crop of farmers at Ketama, a town in the western Rif Mountains, for generations. It is legal to grow it there, since it is the only crop that will grow on the steep hillsides, but illegal to transport it. 'As soon as it leaves the vicinity of Ketama the chase is on; if the shipment gets through the blockade, it reaches the consumer directly, by the normal channels. If it is captured by the authorities, the route to the consumer is, of necessity, more circuitous.' (Paul Bowles in *The Book of Grass*.) Shortages in Tangier and Marrakesh can be traced directly to sporadic bursts of activity against the mule-trains by the Government, usually American inspired.

At Ketama, you can buy freshly harvested, biro-thick stems of uncleaned kif as long as your arm, direct from the farmers, for 10 dirhams (18/-) a kilo. Cleaned: 20–30 dirhams (36/- to 54/-). In Marrakesh, the same stuff will cost you 50–70 dirhams (£4–£6.13.0). A small packet of kif mixed with tobacco is about 1.50 dirhams (2/6)—about three tablespoons. Hash candy and hash cookies are 1 dirham (1/8).

Pollen—a speciality from Ketama, sometimes available in Tangier. A week's supply will fit into a matchbox and cost you 13/6. Sprinkle it on your bread and jam, stir it into your mint tea, mix it with melted chocolate. Pressed (after damping with a little flour and water) between two sellotaped sheets of paper and sent in an envelope, it makes an ideal present for loved ones left behind in the big city.

Special recommendation: Marjoon—a fudge, blended with the leaves—

not the buds —of the plant and which sometimes contains opium as an extra taste treat.

Istanbul
Plentiful, but beware! (See *Pot Trail Casualties*, pp. 226-30).

The best hash comes from Antep and Bursa. Direct from grower, 30 dollars per kilo, rising to 100 dollars in Istanbul, where it is usually mixed with inferior quality grass.

Poorer quality can be bought for 50–60 dollars per kilo. Any offences connected with drugs get extensive publicity in Turkish newspapers. Increasing concern expressed by Turkish officials parallels growing American influence and aid.

Pakistan
Grass: 15 dollars per kilo.

Nepal
The famous Government shop markets the even more famous Nepalese 'blue' hash for one rupee per tola; 7/- will buy a chunk of the best hash in the world. If it's too oily, burn it out over a candle. Hash candies, 6d a block. Hash cakes, 10d.

Afghanistan
Kabul: Hash sold in Spearmint-like packets. ('It helps you to do almost anything.') Hash is cheapest in the north, at Mazar-i-Sharif, 12 dollars per kilo. Nepalese hash is available here for 30 dollars a kilo. From Herat, delicious hash cakes at 3/- each.

India
The law, and consequently the prices vary from state to state. Calcutta boasts an opium and 'charas' shop. In Madras, you can buy bubble gum-sized packets for 1/-.

Some Methods of Smoking

Avoid gaudy hookahs in tourist shops. If you don't have a genuine nargileh from Egypt, make your own water pipe from Butagaz refills: pierce a hole in the top wide enough for tube to stick through. A small hole ¾ up one side, a larger one ¾ up the other side. Dent tin inwards around both holes at the sides. Push tube or sebsi through the hole at the top until it rests an inch or so from the bottom of tin. Seal this hole with wax or plasticine and add container at the top for hash (e.g. chilum). Pour in water, and start smoking. When you smoke this pipe be careful to keep it upright, put mouth to 3rd hole, block 2nd hole with finger and draw, slowly at first until you hear smoke bubbling through water. Then draw more strongly until lungs are filled with one long final draw.

Chilums

Beautifully carved, soft stone chilums can be bought in India, and for smoking are second only to a good water pipe.

Carrot
chilum

Select suitably-sized and shaped carrot—4 ins long or so and as evenly conical as possible—hollow out with a long thin pointed knife. To smoke, wrap damp rag around bottom, covering hole. Make sure that air can pass through silver paper ball or stone. Hold between thumb and four fingers (pointing straight up and bunched together at tips) of left hand. Wrap right hand around the back of left hand, leaving a hole for mouth between thumb and first finger of left hand, closing any other gaps by holding more tightly and adjusting grip. Test by drawing strongly before lighting. Keep chilum upright, head to one side and get someone else to light it. Beware of hair going up in flames. Constant strong drawing is necessary to keep it alight. The advantage of a carrot is that you can throw it away after use. After ten smokes or so it becomes too soggy for use. If you want a carrot chilum that lasts indefinitely, scrape off the outside skin, and bake it in a very low oven for 2–4 hours.

Toilet
Roll
Joint

Simply cover one end of a toilet roll as tightly as possible with your right hand, stick the joint between the 1st and 2nd fingers of this hand, as close to where the fingers join the palm as possible. Draw down the toilet roll so that it fills with smoke, and then, still drawing, take your right hand and the joint away from the end of the roll. The smoke rushes into your lungs and you get zonked immediately.

Some
Places
to
Stay

'Passengers must not gambol, make phlegm, or the smoking of hash and what have we.'

Notice in a Thai Hotel

From Istanbul eastwards, the standards of hotels progressively improve. The Gulhane consists of a tent on the roof, and 40 people camping on the floor; by Katmandu, you have, for much the same price, beds, mattresses and even curtains; by Bangkok, you have *double* beds, a private shower and hot and cold running prostitutes.[10]

On the road, you will receive much more up to date information than that which follows. Remember that prices vary with the patron's mood and your bargaining ability. Never pay more than one dollar a night. You will usually find that the cheapest hotels are the easiest to locate.

Istanbul

Hotel	Price per night
Gulhane Oteli	$.30 (roof)
	$.40 (bed)
New Gulhane	$.55
Tourist Hotel	$.75 (hot showers)
Camping	$.85 (Erzerum: Sehir Palas)

Two rumours circulate in Istanbul about the Gulhane. (1) that the proprietor tips off guests before any police raid, and (2) that the proprietor calls the police at the first whiff of hash. Both rumours are true.

Teheran

Hotel	Price per night
Yanezmir	$.60
Amir Kabir	$.75
Baghdad	$.50
Gulha	$.55

In Iran, Sikh temples are now closed to 'hippies'. Near the railway station in Maidan-E-Rah-E-Ahan, there are several hotels— $.35.

Kabul

Hotel	Price per night
Bamian	$.35

[10] A somewhat infelicitous epithet for the gracious Thais, who often exchange their affections for free after the first night.

Noor	$.25 (floor)
	$.30 (bed)
Benazir	$.60

Delhi

All hotels in the new town are expensive, but First Class railway waiting rooms are free. Some Indians let their houses out to 'hippie-sahibs' for prestige purposes.

Hotel	Price per night
Sikh temples	free

Old Delhi

Crown	$.85
Y.M.C.A.	$1.25

Rosemary says to stay in Janpath Lane, or at the Banerjeer at 18 Fire Brigade Lane. She says not to miss the beach at Goa, or the lotus living by the sea in Ceylon. There is a temple (not Sikh) 10 miles out of Delhi, interesting to stay at. Almost every town in India has a Sikh temple. In Srinagar and Benares stay on the houseboats—2 rupees a night, and no limit to the number of people.

Calcutta

Hotel	Price per night
Red Shield, Salvation Army Hotel	$.85

Katmandu

Hotel	Price per night
Jed Singhs	$.50
The Camp	$.35
The Tourist Corner	$.85
Matchbox	$.25
Bed with a Nepalese family	$.15

There are places all over the town to stay. Just outside the town is Sivoy Ambhu—the Monkey Temple.

Rangoon

Hotel	Price per night
Strand	Free,

if you can convince United Burmese Airways officials you are not travelling student concession. It's worth it for the palm court orchestra. Otherwise, accommodation under the counter in the office of UBA is free.

Bangkok

Hotel	Price per night
Thai Son Greet	$.85 (double)

Buddhist temples are free, although you may be invited to teach some of the monks English. To avoid outraging your hosts, mosquitoes should be killed discreetly.

Vientiane

Hotel	Price per night
Danish Red's crash pad,	free (3 nights maximum)

Singapore

Sikh temples are free. There are countless clean Chinese hotels from 3/– to 7/– a night.

Tangier

Hotel	Price per night
Chauen	$.50
Royal	$.70
Blue Angel	$.70
Olid	$1.00

By asking at the Café Centrale it is very easy to obtain rooms anywhere in the Medina for no more than 3/– a night.

Marrakesh

Hotel	Price per night
Essaouira	$.25
Hôtel de France	$1.00 to $1.75
Oikaimdem	$1.75
El Ward	$1.25
C.T.M.	$2.15 (central heating)

All these hotels are in or near the Medina.

Date/Walnut factory	$.10 roof, mats supplied.
	$.30 double room, mats supplied.
	Watch out for bugs

If you're staying a month or more rent a house. For your $12.00 or so a month you will get three or four rooms, a lavatory, electricity and running water. You can paint all over the walls and entertain as many guests as you like. Mats, blankets and utensils are all very cheap.

Ibiza/Formentera

Hotel	Price per night
Caves	Free

INDEX

Cochran, Eddie, 98
Cock, 181
Cohen, Dr Allen, 144
Cohen, Leonard, 73
Cohn-Bendit brothers, 21, 43, 44, 76, 265 n
Cohn-Bendit, Danny, 11, 44, 255: BBC broadcast, 48
College des Beaux Arts Students, 45, 48
Colombo, Judge, 107
Columbia University captured by students, 57, 59, 60, 88
Comets, the, 97
Comité d'Information Révolutionnaire, 179
Communes, 226 and n
Communications Company, 147
Communist Party: and Paris rising, 43; outlawed in Germany, 41
Computers, Managers and Society (Rose), 271
Computers, use of, 271
Cook, Otis, 232–4, 255: love-in in Marrakesh, 232–3; odyssey, 236–250; Los Angeles, 236–7; Hong Kong, 237–8; Katmandu, 238–240; Afghanistan, 240–41; Copenhagen, 241–2; France, 243–4, 248; Morocco, 244–8; England, 248–50
Cool, 237
Coon, Caroline, 132, 133 n
Cornell University, 59, 60: Willard Straight Hall, 59
Cosmic Circuit, 197
Costa Rica, 225–6: 'Hippy Republic', 226
Coult, Dr Allan, 165
Counter culture, 62–7: and new technology, 63; creation by chance, 65–6; theatre groups, 64–5
Country Joe, 100
Craddock, Crash, 97
Crancer, Alfred, 137–8
Cream, 233
Creamcheese, Suzy, 31, 109–11
Crumb, Robert, 189
Cutler, Sam, 100–115
Cybernation, 272

DADA, INFLUENCE ON UNDERGROUND, 65 n
Dagga, 223
Daily Mirror, 128, 131, 137, 260

Daily Sketch, 33
Daily Telegraph, 15, 23, 269
Daley, Mayor of Chicago, 38, 53, 55–6, 162, 182, 257 n, 283
Dallas Morning News, 198 n
Dallas Notes, 136, 156, 184, 190, 255
Daltrey, Roger, 119–20
D'Arcangelo, Angelo, 74, 91
Darin, Bobby, 97
Davies, Robert H., 271
Day-Glo, 27
Death of a President (Manchester), 158
De Bono, Edward, 66, 163, 276 n
De Grazia, Sebastian, 261 n, 272 n
Delfont, Bernard, 262 n
Dellinger, Dave, 256
Delta, 26 n, 28 n
Demaio, Don, 195
De Ridder, Willem, 178
Deviants, the, 269
Dhulikhel, 238, 240
Digger Bill, 55
Direct Action Committee, 24
Disney, Walt, 189
Distant Drummer, 190, 195
Dixon commune, New Mexico, 266
Djellaba, 208
Dock of the Bay, 185
Doggs Troupe Moonmen, 256
Domhoff, William, 195, 277
Domino, Fats, 97
Donovan, 91, 95, 100
Doors, the, 54, 85, 100
Draft card burnings, 20, 157 and n
Drifters, the, 98
Driving ability and marijuana, 137
Drop City, 265
Drop-outs, 61, 168, 267–70: and Frisbee, 273
Dupree, Simon, 86
Durgnat, Ray, 170
Dutschke, Rudi, 11, 40, 42, 43
Duvalier, President, 181
Dylan, Bob, 54, 99, 104, 125, 162, 181, 249, 262: Isle of Wight concert, 275

EAST VILLAGE: Foundation for Runaway Children, 82; hippies, 37, 39
East Village Other (EVO), 55, 78, 91, 104, 153, 156, 159–62, 164, 182, 189, 191 n, 217: on pot, 154; on Vietnam, 154; survey of readers, 194

316

Hoyland, John, 105
Huizinga, J., 273 and n
Human Be-In, 33-4
Human Family theatre group, 64
Humbert, Humbert, 95
Humperdinck, Engelbert, 121
Humphrey, Hubert, 55
Hunnins, F. C., 281 n
Hunt, Marsha, 110-11
Hurford, John, 189
Hurriyet, 204
Hustler, The, 174
Hutchinson, James 'Groovy', 37
Hyde Park Diggers, 36, 267 n

IBIZA, 205, 211, 307
I Ching, Chinese book of changes, 276
Image, 176
'Imperialism' pop market, 50
India, 303: cannabis carriers in gaol, 226, 227; places to stay, 306
Indian hemp, 126; *see also* Cannabis
Indian Hemp Drugs Commission, 1894, 128, 131
Indica bookshop, 31
Ingrams, Richard, 255
International Narcotic Control Board, 129
International Organ, 191
International Situationists, 45-6, 62
Iran, places to stay, 305
Isle of Wight concert, 1969, 268
IT (formerly *International Times*), 31, 32 n, 42, 49, 78, 88, 154, 156, 169-72, 178, 181, 191, 268 n

JACOBS, PAUL, 61, 265 n
Jagger, Mick, 31, 36, 95, 106, 113-116, 121, 170, 175, 259
Jefferson Airplane, 34, 39, 100, 121, 135
Jewell, Derek, 87-9
Johnson, Paul, 80
Johnson, President Lyndon B., 53, 54, 158, 159 n, 218: War on Poverty, 25
Joints, 236
Jones, Brenda, 232
Jones, Brian, 113, 114, 121, 135
Jones, Mervyn, 282 n
Jones, Steve, 151, 181
Joplin, Janis, 117
Junkies, 138, 148

KAI HERMANN, 281
Kaleidoscope, 153, 187, 190, 195
Karloff, Boris, 158
Katmandu, 203, 205, 207, 209, 216, 221, 238-40, 244, 301: places to stay, 306
Katzman, Allan, 160
Keeler, Christine, 71
Kennedy, President John F., 24, 74, 158, 218
Kennedy, Robert, 54-5
Kerouac, Jack, 23, 24, 34-5: 'On the Road', 35, 215
Kesey, Ken, 11: acid tests, 34-5
Keynes, Lord, 271
Kif, 208, 234-5, 246, 247, 302
Kind, Dr William, 72 n
King Crimson, the, 109
King, Martin Luther, 155
King Mob Echo, 22 n, 176
Kings Road, 48
Kinks, the, 98
Kip (Dutch for policeman), 28
KK organisation, 231
Knullar Ltd., 169
Kois, John, 187 n, 195
Kommunes (Berlin), 21-2, 41, 63, 256
Kornbluth, Jesse, 186 n
Korner, Alexis, 113
Krassner, Paul, 39-40, 53 n, 74, 76, 157-8, 162, 172
Kudsu, 184, 190
Kupferberg, Tuli, 20, 35, 78, 106, 155, 160, 273

LADY CHATTERLEY'S LOVER, 78
Laing, R. D., 179
La Mama Troupe, 64
Lambi, 181
Landau, Paul, 61, 265 n
Lane, Mark, 160
Langhans, founder of Kommune K, 41
Last Exit to Brooklyn, 78
Lateral thinking, 66, 163, 276 n
Leary, Timothy, 11, 35-6, 135, 139, 143-6, 157, 159, 163, 167, 237: arrest, 160; 'drop out' manifesto, 168
Lebel, Jean-Jacques, 71, 159, 170, 179, 257: and working classes, 259; occupation of the Odéon, 44-5
LEMAR INTERNATIONAL, 133 and n

318

319

Twitty, Conway, 97, 98
Two Virgins, LP, 175
Tynan, Kenneth, 12, 78 n

Ubu News, 172
UFO (Underground Freak Out),
  30–32, 37, 50, 75, 170, 255, 276
Underground, the, 18–19, 26, 29,
  31–3, 49: and pop personalities,
  84; and working class, 257–9;
  attitude to work, 256–69; counter
  culture, 62; 'new culture' enterprises, 49–50; Press, *see* separate
  entry; principle of indeterminacy,
  65–6; sex habits, 275; sexual
  freedom, 76; sexual morality,
  73–4; Television workshop, 194;
  theatre groups, 64–5
Underground Digest, 186
Underground Press the, 42, 46, 83,
  85, 105, 106, 133, 151–99, 275:
  analysis of content, 152; Black
  power, 155–6; directory, 289–98;
  film, 193; graphic and comic
  strip artists, 188–9; international
  circulation, 153–4; objectives,
  196–7; papers magnified into
  posters, 188; police, 155; pop,
  156; pot, 154–5; students, 156;
  television, 194; use of term, 153;
  Vietnam, 154, 159
Underground Press Syndicate
  (UPS), 153–4, 160, 161, 163, 173,
  174, 180–2, 185–7, 193, 289–91;
  anthologies, 186; reprints, 186
Universal Tonguebath, A Groupie's
  Vision, 86 n
US National Institute of Mental
  Health, 129
US National Students Association
  studies on drugs, 126
US Peace Corps, 218–21
Uses of Lateral Thinking, The (de
  Bono), 66 n, 276 n

VANCOUVER FREE PRESS, *see Georgia
  Straight*
Van der Aar, Hans, 226, 228–30
Van Duyn, Roel, 29
Vaughan, Frankie, 37
Vientiane, 307
Vietnam, 43, 61; and Underground
  Press, 154, 159; as One Great
  Youth Unifier, 19; London de-

monstrations, 21, 48, 51; marijuana
  among US forces, 142, 143
Vietniks, 207
Village Voice, The, 156–7, 159, 164,
  172, 182, 257 n, 265 n
Vincent, Gene, 97
Vinkenoog, Simon, 11, 30, 159, 170
Violence, 159, 281–5: France,
  282–3; Germany, 281; USA,
  282–5
Vito, 180–81
Vogue, 18
Von Amsberg, Claus, 27

Walker Report, The, 53 n, 283–4
Wall Street Journal, 194 n
Wallace, George, 162, 185
Warhol, Andy, 89; attempted assas-
  sination, 164, 165
Warren Commission, 160
Washington Free Press, 186 n, 190
Washington, University of, Pharma-
  cology Department, 137
Watts, Alan, 167, 215
Wayne, John, 98
Weberman, A. J., 162
Weinstock, Arnold, 262 n
Wenner, Jan, 175, 196
'We Shall Overcome', 25
White Negro, The (Mailer), 23
White Panther Party, 62, 106, 186 n,
  190
Whiter Shade of Pale, A, 100–101
Who, the, 54, 98, 103; at Albert
  Hall, 1969, 115–20
Widgery, David, 173
Wilcock, John, 78 n, 151, 157, 159–
  160, 162–4, 172, 173, 185, 278
Wild Child, 110
Wilson, Colin, 23
Wilson, Harold, 262
Wilson, S. Clay, 189
Wisconsin State University, 58
WITCH (Women's International
  Terrorist Conspiracy from Hell),
  89–90
Witte Krant, 177
Woburn Abbey Festival of the
  Flower Children, 32–3
Wolf, Daniel, 156, 157
Wolfe, Tom, 35 n
Woman of the Year, The, 74
Woman's Weekly, 85
Woodstock Festival, 38, 185

RICHARD NEVILLE was born in 1941. While at the University of New South Wales he edited the student newspaper *Tharunka* ("Message stick" in aborigine). He was sentenced to six months' hard labor for publishing an obscene magazine (OZ) but acquitted after two years of much-publicized. legal battles. He left for London in April 1966 on foot, arriving six months later. He launched OZ in London after reading in an evening newspaper that he was about to do so, and continues to edit it.